THE ITALIAN RENAISSANCE

The Italian Renaissance

The Essential Sources

Edited by Kenneth Gouwens

Blackwell
Publishing

350 Main Street, Malden, MA 02148-5018, USA
108 Cowley Road, Oxford OX4 1JF, UK
550 Swanston Street, Carlton South, Melbourne, Victoria 3053, Australia
Kurfürstendamm 57, 10707 Berlin, Germany

First published 2004 by Blackwell Publishing Ltd

Library of Congress Cataloging-in-Publication Data
Library of Congress data has been applied for.
ISBN 0-631-23164-1 (hardback); ISBN 0-631-23165-X (paperback)

A catalogue record for this title is available from the British Library.

Set in 10/12 pt Photina
by Kolam Information Pvt. Ltd, Pondicherry, India
Printed and bound in the United Kingdom
by MPG Books Ltd, Bodmin, Cornwall

For further information on
Blackwell Publishing, visit our website:
http://www.blackwellpublishing.com

Contents

List of Illustrations	vii
Acknowledgments	ix
Introduction	1

Part I	**Introductory Readings**		**11**
	1	Dante Alighieri (1265–1321)	14
		Inferno, cantos 1, 26	15
	2	Petrarch (Francesco Petrarca, 1304–1374)	24
		The Ascent of Mont Ventoux	26
		Two letters to Cicero	34
		Il Canzoniere, poems 1–5, 30, 189, 272, 365	38
	3	Leonardo Bruni (ca. 1370–1444)	43
		Life of Petrarch	44
Part II	**The Limits of Intra-Italian Statecraft**		**49**
	4	Pope Pius II (Aeneas Silvius Piccolomini, 1405–1464)	52
		Commentaries VIII	53
	5	Niccolò Machiavelli (1469–1527)	71
		The Prince, dedicatory letter and chapters 7, 15, 17–18, 25–6	73

Part III   Urban Life and Values   91

    6   Giovanni Boccaccio (1313–1375)   96
        Decameron II, 5 (story of Andreuccio)   97

    7   Alessandra Macinghi Strozzi (1407–1471)   108
        Selected letters   109

    8   Francesco Vettori (1474–1539)   126
        Two letters between Machiavelli and Vettori   127

Part IV   Gender and Society   135

    9   Boccaccio   139
        Decameron X, 10 (story of Griselda)   141

   10 Francesco Barbaro (1390–1454)   150
        On Wifely Duties, preface; II, 1, 3–5, 9   151

Part V   The Power of Knowledge   171

   11 Lorenzo Valla (1407–1457)   176
        On the Donation of Constantine   177

   12 Marsilio Ficino (1433–1499)   187
        Three Books on Life I, 7; II, 10–13   188

   13 Laura Cereta (1469–1499)   197
        Two "familiar" letters   198

   14 Pietro Alcionio (ca. 1490–1528)   206
        An Oration Concerning the Sack of Rome   207

Part VI   Patronage, Art, and Culture   219

   15 Isabella d'Este (1474–1539)   224
        Selected letters on collecting art   225

   16 Benvenuto Cellini (1500–1571)   244
        Autobiography I, 34–9   245

Part VII   The End of the Renaissance   257

   17 Baldassare Castiglione (1478–1529)   260
        Book of the Courtier IV, 4–26   263

   18 Pierio Valeriano (1477–1558)   278
        On the Ill Fortune of Learned Men I, 1–14   279

Index   288

Illustrations

Plates

1   Carracci, *Hercules at the Crossroads* (1596)   4

2   Carpaccio, *St. Augustine in His Study* (1502–7)   32

3   Detail, Tomb of Pius II, now in the Church of Sant' Andrea della Valle, Rome, perhaps begun by Paolo Taccone and completed by a follower of Andrea Bregno (ca. 1465).   54

4   Attrib. to Rosso Fiorentino (1494–1540), *Portrait of Niccolò Machiavelli*   74

5   Donatello, *Judith and Holofernes* (ca. late 1450s)   94

6   Sofonisba Anguissola, *A Game of Chess* (1555)   138

7   Pesellino (1422–57), *Story of Griselda* (detail)   140

8   Perugino, *Christ Handing the Keys to St. Peter* (1481–2), Sistine Chapel   174

9   Sebastiano del Piombo (ca. 1485–1547), *Portrait of Clement VII* (ca. 1526)   208

10   Cellini, *Perseus with the Head of Medusa* (1545–53)   222

11   Leonardo da Vinci (1452–1519), *Study for a Portrait of Isabella d'Este*   239

12   Raphael (1483–1520), *Portrait of Baldassare Castiglione*   261

Map

1   Renaissance Italy   6

Acknowledgments

In preparing this book, I have benefited immensely from the advice and example of Paula Findlen, whose secondary collection, *The Italian Renaissance: Essential Readings* (Blackwell, 2002), it accompanies. Thanks to her thoughtful suggestions, keen eye, and talent for conveying complex ideas clearly and concisely, this has become a far better book. Sarah Ross, a doctoral student of Renaissance History at Northwestern University, also read and critiqued the entire manuscript. Meredith Gill, an art historian at the University of Notre Dame, vetted the descriptions accompanying the plates, making those texts both more accurate in detail and more graceful in style. My wife, Joan Meznar, herself an historian, offered encouragement and advice throughout the project and played no small part in its timely completion. My editors at Blackwell – Tessa Harvey, Tamsin Smith, Angela Cohen, and Brigitte Lee – have combined efficiency and responsiveness with patience and flexibility. I owe thanks also to the anonymous readers of the book proposal, whose comments much improved its structure and expanded its range. A research grant from the University of Connecticut defrayed the cost of permissions for the plates. Students in my classes at UConn tested earlier versions of this reader and offered advice that ranged from enthusiastic endorsements to searing indictments. I am grateful for their candor and have more often than not followed their suggestions. Finally, I would like to acknowledge a long-standing debt to Dr. Helen Brooks, the coordinator of Stanford's "Humanities Special Programs" teaching staff on which I served for three years while completing my dissertation. Under Helen's careful guidance, I first learned how to design and lead effective class discussions of primary-source readings. With lasting gratitude, I dedicate this book to her.

The editor and publishers gratefully acknowledge the following for permission to reproduce copyright material:

Alcionio, Pietro, "An Oration Concerning the Sack of Rome," translated by Kenneth Gouwens.

Barbaro, Francesco, extract from *On Wifely Duties*, from *The Earthly Republic*, edited by Ronald G. Witt and Benjamin G. Kohl. Published by The University of Pennsylvania Press and Manchester University Press, 1978. Copyright © University of Pennsylvania Press. Reprinted with permission.

Boccaccio, Giovanni, extracts from the *Decameron*, translated and edited by Mark Musa and Peter Bondanella. Copyright © 1982 Mark Musa. Published by New American Library, New York.

Bruni, Leonardo, extract from the *Life of Petrarch*, from *The Three Crowns of Florence: Humanist Assessment of Dante, Petrarca and Boccaccio*, translated by Alan F. Nagel, edited by David Thompson and Alan F. Nagel. Copyright © 1972 David Thompson. Published by Harper and Row, New York.

Castiglione, Baldassare, extract from the *Book of the Courtier*, translated by Charles Singleton. Copyright © 1959 Charles S. Singleton and Edgar de N. Mayhew. Used by permission of Doubleday, a division of Random House, Inc.

Cellini, Benvenuto, extract from the *Autobiography of Benvenuto Cellini*, translated by John Addington Symonds. Published by Doubleday, Garden City, 1961. Used by permission of Doubleday, a division of Random House, Inc.

Cereta, Laura, "Two familiar letters," from *Collected Letters of a Renaissance Feminist*, translated and edited by Diana Robin. Published by The University of Chicago Press, 1997. Reprinted by permission of the publisher.

Alighieri, Dante, *The Inferno*, cantos 1 and 26, translated by Robert Hollander and Jean Hollander. Copyright © 2000 by Robert Hollander and Jean Hollander. Used by permission of Doubleday, a division of Random House, Inc.

D'Este, Isabella, "Selected letters on collecting art," from *Patrons and Artists in the Italian Renaissance*, edited by D. S. Chambers. Published by Macmillan, London, 1971. Reprinted by permission of the publisher.

Ficino, Marsilio, extracts from *Three Books on Life*, translated by Carol V. Kaske and John R. Clark (Binghamton, NY, 1989; Tempe, AZ, 1998). Copyright Arizona Board of Regents for Arizona State University. Reprinted by permission of the publisher.

Machiavelli, Niccolò, extracts from *The Prince*, second edition, translated by Harvey Mansfield. Published by The University of Chicago Press, 1998. Reprinted by permission of the publisher.

Machiavelli, Niccolò, "Exchange of letters with Francesco Vettori, November 23 and December 13, 1513," from *Machiavelli and His Friends: Their Personal Correspondence*, translated by James B. Atkinson and David Sices. Copyright © 1996 Northern Illinois University Press. Published by Northern Illinois University Press, Dekalb. Reprinted by permission of the publisher.

Petrarch, "Two letters to Cicero," from *Letters on Familiar Matters: Rerum Familiarum Libri XVII–XXIV*, translated by Aldo S. Bernardo. Copyright © 1984 The Johns Hopkins University Press. Reprinted by permission of The Johns Hopkins University Press.

Petrarch, "Letter on the Ascent of Mont Ventoux," from *Renaissance Philosophy of Man*, edited by Ernst Cassirer et al. Published by The University of Chicago Press, 1949. Reprinted by permission of the publisher.

Petrarch, extracts from *Il Canzoniere*, from *Petrarch's Songbook*, translated by James Wyatt Cook. Published by Medieval and Renaissance Texts and Studies, Binghamton, NY, 1995. Reprinted by permission of James Wyatt Cook.

Pius II, extract from *Commentaries*, from *Memoirs of a Renaissance Pope*, translated by Florence Alden Gragg. Published by Putnam, New York, 1959.

Strozzi, Alessandra Macinghi, extracts from *Letters of Alessandra Strozzi: Bilingual Edition*, translated and edited by Heather Gregory. Copyright © 1997 The Regents of the University of California. Published by The University of California Press. Reprinted by permission of the publisher.

Valeriano, Pierio, extract from *On the Ill fortune of Learned Men*, from *Pierio Valeriano on the Ill Fortune of Learned Men: A Renaissance Humanist and His World*, translated and edited by Julia Haig Gaisser. Published by The University of Michigan Press, Ann Arbor, 1999. Reprinted by permission of the publisher.

Valla, Lorenzo, extract from *The Treatise of Lorenzo Valla on the Donation of Constantine*, translated by Christopher Bush Coleman. Published by Yale University Press, 1922. Reprinted by permission of the publisher.

Footnotes in the present volume are for the most part drawn verbatim from those in the texts listed above. The present editor gratefully acknowledges the labors of previous annotators and has thus endeavored to intervene minimally in the content of their notes, which have of necessity been abbreviated and altered in places.

The publishers apologize for any errors or omissions in the above list and would be grateful to be notified of any corrections that should be incorporated in the next edition or reprint of this book.

Introduction

Structure and Purposes

This reader has been designed to accompany the collection of scholarly essays edited by Paula Findlen, *The Italian Renaissance: Essential Readings* (Blackwell, 2002). It is divided into seven major sections: (1) introductory readings; (2) statecraft; (3) urban life and values; (4) gender and society; (5) the power of knowledge; (6) patronage, art, and culture; and (7) the end of the Renaissance. Each primary-source reading is preceded by a short introduction that provides background and context. The questions that accompany each selection are intended both to facilitate students' reading comprehension and to provide a springboard for in-class discussion.

The readings contained in this volume represent a range of genres, from poetry, oratory, and dialogue to autobiography, the short story, and the personal letter. Letters receive particular attention for reasons both conceptual and pragmatic. Petrarch as well as many later humanists including Laura Cereta favored the personal Latin letter, which allowed for expression of one's own feelings as well as for the discussion of ethics on a practical level through an implied encounter with another human being.[1] For purposes of this reader, the genre has the additional advantage of concision, so that texts can be presented without extensive editorial pruning. This practical consideration is no small matter. In pursuit of comprehensiveness, many collections have ended up heavy-laden with brief, decontextualized passages. This

---

1   On the importance of the personal Latin letter to Petrarch and his followers, see Ronald G. Witt, *"In the Footsteps of the Ancients": The Origins of Humanism from Lovato to Bruni* (Leiden, 2000), esp. chap. 6: "Petrarch, Father of Humanism?"

reader, by contrast, includes shorter texts in their entirety and, when excerpting longer works (such as Machiavelli's *Prince*), reproduces distinct sections of them without internal omission or condensation. As a result, fewer texts can be represented within the space of these pages, but those that do appear gain significantly in coherence, complexity, and integrity. In this way, writers from the Italian Renaissance – a movement vaunted, whether justifiably or not, for individualism – are allowed to speak to us in something more closely resembling their own individual voices.

The selections that follow will be most effective when studied in tandem with the secondary essays in the Findlen collection, but they should also be useful in their own right for what they can disclose about the culture of the Italian Renaissance. Primary sources are the main focus of professional historians, who must develop an awareness not only of what makes those sources valuable as evidence, but also of the limitations on what they can tell us about the past. All narratives are "biased": that is, all are written from a particular point of view. But since that is true of all human expression, simply stating that a source is biased does not get us very far. More difficult – and, correspondingly, more rewarding – is the task of determining what we *can* in fact know from a source despite its biases. Discerning the author's point of view is a good starting point, but one must move beyond that to examine the values that the author assumes the reader will share, and the cultural context in which the text's assumptions made sense. The more aware we become of the fragmentary nature of our evidence and the constraints upon the historian's efforts to interpret it, the better we will appreciate the preciousness of those vestiges of Renaissance culture that we can recover, as well as the importance of approaching such cultural artifacts with respect for the society and the individuals that produced them.

The Political Environment

The Italian Renaissance first took hold in the city-states of northern and central Italy. By the mid-sixteenth century, however, these city-states had for the most part been subsumed into larger political units. A brief synopsis of this transformation may provide some useful background for the chapters that follow.

From city-states to territorial states

In the two centuries following the reign of Frederick II (d. 1250), the emperor who had tried without success to reduce all Italy to his sway, the northern and central portions of the peninsula enjoyed considerable *de facto* political autonomy. On occasion, a pope could significantly influence local affairs, as Boniface VIII did in the events leading to Dante's exile from Florence in 1302; but the papacy's move from Rome to Avignon in 1309, followed by decades of schism beginning in 1378, greatly diminished its effectiveness as a political force in Italy. Meanwhile the emperors, technically overlords of much of Italy, lacked the power to make that ideal a reality. When the Holy Roman Emperor Henry VII announced in 1307 that he would come to Italy to be crowned in Rome, Dante hailed his arrival and wrote letters to Italian rulers, urging them to support Henry's stated desire to bring peace to the peninsula. In the event, however, Henry's trip to Italy was a fiasco: in Rome, he ended up having to crown himself, and an irate crowd disrupted the celebratory banquet by pelting rocks in through the window. Upon his death in 1313 Italy was if anything more factionalized than before.

With both papacy and empire thus limited in their ability to reach out and clutch someone, the Italian city-states could develop as independent polities that ran by their own rules. In his masterly *Civilization of the Renaissance in Italy* (1860), Jacob Burckhardt argued that the "illegitimacy" of local governments underlay the political and cultural dynamism of the fourteenth and fifteenth centuries. Whereas in oligarchical republics such as Florence groups of merchants arrogated to themselves the right to govern, in many city-states tyrants seized power: men with no legitimate claim to have inherited power, who instead held it by force, through their own individual prowess. Untrammeled by tradition, these tyrants fostered the development of a society in which talent and ability, rather than morals and nobility, held sway – a change in values that Burckhardt viewed as conducive to innovation and excellence also in cultural production.

Few historians today accept Burckhardt's interpretation uncritically, but surely there is something to the view that Italian city-states, which grew in size and wealth in the High Middle Ages, benefited from the absence of foreign domination. In the early 1400s, when Leonardo Bruni was writing in praise of the Florentine Republic and criticizing the duchy of Milan, the chief enemies of the Italian city-states were still one another. The more powerful ones, including Florence, pursued policies of territorial expansion, but until the last decade of the Quattrocento, they did so by and large without foreign military interference.

In 1454, in the Peace of Lodi, Florence, Milan, and the Kingdom of Naples joined in opposition to Venice and the papacy (which Martin V had returned to Rome in 1420). The resultant "balance of power" (a term used before the end of the century to describe the situation), engineered in no small part by Cosimo "The Elder" de' Medici (d. 1464), was to last until the invasion of Italy in 1494 by a French army led by King Charles VIII – an event that marked the beginning of the end of the political autonomy that had distinguished earlier Renaissance Italy.

From territorial states to subject territories

The renewed power and influence of the papacy following its return to Rome threatened in time to destabilize the peninsula. The popes derived both revenue and troops from subject territory in central Italy (known as the "Papal States"), which they now sought to build up once again. The Peace of Lodi did not prevent the papacy from being a wild card in Italian politics:

Plate I   Carracci, *Hercules at the Crossroads* (1596), Museo Nazionale di Capodimonte, Naples. *Source:* Alinari/Art Resource, NY.

This oil painting on canvas by Annibale Carracci (1560–1609) initially served as the centerpiece of the ceiling decorations in the *Camerino* of the Palazzo Farnese in Rome, a small room that Cardinal Odoardo Farnese used as his study. A great-great-grandson of Pope Paul III (d. 1549) and the grandnephew of two cardinals, Odoardo had been elevated to the cardinalate at age 17 and was in his early twenties when he commissioned Carracci's work for the ceiling. The story of the choice of Hercules, which dated from antiquity, had been virtually ignored throughout the Middle Ages, but it enjoyed renewed popularity in the Renaissance. Petrarch knew the story through the dialogue *On Duties* (*De officiis*) by the Roman philosopher and statesman Cicero, who had appropriated it from the Greek author Xenophon. In Petrarch's telling, the adolescent Hercules confronted a critical choice between the path of laziness and indulgence (*voluptas*) on the one hand, and that of excellence and moral virtue (*virtus*) on the other. After deliberating for some time, he opted for the difficult path of virtue. Through his own effort he ascended that steep road, going beyond the peak of human glory to the point where he gained the reputation of a divinity (or, in Cicero's words, "obtained a place among the gods").

By the time Carracci gave this story its definitive artistic treatment, it had long been a commonplace in Renaissance literature and art. In the context of Odoardo's study, this painting of the beardless, adolescent Hercules was probably intended both to compliment the young cardinal and to inspire him to imitate the heroic example of choosing the path of virtue. At Hercules' feet sits a poet, with a laurel wreath, perhaps representing the eternal fame to be gained by choosing the right path.

These ideals of heroism, achievement, and recognition leave little room for the emphasis in Christianity upon human weakness and the need for divine grace. In the gospel of Matthew, Jesus had described a very different sort of crossroads: "Enter through the narrow gate; for the gate is wide and the road is easy that leads to destruction, and there are many who take it. For the gate is narrow and the road is hard that leads to life, and there are few who find it" (Matthew 7:13–14, NRSV). Thus for Renaissance Christians, the pagan virtues need not even lie along the same path as the ascent toward God. Moreover, because of human weakness and inclination to sin, the Christian's ascent is only possible with divine assistance. In his writings (e.g., the letter on the "Ascent of Mont Ventoux"), Petrarch invoked both visions of crossroads, and the tensions between them neatly encapsulate a major theme of Italian Renaissance thought and cultural production: that is, the effort to combine classical and Christian wisdom into a harmonious whole.

RENAISSANCE ITALY

SWISS
FEDERATION

HOLY ROMAN EMPIRE

N

DUCHY
OF
SAVOY

DUCHY
OF
MILAN

REPUBLIC
OF VENICE

Turin

Milan

Brescia

SALUZZO

MARQUISATE
OF MANTUA

Mantua

Trieste

KINGDOM
OF
HUNGARY

Genoa

Parma

Venice

MONFERRATO

DUCHY
OF FERRARA &
MODENA

Ferrara

ISTRIA
(VENETIAN)

REPUBLIC
OF GENOA

Bologna

Ravenna

OTTOMAN
EMPIRE

REPUBLIC
OF LUCCA

Lucca

Florence

REPUBLIC
OF FLORENCE

Pesaro

Urbino

DALMATIA
(VENETIAN)

CORSICA
(GENOESE)

Siena

REPUBLIC
OF SIENA

PAPAL
STATES

Perugia

*ADRIATIC
SEA*

Rome

SARDINIA
(ARAGONESE)

Naples

KINGDOM
OF
NAPLES
(ARAGONESE)

Bari

*TYRRHENIAN
SEA*

Taranto

Brindisi

Otranto

Palermo

Messina

*IONIAN
SEA*

KINGDOM OF
SICILY
(ARAGONESE)

*MEDITERRANEAN
SEA*

| 0 | 50 | 100 Mi. |
| 0 | 50 | 100 | 150 Km. |

Pope Sixtus IV was among those responsible for the Pazzi Conspiracy that resulted in the assassination of Giuliano de' Medici (brother of Lorenzo "The Magnificent"); and two popes from the Borgia family in Valencia, Calixtus III (r. 1455–8) and Alexander VI (r. 1492–1503), increased the influence of Spanish interests upon Italian politics.

Also during the second half of the Quattrocento, the westward expansion of the Ottoman Turks became an object of intense concern. After conquering Constantinople in 1453, the Turks were perceived to be menacing western Christendom. In response, Pope Pius II (r. 1458–64) sought to launch a new Crusade to push back the forces of Islam and to retake the Holy Land, but neither he nor later pontiffs could muster support adequate for a united counter-offensive. By the pontificate of Clement VII (r. 1523–34), the Turkish threat to Roman Christendom had become acute: in 1526, troops of the sultan Süleyman "The Magnificent" (r. 1520–66) won a decisive victory in the battle of Mohács in Hungary. Three years later, troops of the Holy Roman Emperor Charles V (who was also king of Hungary after 1526) were

Map I Renaissance Italy

The map facing this page represents some of the more significant territories on the Italian peninsula in the period of the Renaissance. The cities here identified have been chosen either for their historical significance (e.g., Rome, Florence) or because of their prominence in selections in this reader (Baldassare Castiglione's *Courtier* is set in Urbino; Laura Cereta was born and educated in Brescia; Giovanni Boccaccio's fictive merchant Andreuccio went to Naples from Perugia; and Alessandra Macinghi Strozzi and her family moved to Pesaro after her husband was exiled from Florence).

Territories of particular strategic importance were often contested over many decades, having different rulers as the political dynamics of the peninsula shifted. Consider, for example, the duchy of Urbino in the early sixteenth century. In 1508 Pope Julius II confirmed the inheritance of the duchy by his kinsman Francesco Maria Della Rovere. In 1516, Pope Leo X dispossessed Della Rovere in favor of his own nephew, Lorenzo de' Medici (d. 1519). Della Rovere was reinvested with the duchy by Pope Adrian VI (r. 1522–23), but the next pontiff, Clement VII (r. 1523–34) – a cousin of Leo X – opposed the duke and did not formally enfief him until pressured to do so by the Emperor Charles V in 1529. In the mid-1520s, although lacking formal recognition, Della Rovere was de facto ruler of Urbino, protecting his position as necessary by military force. In addition, Della Rovere and Clement VII each sought to strengthen his own hand against the other by seeking alliances with foreign powers including France, Spain, and England, or by petitioning them for financial support in times of war.

The point of this story, for our purposes, is that *any* map of Italy in the Renaissance can provide only an approximation of how political boundaries stood at a given moment. Those consulting the map that faces this page should therefore keep in mind its limitations. It will be most useful for determining the geographical relationship among the cities (and, to a lesser extent, among the territorial states) that figure prominently in the pages that follow.

defending Vienna from Turkish attack. If the danger was sensed throughout Europe, it was felt particularly intensely in Venice and other Italian polities that depended upon trade routes in the eastern Mediterranean.

Further complicating the situation, and more immediately threatening to the Italian city-states' autonomy, were the invasions of their peninsula by northern European armies beginning in 1494, when King Charles VIII of France led an army as far south as Naples. The Spanish crown, too, soon sought to assert its hereditary claims in southern Italy. In 1500, King Louis XII of France and King Ferdinand of Aragon agreed in the Treaty of Granada that together they would conquer Naples and divide its kingdom between them; but within four years the Spaniards had driven out the French, and so Ferdinand added it to his domains (he was king of Naples from 1504 until his death in 1516). Meanwhile, not to be excluded, the French fielded armies in northern Italy. These Spanish and French troops were, in fact, the first large standing armies in Europe since antiquity, and in scale they dwarfed any force that an individual Italian territorial state could assemble.

The sustained presence of foreign troops in the peninsula permanently transformed Italian politics. Small to moderate-sized territorial states that had earlier maintained a tenuous balance of power now struggled to preserve their autonomy, which could only be done by keeping either the French or the Spanish from becoming dominant on the peninsula. Thus in 1511 Pope Julius II (r. 1503–13), who had previously been allied with the French in a war against Venice, formed the "Holy League," including the papacy, Spain, Venice, and England, to check French power in northern Italy. The situation became critical during the reigns of Francis I (king of France, 1515–47) and Charles V (Holy Roman Emperor, 1519–56; king of Spain, 1516–56). In 1525, Charles's troops decisively defeated the French at Pavia, taking Francis I prisoner. Following his release a year later, the French king again took part in an alliance with the papacy and several Italian powers against the emperor, but its activities in the peninsula were limited, and Spain increasingly gained the upper hand, especially after Imperial troops sacked Rome in 1527. Three years later, Pope Clement VII – once more allied with Charles V – officially crowned him Holy Roman Emperor.[2]

By the 1530s, with the Spanish overwhelmingly victorious in Italy, the focus of conflict moved elsewhere. In a strikingly cynical effort to contain Charles V's power, the French formed an alliance with the Turks against the emperor. Closer to home, the fragmentation caused by the Reformation was increasingly a central concern, first in the German lands of the Holy Roman Empire, but soon elsewhere as well. Yet the ultimately unsuccessful struggle

2 Before 1530, Charles V was technically "Holy Roman Emperor-Designate" rather than officially being the emperor. Following convention, the present reader describes him as "emperor" from 1519, when he was elected to succeed his grandfather, Maximilian, in that role.

for Italian autonomy in the years 1494–1530 did have a lasting effect not only upon Italian politics, but upon political thought. The historian Francesco Guicciardini, a wealthy Florentine who served as Lieutenant-General of the papal forces during the Imperial campaigns of 1526–7, came to believe that the course of events was unpredictable and capricious. His fellow Florentine Niccolò Machiavelli, on the other hand, sought in *The Prince* to identify some rules governing political action that could prove effective even in his own seemingly unpredictable times. At the end of the sixteenth century, the Italian economy remained strong. While the Catholic Reformation strove to contain creativity within orthodox channels, Italian culture continued to produce great artists and intellectuals. Yet at least in the sphere of politics – and in art and literature, to the extent that politics influenced them – the conditions in which Renaissance culture first took hold had long since ceased to obtain, and a new age had begun.

Part I

Introductory Readings

Introduction to Part I

Neither political nor economic conditions can account for the emergence of a figure like Francesco Petrarca, or "Petrarch." Often described as one of the "three crowns of Florence" (the other two being Dante and Boccaccio), Petrarch has long held a position of special prominence as a key early advocate of the revival we term the Italian Renaissance. What did he do that was different and new, or at least was perceived as being so? As a step toward answering this question, the selections below situate Petrarch with respect to Dante Alighieri, widely considered the greatest poet in the Italian language. Creating a metaphor as useful as it is awkward, a student once wrote of Dante that he "stands with one foot firmly placed in the Middle Ages, while with the other he salutes the rising star of the Renaissance." But if scholars have long identified both "medieval" and "Renaissance" aspects in Dante's thought and literary style, Petrarch is most often cast as having "opened the way" (as Leonardo Bruni phrased it) to the Renaissance revival of classical learning. The selections provide a glimpse of how these two outstanding writers could creatively appropriate common material – here, including the medieval allegory of a Christian's journey toward the blessed life, and the ancient story of the voyage of Ulysses – and put that material to tellingly different purposes.

1

Dante Alighieri (1265–1321)

Dante wrote his famous allegorical poem, the *Divine Comedy*, after being exiled from his native Florence in 1302. Soon after Dante's family had gained the rights of citizenship as a result of a broadening of the government in 1293, he had become active in politics. In 1300 he even served a two-month term as one of the six priors (or chief executive officers) of the Florentine government. But two years later, a rival faction took power, forcing Dante and others into exile. Although he never saw Florence again, it figures prominently in the *Divine Comedy*, in which he bitterly criticizes the city and certain of its citizens.

In the three parts of the *Divine Comedy*, a pilgrim named "Dante" narrates his journey through hell, purgatory, and finally paradise. Frequently reprinted in the Renaissance, the poem significantly influenced themes and images in both art and literature. Some fifteenth-century humanists, such as Cristoforo Landino, lectured or wrote learned commentaries interpreting it, while others, such as Matteo Palmieri, emulated it by writing their own visionary poems.

The two selections below are drawn from the initial third of the poem. In canto 1, after failing to ascend a difficult path on his own, the pilgrim "Dante" meets the shade (or spirit) of Virgil, the great epic poet of classical Rome, who will serve as his initial tour guide. Virgil's own greatest work, the *Aeneid*, had narrated the founding of Rome by the Trojan Aeneas, whose journeyings toward Italy began after the Greeks had conquered Troy. In canto 26, the characters Virgil and "Dante" have descended into the eighth of the nine circles of hell, whose residents include those who have counseled others to do evil. Here they speak with the shade of the famous Greek warrior, Ulysses, who had devised the trickery of the Trojan horse.

Questions

1 What meanings, allegorical and personal, might there be in the pilgrim Dante's failed attempts to ascend the path?
2 Why is Virgil an appropriate guide for the initial phases of the journey? What are his shortcomings as a guide likely to be?
3 In what sense is Ulysses (as Dante presents him) a counselor of evil or of fraud? Why has the poet placed him so far down in the depths of hell?
4 Dante adds a new wrinkle to the Ulysses story, a final voyage that ends in shipwreck. What kind of journey is it that this Ulysses makes? How does he persuade his men to join him? What are they seeking?
5 Compare and contrast Ulysses' final voyage here with the journey that the pilgrim Dante attempts at the start of canto I. Other than one being on water and the other on land, what important differences are there between the two? How many "correct" paths are there likely to be in Dante's schema, and why?

Inferno

Canto I

Midway in the journey of our life
I came to myself in a dark wood,
3   for the straight way was lost.

Ah, how hard it is to tell
the nature of that wood, savage, dense and harsh –
6   the very thought of it renews my fear!

It is so bitter death is hardly more so.
But to set forth the good I found
9   I will recount the other things I saw.

How I came there I cannot really tell,
I was so full of sleep
12   when I forsook the one true way.

But when I reached the foot of a hill,
there where the valley ended
15   that had pierced my heart with fear,

looking up, I saw its shoulders
arrayed in the first light of the planet
18   that leads men straight, no matter what their road.

Then the fear that had endured
in the lake of my heart, all the night
21   I spent in such distress, was calmed.

And as one who, with laboring breath,
has escaped from the deep to the shore
24   turns and looks back at the perilous waters,

so my mind, still in flight,
turned back to look once more upon the pass
27   no mortal being ever left alive.

After I rested my wearied flesh a while,
I took my way again along the desert slope,
30   my firm foot always lower than the other.

But now, near the beginning of the steep,
a leopard light and swift
33   and covered with a spotted pelt

refused to back away from me
but so impeded, barred the way,
36   that many times I turned to go back down.

It was the hour of morning,
when the sun mounts with those stars
39   that shone with it when God's own love

first set in motion those fair things,
so that, despite that beast with gaudy fur,
42   I still could hope for good, encouraged

by the hour of the day and the sweet season,
only to be struck by fear
45   when I beheld a lion in my way.

He seemed about to pounce –
his head held high and furious with hunger –
48   so that the air appeared to tremble at him.

And then a she-wolf who, all hide and bones,
seemed charged with all the appetites
51   that have made many live in wretchedness

so weighed my spirits down with terror,
which welled up at the sight of her,
54   that I lost hope of making the ascent.[1]

And like one who rejoices in his gains
but when the time comes and he loses,
57   turns all his thought to sadness and lament,

such did the restless beast make me –
coming against me, step by step,
60   it drove me down to where the sun is silent.

While I was fleeing to a lower place,
before my eyes a figure showed,
63   faint, in the wide silence.

When I saw him in that vast desert,
"Have mercy on me, whatever you are,"
66   I cried, "whether shade or living man!"

He answered: "Not a man, though once I was.
My parents were from Lombardy –
69   Mantua was their homeland.

"I was born *sub Julio*,[2] though late in his time,
and lived at Rome, under good Augustus
72   in an age of false and lying gods.

"I was a poet and I sang
the just son of Anchises[3] come from Troy
75   after proud Ilium[4] was put to flame.

"But you, why are you turning back to misery?
Why do you not climb the peak that gives delight,
78   origin and cause of every joy?"

1   The leopard, lion, and she-wolf are taken from the Bible, Jeremiah 5:6. They have been interpreted as foreshadowing the division of Dante's hell into three regions, encompassing respectively the sins of incontinence, violence, and fraud.
2   i.e., under Julius Caesar.
3   Anchises' son was Aeneas.
4   i.e., Troy.

"Are you then Virgil, the fountainhead
that pours so full a stream of speech?"
81   I answered him, my head bent low in shame.

"O glory and light of all other poets,
let my long study and great love avail
84   that made me delve so deep into your volume.

"You are my teacher and my author.
You are the one from whom alone I took
87   the noble style that has brought me honor.

"See the beast that forced me to turn back.
Save me from her, famous sage –
90   she makes my veins and pulses tremble."

"It is another path that you must follow,"
he answered, when he saw me weeping,
93   "if you would flee this wild and savage place.

"For the beast that moves you to cry out
lets no man pass her way,
96   but so besets him that she slays him.

"Her nature is so vicious and malign
her greedy appetite is never sated –
99   after she feeds she is hungrier than ever.

"Many are the creatures that she mates with,
and there will yet be more, until the hound
102   shall come who'll make her die in pain.[5]

"He shall not feed on lands or lucre
but on wisdom, love, and power.
105   Between felt and felt shall be his birth.

"He shall be the salvation of low-lying Italy,
for which maiden Camilla, Euryalus,
108   Turnus, and Nisus died of their wounds.

"He shall hunt the beast through every town
till he has sent her back to Hell
111   whence primal envy set her loose.

---

5   Verses 100–11 refer to a promising Italian political leader, Can Grande della Scala (1290–1329), who was born in Verona (and hence between the two towns of Feltre and Montefeltro, the "felt and felt" of verse 105).

"Therefore, for your sake, I think it wise
you follow me: I will be your guide,
114   leading you, from here, through an eternal place

"where you shall hear despairing cries
and see those ancient souls in pain
117   as they bewail their second death.

"Then you will see the ones who are content
to burn because they hope to come,
120   whenever it may be, among the blessed.

"Should you desire to ascend to these,
you'll find a soul more fit to lead than I:
123   I'll leave you in her care when I depart.

"For the Emperor who has his seat on high
wills not, because I was a rebel to His law,
126   that I should make my way into His city.

"In every part He reigns and there He rules.
There is His city and His lofty seat.
129   Happy the one whom He elects to be there!"

And I answered: "Poet, I entreat you
by the God you did not know,
132   so that I may escape this harm and worse,

"lead me to the realms you've just described
that I may see Saint Peter's gate
and those you tell me are so sorrowful."
136   Then he set out and I came on behind him.

Canto 26

Take joy, oh Florence, for you are so great
your wings beat over land and sea,
3   your fame resounds through Hell!

Among the thieves, I found five citizens of yours
who make me feel ashamed, and you
6   are raised by them to no great praise.

But if as morning nears we dream the truth,
it won't be long before you feel the pain
9   that Prato, to name but one, desires for you.

Were it already come, it would not be too soon.
But let it come, since come indeed it must,
12   and it will weigh the more on me the more I age.

We left that place and, on those stairs
that turned us pale when we came down,
15   my leader now climbed back and drew me up.

As we took our solitary way
among the juts and crags of the escarpment,
18   our feet could not advance without our hands.

I grieved then and now I grieve again
as my thoughts turn to what I saw,
21   and more than is my way, I curb my powers

lest they run on where virtue fails to guide them,
so that, if friendly star or something better still
24   has granted me its boon, I don't refuse the gift.

As when a peasant, resting on a hillside –
in the season when he who lights the world
27   least hides his face from us,

at the hour when the fly gives way to the mosquito –
sees fireflies that glimmer in the valley
30   where he perhaps ploughs fields and harvests grapes,

with just so many flames the eighth crevasse
was everywhere aglow, as I became aware
33   once I arrived where I could see the bottom.

And as the one who was avenged by bears[6]
could see Elijah's chariot taking flight,
36   when the horses reared and rose to Heaven,

but made out nothing with his eyes
except the flame alone
39   ascending like a cloud into the sky,

so each flame moves along the gullet
of the trench and – though none reveals the theft –
42   each flame conceals a sinner.

---

6   Verses 34–9 refer to the Hebrew prophet Elisha (see II Kings 2:11–24).

Rising to my feet to look, I stood up
on the bridge. Had I not grasped a jutting crag,
45   I would have fallen in without a shove.

My leader, when he saw me so intent, said:
"These spirits stand within the flames.
48   Each one is wrapped in that in which he burns."

"Master," I replied, "I am the more convinced
to hear you say it. That is what I thought,
51   and had it in my mind to ask you this:

"Who is in the flame so riven at the tip
it could be rising from the pyre
54   on which Etèocles was laid out with his brother?"

He replied: "Within this flame find torment
Ulysses and Diomed. They are paired
57   in God's revenge as once they earned his wrath.

"In their flame they mourn the stratagem
of the horse that made a gateway
60   through which the noble seed of Rome came forth.

"There they lament the wiles for which, in death,
Deidamia mourns Achilles still,
63   and there they make amends for the Palladium."

"If they can speak within those flames,"
I said, "I pray you, master, and I pray again –
66   and may my prayer be a thousand strong –

"do not forbid my lingering awhile
until the twin-forked flame arrives.
69   You see how eagerly I lean in its direction."

And he to me: "Your prayer deserves
much praise. Therefore, I grant it,
72   but on condition that you hold your tongue.

"Leave speech to me, for I have understood
just what you want. And, since they were Greeks,
75   they might disdain your words."

Once the flame had neared, when he thought
the time and moment right,
78   I heard my leader speaking in this way:

"O you who are twinned within a single fire,
if I have earned your favor while I lived,
81   if I have earned your favor – in whatever measure –

"when, in the world, I wrote my lofty verses,
then do not move away. Let one of you relate
84   just where, having lost his way, he went to die."

And the larger horn of that ancient flame
began to murmur and to tremble,
87   like a flame that is worried by the wind.

Then, brandishing its tip this way and that,
as if it were the tongue of fire that spoke,
90   it brought forth a voice and said: "When I

"took leave of Circe, who for a year and more
beguiled me there, not far from Gaëta,
93   before Aeneas gave that name to it,

"not tenderness for a son, nor filial duty
toward my agèd father, nor the love I owed
96   Penelope that would have made her glad,

"could overcome the fervor that was mine
to gain experience of the world
99   and learn about man's vices, and his worth.

"And so I set forth on the open deep
with but a single ship, with that handful
102   of shipmates who had not deserted me.

"One shore and the other I saw as far as Spain,
Morocco – the island of Sardegna,
105   and other islands set into that sea.

"I and my shipmates had grown old and slow
by the time we reached the narrow strait
108   where Hercules marked off the limits,[7]

"warning all men to go no farther.
On the right-hand side I left Seville behind,
111   on the other I had left Ceüta.

---

7   i.e., the "Pillars of Hercules," known today as the Straits of Gibraltar.

" 'O brothers,' I said, 'who, in the course
of a hundred thousand perils, at last
114   have reached the west, to such brief wakefulness

" 'of our senses as remains to us,
do not deny yourselves the chance to know –
117   following the sun – the world where no one lives.

" 'Consider how your souls were sown:
you were not made to live like brutes or beasts,
120   but to pursue virtue[8] and knowledge.'

"With this brief speech I had my companions
so ardent for the journey
123   I could scarce have held them back.

"And, having set our stern to sunrise,
in our mad flight we turned our oars to wings,
126   always gaining on the left.

"Now night was gazing on the stars that light
the other pole, the stars of our own so low
129   they did not rise above the ocean floor.

"Five times the light beneath the moon
had been rekindled and as often been put out
132   since we began our voyage on the deep,

"when we could see a mountain, distant,
dark and dim. In my sight it seemed
135   higher than any I had ever seen.

"We rejoiced, but joy soon turned to grief:
for from that unknown land there came
138   a whirlwind that struck the ship head-on.

"Three times it turned her and all the waters
with her. At the fourth our stern reared up,
the prow went down – as pleased Another –
142   until the sea closed over us."

---

8   The word *virtute*, here translated "virtue," can also mean "excellence" or "prowess."

2

Petrarch (Francesco Petrarca, 1304–1374)

Petrarch is a key figure in the development of Renaissance Humanism, which was an intellectual and cultural movement rooted in the love of antiquity and the desire for its rebirth. He was not the first humanist – two generations of scholars before him had sought to imitate literary models drawn from the classical past – but he broadened the revival to include Christian writers, such as Augustine of Hippo (d. 430), whose *Confessions*, a spiritual autobiography, particularly captivated him. A charismatic figure, Petrarch became an advocate for the humanist movement, and its subsequent growth in popularity was owed in no small part to the influence of his example. Unlike Dante, he conceived of himself as helping to initiate a new age, built upon a revival of the learning of classical and early Christian antiquity. This revival, he believed, would put an end to the barbarism of the intervening centuries, which he influentially termed the "Dark Ages."

Born in Arezzo, Petrarch spent much of his youth in Avignon, France, where his father (a Florentine, exiled for political reasons much as Dante had been) went in 1312 to work as a notary in the papal bureaucracy. Initially sent to study law in Montpellier and then in Bologna, after his father's death in 1326 Petrarch lived off his inheritance and devoted himself primarily to writing poetry and prose. Although the poems he wrote in Italian are today the most widely read of his works, he sought to revive the classical Latin language, as opposed to the "barbarous" style of Latin used by Scholastic theologians in his own day. In a variety of genres, including philosophical dialogues, epic poetry, invectives, and letters, he imitated the writings of the ancient Romans. This effort to emulate classical Latin vocabulary and style was integral to the revival of antiquity in two key ways: (1) through imitating the ancients' ways of expressing themselves in words, one could to some extent recover their culture; and (2) by telling stories of exemplary behavior in aesthetically pleasing language, he believed, one could help sway people toward moral improvement.

The selections below illustrate three aspects of Petrarch's writings. His letter on the ascent of Mont Ventoux, dated 1336 but actually written (or, at least, revised) later, describes the climb allegorically, likening it to the believer's progress toward "the blessed life." His letters to Cicero, by contrast, imagine conversing with an historical individual. In 1345, Petrarch had discovered manuscripts of Cicero's personal letters to his friend Atticus. Here the great rhetorician and philosopher of antiquity came across as ambitious, vain, and at times petty – but also therefore more approachable, a human being with whom one could have a personal interaction of sorts across time. The poems, finally, draw upon themes of courtly love, yet make a unique personal statement. Linking his lady (Laura) with gold ("*l'auro*") and with the laurel ("*lauro*"), which symbolizes poetic fame, he dramatizes the tensions between the poet's quest for glory and the urgency of following a spiritual path.

Questions

1   Why, according to Petrarch, does he set out to climb Mont Ventoux, and why does he take with him his brother (who, as it happens, later became a monk)? In what ways, if any, is the Petrarch we see at the end of the letter a changed man?

2   In addition to its allegory of the uphill journey toward the spiritual life, the letter tells the stories of the conversions to Christianity of Augustine and of Anthony. To what extent does Petrarch's experience, as recounted in the letter, run parallel to theirs? Of what significance are the differences? How does he portray his spiritual condition at the time of writing?

3   In the two letters to Cicero, how does Petrarch treat the imagined recipient? What sort of reaction does he imagine Cicero having had to the first letter?

4   Consider the figure of Laura in Petrarch's poetry:

(a)   Poem 3 tells of his first sighting of her, at a church service on Good Friday. How, if at all, might Laura be related to the poet's religious quest?

(b)   Poem 30 opens with a description of the lady (Laura) sitting under a laurel, but its subject quickly becomes the effects of time and aging upon the poet. What roles do the lady and the tree play with respect to that theme?

> 5   Poem 189 explicitly evokes the voyage of Ulysses. How is the image of
>   a storm at sea deployed here, and in poem 272?
> 6   Petrarch may well have intended his poetry-book to begin with no. 1
>   and end with no. 365. What themes do these two poems emphasize?
>   How might this "frame" affect our reading of the poems in between?

The Ascent of Mont Ventoux

Letter to Francesco Dionigi de'Roberti of Borgo San Sepolcro, professor of
theology in Paris. Malaucène, April 26, 1336. (*Fam.*, IV, 1, in *Le Familiari*,
ed. V. Rossi, I, 153–61; *Opera* [Basel, 1581], pp. 624–7.)

*To Dionigi da Borgo San Sepolcro, of the Order of Saint Augustine, Professor of
Theology, about his own troubles*

Today I ascended the highest mountain in this region, which, not without
cause, they call the Windy Peak. Nothing but the desire to see its conspicuous
height was the reason for this undertaking. For many years I have been
intending to make this expedition. You know that since my early childhood,
as fate tossed around human affairs, I have been tossed around in these parts,
and this mountain, visible far and wide from everywhere, is always in your
view. So I was at last seized by the impulse to accomplish what I had always
wanted to do. It happened while I was reading Roman history again in Livy
that I hit upon the passage where Philip, the king of Macedon – the Philip
who waged war against the Roman people – ascends Mount Haemus in
Thessaly, since he believed the rumor that you can see two seas from its top:
the Adriatic and the Black Sea. Whether he was right or wrong I cannot
make out because the mountain is far from our region, and the disagreement
among authors renders the matter uncertain. I do not intend to consult all of
them: the cosmographer Pomponius Mela does not hesitate to report the fact
as true; Livy supposes the rumor to be false. I would not leave it long in doubt
if that mountain were as easy to explore as the one here. At any rate, I had
better let it go, in order to come back to the mountain I mentioned at first. It
seemed to me that a young man who holds no public office might be excused
for doing what an old king is not blamed for.

I now began to think over whom to choose as a companion. It will sound
strange to you that hardly a single one of all my friends seemed to me suitable

in every respect, so rare a thing is absolute congeniality in every attitude and habit even among dear friends. One was too sluggish, the other too vivacious; one too slow, the other too quick; this one too gloomy of temper, that one too gay. One was duller, the other brighter than I should have liked. This man's taciturnity, that man's flippancy; the heavy weight and obesity of the next, the thinness and weakliness of still another were reasons to deter me. The cool lack of curiosity of one, like another's too eager interest, dissuaded me from choosing either. All such qualities, however difficult they are to bear, can be borne at home: loving friendship is able to endure everything; it refuses no burden. But on a journey they become intolerable. Thus my delicate mind, craving honest entertainment, looked about carefully, weighing every detail, with no offense to friendship. Tacitly it rejected whatever it could foresee would become troublesome on the projected excursion. What do you think I did? At last I applied for help at home and revealed my plan to my only brother, who is younger than I and whom you know well enough. He could hear of nothing he would have liked better and was happy to fill the place of friend as well as brother.

We left home on the appointed day and arrived at Malaucène at night. This is a place at the northern foot of the mountain. We spent a day there and began our ascent this morning, each of us accompanied by a single servant. From the start we encountered a good deal of trouble, for the mountain is a steep and almost inaccessible pile of rocky material. However, what the Poet says is appropriate: "Ruthless striving overcomes everything."[1]

The day was long, the air was mild; this and vigorous minds, strong and supple bodies, and all the other conditions assisted us on our way. The only obstacle was the nature of the spot. We found an aged shepherd in the folds of the mountain who tried with many words to dissuade us from the ascent. He said he had been up to the highest summit in just such youthful fervor fifty years ago and had brought home nothing but regret and pains, and his body as well as his clothes torn by rocks and thorny underbrush. Never before and never since had the people there heard of any man who dared a similar feat. While he was shouting these words at us, our desire increased just because of his warnings; for young people's minds do not give credence to advisers. When the old man saw that he was exerting himself in vain, he went with us a little way forward through the rocks and pointed with his finger to a steep path. He gave us much good advice and repeated it again and again at our backs when we were already at quite a distance. We left with him whatever of our clothes and other belongings might encumber us, intent only on the ascent, and began to climb with merry alacrity. However, as almost always happens, the daring attempt was soon followed by quick fatigue.

1 Virgil, *Georgica* i.145–6; Macrobius, *Saturnalia* v.6.

Not far from our start we stopped at a rock. From there we went on again, proceeding at a slower pace, to be sure. I in particular made my way up with considerably more modest steps. My brother endeavored to reach the summit by the very ridge of the mountain on a short cut; I, being so much more of a weakling, was bending down toward the valley. When he called me back and showed me the better way, I answered that I hoped to find an easier access on the other side and was not afraid of a longer route on which I might proceed more smoothly. With such an excuse I tried to palliate my laziness, and, when the others had already reached the higher zones, I was still wandering through the valleys, where no more comfortable access was revealed, while the way became longer and longer and the vain fatigue grew heavier and heavier. At last I felt utterly disgusted, began to regret my perplexing error, and decided to attempt the heights with a wholehearted effort. Weary and exhausted, I reached my brother, who had been waiting for me and was refreshed by a good long rest. For a while we went on together at the same pace. However, hardly had we left that rock behind us when I forgot the detour I had made just a short while before and was once more drawing down the lower regions. Again I wandered through the valleys, looking for the longer and easier path and stumbling only into longer difficulties. Thus I indeed put off the disagreeable strain of climbing. But nature is not overcome by man's devices; a corporeal thing cannot reach the heights by descending. What shall I say? My brother laughed at me; I was indignant; this happened to me three times and more within a few hours. So often was I frustrated in my hopes that at last I sat down in a valley. There I leaped in my winged thoughts from things corporeal to what is incorporeal and addressed myself in words like these:

"What you have so often experienced today while climbing this mountain happens to you, you must know, and to many others who are making their way toward the blessed life. This is not easily understood by us men, because the motions of the body lie open, while those of the mind are invisible and hidden. The life we call blessed is located on a high peak. 'A narrow way,'[2] they say, leads up to it. Many hilltops intervene, and we must proceed 'from virtue to virtue' with exalted steps.[3] On the highest summit is set the end of all, the goal toward which our pilgrimage is directed. Every man wants to arrive there. However, as Naso says: 'Wanting is not enough; long and you attain it.'[4] You certainly do not merely want; you have a longing, unless you are deceiving yourself in this respect as in so many others. What is it, then, that keeps you back? Evidently nothing but the smoother way that leads through the meanest earthly pleasures and looks easier at first sight. How-

2   Matt. 7:14 (Sermon on the Mount).
3   A typical metaphor familiar to ecclesiastical writers; cf., e.g., Anselm of Canterbury, *Letters* i.43, where it is used as a friendly wish in salutations.
4   Ovid, *Ex Ponto* iii.1.35.

ever, having strayed far in error, you must either ascend to the summit of the blessed life under the heavy burden of hard striving, ill deferred, or lie prostrate in your slothfulness in the valleys of your sins. If 'darkness and the shadow of death'[5] find you there – I shudder while I pronounce these ominous words – you must pass the eternal night in incessant torments."

You cannot imagine how much comfort this thought brought my mind and body for what lay still ahead of me. Would that I might achieve with my mind the journey for which I am longing day and night as I achieved with the feet of my body my journey today after overcoming all obstacles. And I wonder whether it ought not to be much easier to accomplish what can be done by means of the agile and immortal mind without any local motion "in the twinkling of the trembling eye"[6] than what is to be performed in the succession of time by the service of the frail body that is doomed to die and under the heavy load of the limbs.

There is a summit, higher than all the others. The people in the woods up there call it "Sonny," I do not know why. However, I suspect they use the word in a sense opposite to its meaning, as is done sometimes in other cases too. For it really looks like the father of all the surrounding mountains. On its top is a small level stretch. There at last we rested from our fatigue.

And now, my dear father, since you have heard what sorrows arose in my breast during my climb, listen also to what remains to be told. Devote, I beseech you, one of your hours to reading what I did during one of my days. At first I stood there almost benumbed, overwhelmed by a gale such as I had never felt before and by the unusually open and wide view. I looked around me: clouds were gathering below my feet, and Athos and Olympus grew less incredible, since I saw on a mountain of lesser fame what I had heard and read about them. From there I turned my eyes in the direction of Italy, for which my mind is so fervently yearning. The Alps were frozen stiff and covered with snow – those mountains through which that ferocious enemy of the Roman name once passed, blasting his way through the rocks with vinegar if we may believe tradition. They looked as if they were quite near me, though they are far, far away. I was longing, I must confess, for Italian air, which appeared rather to my mind than my eyes. An incredibly strong desire seized me to see my friend[7] and my native land again. At the same time I rebuked the weakness of a mind not yet grown to manhood, manifest in both these desires, although in both cases an excuse would not lack support from famous champions.

Then another thought took possession of my mind, leading it from the contemplation of space to that of time, and I said to myself: "This day marks

5   Ps. 106(107):10; Job 34:22.
6   I Cor. 15:52; Augustine, *Confessions* vii.1.1.
7   A reference to Bishop Giacomo Colonna, who had gone to Rome in 1333.

the completion of the tenth year since you gave up the studies of your boyhood and left Bologna. O immortal God, O immutable Wisdom! How many and how great were the changes you have had to undergo in your moral habits since then." I will not speak of what is still left undone, for I am not yet in port that I might think in security of the storms I have had to endure. The time will perhaps come when I can review all this in the order in which it happened, using as a prologue that passage of your favorite Augustine: "Let me remember my past mean acts and the carnal corruption of my soul, not that I love them, but that I may love Thee, my God."[8]

Many dubious and troublesome things are still in store for me. What I used to love, I love no longer. But I lie: I love it still, but less passionately. Again have I lied: I love it, but more timidly, more sadly. Now at last I have told the truth; for thus it is: I love, but what I should love not to love, what I should wish to hate. Nevertheless I love it, but against my will, under compulsion and in sorrow and mourning. To my own misfortune I experience in myself now the meaning of that most famous line: "Hate I shall, if I can; if I can't I shall love though not willing."[9] The third year has not yet elapsed since that perverted and malicious will, which had totally seized me and reigned in the court of my heart without an opponent, began to encounter a rebel offering resistance. A stubborn and still undecided battle has been long raging on the field of my thoughts for the supremacy of one of the two men within me.[10]

Thus I revolved in my thoughts the history of the last decade. Then I dismissed my sorrow at the past and asked myself: "Suppose you succeed in protracting this rapidly fleeing life for another decade, and come as much nearer to virtue, in proportion to the span of time, as you have been freed from your former obstinacy during these last two years as a result of the struggle of the new and the old wills – would you then not be able – perhaps not with certainty but with reasonable hope at least – to meet death in your fortieth year with equal mind and cease to care for that remnant of life which descends into old age?"

These and like considerations rose in my breast again and again, dear father. I was glad of the progress I had made, but I wept over my imperfection and was grieved by the fickleness of all that men do. In this manner I seemed to have somehow forgotten the place I had come to and why, until I was warned to throw off such sorrows, for which another place would be more appropriate. I had better look around and see what I had intended to see in coming here. The time to leave was approaching, they said. The sun was already setting, and the shadow of the mountain was growing longer and longer. Like a man aroused from sleep, I turned back and looked toward the west. The boundary wall between France and Spain, the ridge of the Pyrenees,

8   Augustine, *Confessions* ii.1.1.   9   Ovid, *Amores* iii.11.35.
10   Cf. Augustine, *Confessions* viii.5; x.22–30.

is not visible from there, though there is no obstacle of which I knew, and nothing but the weakness of the mortal eye is the cause. However, one could see most distinctly the mountains of the province of Lyons to the right and, to the left, the sea near Marseilles as well as the waves that break against Aigues Mortes, although it takes several days to travel to this city. The Rhone River was directly under our eyes.

I admired every detail, now relishing earthly enjoyment, now lifting up my mind to higher spheres after the example of my body, and I thought it fit to look into the volume of Augustine's *Confessions* which I owe to your loving kindness and preserve carefully, keeping it always in my hands, in remembrance of the author as well as the donor. It is a little book of smallest size but full of infinite sweetness. I opened it with the intention of reading whatever might occur to me first: nothing, indeed, but pious and devout sentences could come to hand. I happened to hit upon the tenth book of the work. My brother stood beside me, intently expecting to hear something from Augustine on my mouth. I ask God to be my witness and my brother who was with me: Where I fixed my eyes first, it was written: "And men go to admire the high mountains, the vast floods of the sea, the huge streams of the rivers, the circumference of the ocean, and the revolutions of the stars – and desert themselves."[11] I was stunned, I confess. I bade my brother, who wanted to hear more, not to molest me, and closed the book, angry with myself that I still admired earthly things. Long since I ought to have learned, even from pagan philosophers, that "nothing is admirable besides the mind; compared to its greatness nothing is great."[12]

I was completely satisfied with what I had seen of the mountain and turned my inner eye toward myself. From this hour nobody heard me say a word until we arrived at the bottom. These words occupied me sufficiently. I could not imagine that this had happened to me by chance: I was convinced that whatever I had read there was said to me and to nobody else. I remembered that Augustine once suspected the same regarding himself, when, while he was reading the Apostolic Epistles, the first passage that occurred to him was, as he himself relates: "Not in banqueting and drunkenness, not in chambering and wantonness, not in strife and envying; but put ye on the Lord Jesus Christ, and make no provision for the flesh to fulfil your lusts."[13] The same had happened before to Anthony: he heard the Gospel where it is written: "If thou wilt be perfect, go and sell that thou hast, and give to the poor, and come and follow me, and thou shalt have treasure in heaven."[14] As his biographer Athanasius says, he applied the

11   Augustine, *Confessions* x.8.15.   12   Seneca, *Epistle* 8.5.
13   Rom. 13:13–14, quoted by Augustine, *Confessions* viii.12.29.
14   Matt. 19:21, quoted by Athanasius in his *Life of St. Anthony* (Latin version by Euagrius), chap. 2, and from there by Augustine, *Confessions* viii.12.29.

Lord's command to himself, just as if the Scripture had been recited for his sake. And as Anthony, having heard this, sought nothing else, and as Augustine, having read the other passage, proceeded no further, the end of all my reading was the few words I have already set down. Silently I thought over how greatly mortal men lack counsel who, neglecting the noblest part of themselves in empty parading, look without for what can be found within. I admired the nobility of the mind, had it not voluntarily degenerated and strayed from the primordial state of its origin, converting into disgrace what God had given to be its honor.

How often, do you think, did I turn back and look up to the summit of the mountain today while I was walking down? It seemed to me hardly higher than a cubit compared to the height of human contemplation, were the latter not plunged into the filth of earthly sordidness. This too occurred to me at every step: "If you do not regret undergoing so much sweat and hard labor to lift the body a bit nearer to heaven, ought any cross or jail or torture to frighten the mind that is trying to come nearer to God and set its feet upon the swollen summit of insolence and upon the fate of mortal men?" And this too: "How few will ever succeed in not diverging from this path because of

---

Plate 2 Carpaccio, *St. Augustine in His Study (Vision of St. Augustine)* (1502–7), Scuola di San Giorgio degli Schiavoni, Venice. *Source*: Alinari/Art Resource, NY.

This oil on canvas by the Venetian painter Vittore Carpaccio (1465?–ca. 1525) depicts St. Augustine with what some art historians have identified as the facial characteristics of Cardinal Bessarion, the theologian and Neoplatonic philosopher who gave his collection of Greek books to the city of Venice in 1468 (later, they formed the core collection of the Biblioteca Marciana). Beyond its traditional use to indicate the presence of the divine, the shaft of light (here transfixing both Augustine and his dog) would have a further significance for Renaissance Platonists: in the *Platonic Theology* of Marsilio Ficino, for example, light represents metaphorically the emanations from the mind of God that elucidate our own minds, thereby giving rise to the highest kind of spiritual and intellectual understanding. In this painting, St. Augustine's study resembles a Venetian humanist's *studiolo*: note, for example, the full shelf of books on the left, under which appear various classical artifacts and curiosities, including pottery and bronzes. On the altar in the background is a bronze statue of Christ triumphant: something that the historical Augustine would have viewed as an idolatrous graven image. Yet the combination of these elements – the saint, his books, and selected objects drawn from antiquity – reflects not only contemporary Venetian tastes, but also the Renaissance appropriation of a range of images from the past to form a visual rhetoric that could help inspire piety in the present.[1]

1 Here I follow the interpretation of art historian Alexander Nagel.

fear of hardship or desire for smooth comfort?[15] Too fortunate would be any man who accomplished such a feat – were there ever such anywhere. This would be him of whom I should judge the Poet was thinking when he wrote:

> Happy the man who succeeded in baring the causes of things
> And who trod underfoot all fear, inexorable Fate and
> Greedy Acheron's uproar....[16]

How intensely ought we to exert our strength to get under foot not a higher spot of earth but the passions which are puffed up by earthly instincts."

Such emotions were rousing a storm in my breast as, without perceiving the roughness of the path, I returned late at night to the little rustic inn from which I had set out before dawn. The moon was shining all night long and offered her friendly service to the wanderers. While the servants were busy preparing our meal, I withdrew quite alone into a remote part of the house to write this letter to you in all haste and on the spur of the moment. I was afraid the intention to write might evaporate, since the rapid change of scene was likely to cause a change of mood if I deferred it.

And thus, most loving father, gather from this letter how eager I am to leave nothing whatever in my heart hidden from your eyes. Not only do I lay my whole life open to you with the utmost care but every single thought of mine. Pray for these thoughts, I beseech you, that they may at last find stability. So long have they been idling about and, finding no firm stand, been uselessly driven through so many matters. May they now turn at last to the One, the Good, the True, the stably Abiding.

Farewell.

On the twenty-sixth day of April, at Malaucène.

Two letters to Cicero

Rerum Familiarum XXIV, 3

To Marcus Tullius Cicero.

Francesco sends his greetings to his Cicero. After a lengthy and extensive search for your letters, I found them where I least expected, and I then read

15   Cf. Matt. 7:13–15.
16   Virgil, *Georgica* ii.490–2.

them with great eagerness. I listened to you speak on many subjects, complain about many things, waver in your opinions, O Marcus Tullius, and I who had known the kind of preceptor that you were for others now recognize the kind of guide that you were for yourself. Now it is your turn, wherever you may be, to hearken not to advice but to a lament inspired by true love from one of your descendants who dearly cherishes your name, a lament addressed to you not without tears. O wretched and distressed spirit, or to use your own words, O rash and ill-fated elder, why did you choose to become involved in so many quarrels and utterly useless feuds? Why did you forsake that peaceful ease so befitting a man of your years, your profession, and your fate? What false luster of glory led you, an old man, into wars with the young, and into a series of misfortunes that then brought you to a death unworthy of a philosopher? Alas, forgetful of your brother's advice and of your many wholesome precepts, like a wayfarer at night carrying a lantern before him, you revealed to your followers the path where you yourself stumbled most wretchedly. I make no mention of Dionysius, of your brother or of your nephew, and, if you like, even of Dolabella, all men whom you praise at one moment to the high heavens and at the next rail at with sudden wrath. Perhaps these may be excused. I bypass even Julius Caesar, whose oft-tested clemency proved a haven of refuge for those very men who had assailed him; I likewise refrain from mentioning Pompey the Great, with whom you seemed able to accomplish whatever you liked by right of friendship. But what madness provoked you against Mark Anthony? Love for the Republic, I suppose you would say, but you yourself confessed that it had already collapsed. But if it were pure loyalty, if it were love of liberty that impelled you, why such intimacy with Augustus? What would your answer be to your Brutus who says, "If you are so fond of Octavius, you seem not to have fled a tyrant, but rather to have sought a kindlier one." There still remained your last, lamentable error, O unhappy Cicero: that you should speak ill of the very man whom you had previously praised, not because he was doing you any harm, but merely because he failed to check your enemies. I grieve at your destiny, my dear friend, I am filled with shame and distress at your shortcomings; and so even as did Brutus, "I place no trust in those arts in which you were so proficient." For in truth, what good is there in teaching others, what benefit is there in speaking constantly with the most magnificent words about the virtues, if at the same time you do not give heed to your own words? Oh, how much better it would have been, especially for a philosopher, to have grown old peacefully in the country, meditating, as you write somewhere, on that everlasting life and not on this transitory existence; how much better for you never to have held such offices, never to have yearned for triumphs, never to have had any Catilines to inflate your ego. But these words indeed are all in vain. Farewell forever, my Cicero.

From the land of the living, on the right bank of the Adige, in the city of Verona in transpadane Italy, on 16 June in the year 1345 from the birth of that Lord whom you never knew.

Rerum Familiarum XXIV, 4

To the same correspondent.

Francesco sends his greetings to his Cicero. I hope that my previous letter did not offend you; for as you are wont to say, there is truth in what your contemporary says in the *Andria*: "Indulgence begets friends, truth only hatred." Accept then what may somewhat soothe your wounded feelings so that the truth may not always seem hateful; if we are irritated by true criticism, we rejoice in true praise. Allow me to say, O Cicero, that you lived as a man, you spoke as an orator, you wrote as a philosopher; and it was your life that I censured, not your intellect and your tongue since I admire the former and am astounded by the latter. Moreover, nothing was lacking but constancy in your personal life, a desire for the tranquillity necessary for the practice of philosophy, and withdrawal from civil strife, once liberty was spent and the Republic buried and mourned. Note how different is my treatment of you than yours of Epicurus throughout your works, but especially in the *De finibus*, where you approve of his life and ridicule his intellect. I do not ridicule you at all; I pity only your life, as I said, and applaud your talent and your eloquence. O great father of Roman eloquence, not I alone but all who bedeck themselves with the flowers of Latin speech are grateful to you; for it is with the waters from your wellsprings that we irrigate our fields, frankly admitting that we are sustained by your leadership, aided by your judgments, and enlightened by your radiance. In a word, under your auspices, so to speak, we have achieved whatever writing skills and principles we possess. In the realm of poetry we followed another master since necessarily we had to follow one supreme guide in the unencumbered ways of prose and another in the more restricted paths of poetry; we were moved to admire one who spoke and one who sang since, and I beg the indulgence of you both, neither of you could serve both purposes; in your waters he was unequal to you, and you to him in his measured flow. Possibly I would not have ventured to say this first, however much I felt it, but before me the great Anneus Seneca from Cordova said it, or borrowed it from someone else. He laments that the obstacle to his knowing you was not your ages but the fury of civil strife; he could have met you but never did, yet he was always an admirer of your works and those of that other writer. According to him, then, each of you is confined to his own realm of eloquence and is bidden to yield to his colleague in all else. But I am keeping you too long in suspense: you would like to know who the other master is. You know him; you must remember his name: it is Publius Virgilius Maro, a citizen of Mantua, about whom you prophesied great things. For we read that, struck by one of his youthful works, you sought the author's name; you, already advanced in years, saw him while he was still young, and expressed your delight with him, rendering a judgment from the inexhaustible fount of eloquence, which, though mingled with self-praise, was truly honorable and splendid for him: for you called him "the second hope of great Rome." At your words, he was so pleased and committed them so deeply to memory that twenty years later, after your earthly journey had long since ended, he inserted your very words into his divine poem. Had it been given to you to see the work, you would have rejoiced at discerning from the first blossom the promise of the real fruit to come; what is more, you would have congratulated the Latin Muses either for having left a doubtful superiority to the insolent Greek Muses or for having won a decisive victory. There are defenders of both these opinions; and if I have come to know your mind from your works, which I do seem to know as though I had lived with you, your choice will be the latter, and as you gave primacy in oratory to Latium, so would you give it the poetic palm. Doubtless you would have ordered the *Iliad* to yield to the *Aeneid*, something that Propertius did not fear to affirm from the very beginning of Virgil's labors. For in his work on the fundamentals of poetry, he openly declared his feelings and hope for those works in these verses: "Yield, O Roman authors, yield, O Greeks; something greater than the *Iliad* is born." So much for the other master of Latin literature, the other hope of great Rome; now I return to you.

You have heard my opinions about your life and your talent. Do you also wish to hear about your books, how fortune has treated them and how the public and scholars view them? Some splendid volumes still exist that I can hardly list, much less peruse with care; moreover, your works enjoy an immense reputation and your name is on everyone's lips, but rare are those who study you, whether because the times are unfavorable or men's minds dull and sluggish, or, as I think more likely, because greed has bent their minds to other pursuits. Thus, some of your books, I suspect, are lost for us who still live, and I know not whether they will ever be recovered: how great is my grief, how great a shame for our times, how great a wrong to posterity! It was not degrading enough to neglect our own intellects to the detriment of the following age, but we had to destroy the fruit even of your labor with our cruel and unpardonable negligence. What I am deploring with respect to your works has also happened to many works of other illustrious authors. But since at present I am dealing only with yours, here are the titles of those whose loss is most to be deplored: *De republica, De re familiari, De re militari, De laude philosophie, De consolatione,* and *De gloria,* although my feeling is one of faint hope for the last ones rather than total despair. And furthermore, even of the surviving books, large portions are missing; it is as though after winning a great battle against oblivion and sloth, we now had to mourn our leaders, and not only those who had been killed but those who had been maimed or lost. This we deplore in many of your works, but particularly in *De oratore*, the *Academica*, and *De legibus*, all of which have reached us in such fragmentary and mutilated condition that it would perhaps have been better for them to have perished.

In conclusion, you will wish to know about the condition of Rome and of the Roman state, as well as the appearance of your homeland, the degree of harmony among its citizenry, to whom power has been entrusted, and by whose hands and with what wisdom the reins of government are held; also whether the Danube, the Ganges, the Ebro, the Nile, the Don are still our boundaries, or whether in the words of your Mantuan poet, someone has arisen "whose empire shall reach to the ocean's limits, whose fame shall end in the stars," or "whose empire shall expand beyond the Garamants and Indians." I surmise that you are most eager to hear these and similar tidings, owing to your patriotism and your love of country, which led to your death. But it is truly better to pass over such subjects in silence, for believe me, O Cicero, were you to learn your country's condition, you would weep bitter tears, wherever in heaven or in Erebus your lodging may be. Farewell forever.

From the land of the living, on the left bank of the Rhone, in transalpine Gaul, in the same year, on 19 December.

Il Canzoniere

I

    O you that hear in scattered rhymes the sound
Of those sighs that I used to feed my heart
In my first youthful error, when I was
In part a different man than now I am,
    Whoever knows of love by trial, from him   5
If pardon none, compassion then I hope
To find, for this the various style in which
I weep, debate these vain hopes, this vain woe.
    Now I see clearly how to everyone
I long have been a fable, and of that   10
Deep in myself I often am ashamed;
    Shame is the fruit of my delirium;
As is repentance, and the knowledge sure
That worldly joy is but a passing dream.

2

To make a graceful one his fit revenge
And punish in one day a thousand crimes,
Love stealthily took up his bow again
Like one who waits his time and place to harm.
 My Virtue massed her forces in my heart   5
To raise defenses there, and in my eyes,
When suddenly the mortal arrow fell
Where she had always blunted every shot;
 Plunged into turmoil at this first assault
She had not time nor strength enough to seize   10
Weapons with power sufficient to her need,
 Nor to ascend her high and weary hill
And wisely lead me out of that affray
Whence she today would save me, but cannot.

3

It was the day on which the sun's rays paled
At their Creator's passion when, off guard,
All unaware, I taken was and bound,
Tied fast, my lady, by your lovely eyes.
 No need in such a season, so I thought,   5
To frame defence against Love's battery;
Thus, unsuspecting and secure I walked,
When 'midst the common sorrow came my woe.
 Love found me out, defenceless, all disarmed,
Found open wide the way from eyes to heart   10
Through gaps and crazings channeled there by tears;
 No honor, though, to him, or so it seems,
To wound me in that state with passion's dart
And never show the bow to you, all armed.

4

He who with infinite providence and art
Revealed the wondrous mastery of his work,
Who shaped this, and that other hemisphere
And framed more gentle Jupiter than Mars,
 To earth came, to illuminate the leaves   5
That had for ages past concealed the truth,
And John and Peter from their nets he took

And made them citizens of heaven's realm.
    Not on proud Rome but on Judea, God
Pleased ever to exalt humility,   10
The grace of his nativity conferred,
    And now a small town gives to us a sun,
And one that blesses nature and the place
That brought so fair a lady forth on earth.

5

    When I breathe forth my sighs to call on you,
And sound that name which Love wrote in my heart,
Outside, one starts to hear the notes of LAUd,
First accents of a swelling music sweet.
    Your REgal state which I encounter then,   5
Doubles my prowess for the lofty task;
But "sTAy," the end cries out, "to honor her
Must burden shoulders worthier than yours."
    Thus does the word itself instruct those who
Invoke your name, to LAUd and to REvere,   10
O worthy of all reverence, honor's prize;
    Only Apollo himself, perhaps, disdains
Whatever rash, presuming, morTAl tongue
Bespeaks his laurel branches, always green.

30

    A youthful lady under a green laurel
I saw once, whiter and more cold than snow
Untouched by sun for many, many years;
I liked her speech, fair features, and her hair
So much that I keep her before my eyes –   5
And ever shall, though I'm on hill or shore.
    And thus my thoughts will stay along the shore,
Where no green leaf is found upon the laurel;
When I have stilled my heart and dried my eyes,
We'll see fire freeze and into flame burst snow;   10
I don't have strands as many in this hair
As, waiting for that day, there would be years.
    Because time flies, however, and since years
Soon flee until one fetches on death's shore –
Whether with locks of brown or with white hair –   15
I'll follow still the shade of that sweet laurel
Through the most parching sun and through the snow

Until the final day shall close these eyes.
   Never before were seen such lovely eyes
Not in our age nor in man's pristine years;   20
They make me melt just as the sun does snow,
From whence a tearful river floods the shore –
Love leads it to the foot of that hard laurel
Whose branches are of diamond, gold its hair.
   I fear the changing of my face and hair   25
Before, with pity true, she shows her eyes –
My idol, sculpted in the living laurel;
For if my count errs not, it's seven years
Today that I have sighed from shore to shore
By night and day, in heat and in the snow.   30
   Still fire within, though outside whitest snow
With these thoughts only, though with altered hair,
Ever in tears, I'll wander every shore,
Perhaps creating pity in the eyes
Of persons born from hence a thousand years –   35
If, tended well, so long can live a laurel.
   In sun, the gold and topaz on the snow
Are conquered by blond hair close by those eyes
That lead my years so swiftly towards the shore.

189

   My vessel, with oblivion awash,
Drives on in winter midnight through rough seas
Twixt Scylla and Charybdis; sitting at
Its helm, my lord – indeed, my enemy.
   At each oar sits an urgent, wicked thought   5
That seems to sneer both at the tempest and
Its end; a damp, unceasing wind of sighs,
Of hopes and of desires now splits the sail.
   A rain of tears, a thick fog of contempt
Soak through and slacken shrouds already strained –   10
They're formed from error spliced with ignorance.
   My two accustomed lodestars sweet concealed,
And Art and Reason dead amidst the waves,
Whence I begin to lose all hope of port.

272

    Life flees and will not be delayed an hour,
And, by forced marches, Death pursues apace,
And present deeds, and matters past, as well
As what's to come – all these make war on me!
    And it afflicts me to remember them –   5
And wait for them, first here, then there, so that
In truth, if piety did not prevent,
Beyond these cares I would already be.
    If something sweet my wretched heart once had
Comes to my mind, then on the other hand   10
My sailing winds become tumultuous,
    I see a storm in harbor, and by now
My pilot's wearied, split my masts and sails,
And those fair lights I steered for are snuffed out.

365

    I wander weeping for my vanished hours,
For time spent loving a mere mortal thing,
Not rising up to fly, though I had wings
To give no base accounting of myself.
    And you who see my vile and impious deeds,   5
Invisible, immortal King of Heaven,
Bring succor to my frail and wayward soul,
And remedy its defect, by your grace.
    Thus, though I lived in tempest and at war,
May I yet die in harbor and at peace;   10
Though vain my stay, in virtue let me pass.
    In that small scrap of life that I have left,
And at my death, vouchsafe Your ready hand;
In others, well you know, I have no hope.

3

Leonardo Bruni (ca. 1370–1444)

Bruni is most famous today as the originator of "civic humanism," in which Florentine humanists applied their skills and learning to politics. Thus Bruni and his followers praised and dignified Florence as having a special historic role as rightful heir of the ancient Roman Republic. Originally from Arezzo, in his early twenties Bruni went to study law in Florence. There he became active as well in the informal literary discussions presided over by the city's chancellor, the humanist Coluccio Salutati (d. 1406). Starting in 1405, Bruni spent nearly a decade in Rome as a papal secretary, but then returned to Florence, where he began work on his monumental *Histories of the Florentine People*. Renowned both as an historian and as a translator of Greek classics (including orations of Demosthenes and dialogues of Plato) into elegant Ciceronian Latin, Bruni also served as chancellor of Florence (1427–44), overseeing the city's public correspondence through a period that saw the establishment of unofficial Medici control of the city after Cosimo de' Medici's return from exile in 1434. The *Life of Petrarch* (1436) ranks among his best-known works.

Questions

1 Bruni portrays Petrarch as the literary successor of Dante, and as the predecessor of Boccaccio. What does he identify as Petrarch's particular strengths as a writer?
2 While Bruni believed that ideal Latin style was perfect and unchanging, he outlines the use and abuse of the language over time, from

classical Rome to Renaissance Florence. Make a chart of his history of
Latin-writing. What are the high and low points, and how does he
explain why they occurred when they did?
3   According to Bruni, Petrarch "opened the way" to the recovery of the
perfect eloquence of antiquity. How did he do that? And, what implications might this claim have for Bruni and other humanists of his
generation?

Life of Petrarch

Francesco Petrarca, a man of great genius and no less virtue, was born at
Arezzo in the Borgo dell'Orto, shortly before sunrise on the twenty-first of July,
1304. The name of his father was Petracolo; his grandfather was named
Parenzo; they were originally from Ancisa. Petracolo, the father, lived in
Florence and was very active in the Republic: he was sent out as an ambassador of the city on many very serious occasions, often he was employed with
other duties of great importance, and in the court he was for a time a scribe of
the Riformagioni.[1] He was a worthy man, active and quite prudent.

In that disaster suffered by the Florentine citizenry, when there came the
division between White and Black [Guelfs], this man was believed to sympa-
thize with the White party and consequently was driven from Florence along
with the others. Thus he was reduced to living in Arezzo where he stayed,
vigorously aiding his party and his faction according to his hope of returning
home. Then when his hopes lessened, he left Arezzo and went to the Roman
court, which was newly transferred in those times to Avignon. In the court
he was well employed with considerable honor and income. There he
brought up two sons, one named Gherardo and the other Checco, who was
then called Petrarca as we shall observe in this biography.

Petrarca, then, was raised at Avignon and as he began to grow up he
showed a gravity of manner and high intellect. He was very attractive in
appearance, and his handsomeness lasted throughout his life. After learning
letters and finishing his first childhood studies, he gave himself over to the
study of civil law, according to the orders of his father. In these studies he
persevered several years, but he considered this material too low for his
aptitude, for his nature was drawn to higher things and did not much esteem
the law and litigation. Secretly he directed all his study to Cicero, to Virgil

1   Part of the Florentine government.

and Seneca, to Lactantius and to other philosophers, poets and historians. He was already set to write prose, ready for sonnets and edifying canzoni; gentle and gracious in all his speech, he despised the law and its tedious and gross explanatory glossing. He did not pursue the law, and even if the law had pursued him, he would not have accepted it, had his reverence for his father not held him to it.

After the death of his father he became his own master and dedicated himself openly and entirely to those studies of which he had earlier been a disciple in secret for fear of his father. Quickly his fame began to spread; he came to be called not Francesco Petracchi, but Francesco Petrarca, his name made greater out of respect for his virtues. He had such grace of intellect that he was the first to bring back into the light of understanding the sublime studies, so long fallen and ignored. Having grown since then, they have reached their present heights, of which I want to tell briefly. So that I may be better understood, I would like to turn to earlier times.

The Latin tongue and its perfections and greatness flourished most at the time of Cicero, for previously it was neither polished nor precise nor refined; but its perfection increased slowly until at the time of Cicero it reached its summit. After the age of Cicero it began to fall, and sank as in his time it had risen; not many years passed before it had suffered a very great decadence and diminution. It can be said that letters and the study of Latin went hand in hand with the state of the Roman Republic, since it increased until the age of Cicero; and then after the Roman people lost their liberty in the rule of the emperors, who did not even stop at killing and ruining highly regarded men, the good disposition of studies and letters perished together with the good state of the city of Rome. Octavian, who was the least fierce of the emperors, killed thousands of Roman citizens; Tiberius and Caligula and Claudius and Nero left not one who had the appearance of a man. Then followed Galba and Otho and Vitellius, who in a few months undid one another. After these there were no emperors of Roman blood, for the land was so devastated by the preceding emperors that no man of worth remained. Vespasian, who was emperor after vitellius, was from Rieti and so too were Titus and Domitian his sons; the emperor Nerva was from Narni, his adopted son Trajan from Spain; Hadrian too was Spanish, Severus from Africa, Alexander from Asia, Probus from Hungary, Diocletian from Slavonia and Constantine from England. Why do I bother with this? Only to show that as the city of Rome was devastated by perverse tyrannical emperors, so Latin studies and letters suffered a similar destruction and diminution, so that at the last hardly anyone could be found who knew Latin with the least sense of style. And there came over into Italy the Goths and the Lombards, barbarous and foreign nations who in fact almost extinguished all understanding of letters, as appears in the documents drawn up and circulated in those times; for one could find no writing more prosaic or more gross and coarse.

When the Lombards, who had occupied Italy for 240 years, were chased out and the Italian people thus recovered their liberty, the Tuscan cities and others began to recuperate.[2] They devoted work to studies and began to polish their coarse style somewhat. Thus little by little they regained their vigor, although they were weak and lacked real judgment for any fine style, since they paid attention mainly to vernacular rhyme. In this way until the time of Dante few knew the literate style and those few knew it rather poorly, as we said in the *Life of Dante*.

Francesco Petrarca was the first with a talent sufficient to recognize and call back to light the antique elegance of the lost and extinguished style. Admitted it was not perfect in him, yet it was he by himself who saw and opened the way to its perfection, for he rediscovered the works of Cicero, savored and understood them; he adapted himself as much as he could and as much as he knew how to that most elegant and perfect eloquence. Surely he did enough just in showing the way to those who followed it after him. Having given himself to these studies and thus showing his virtue, Petrarca was much honored and favored while still young, and was called by the Pope to be secretary of his court; but Petrarca never agreed, nor did he value money. Nevertheless, so that he could lead an honorable life with leisure, he accepted benefices and became a regular cleric; he did this not so much by his own choice as constrained to it by necessity, for little or nothing remained from his father, and in marrying off his sister almost all the paternal inheritance was spent. Gherardo his brother became a Carthusian monk and persevered in that order to the end of his life.

Petrarca's honors were so great that no man of his age was more highly thought of, not only beyond the mountains but also here in Italy; having gone to Rome, he was solemnly crowned poet. He wrote in one of his own epistles that he came to Rome for the Jubilee in 1350. Returning from Rome, he took his way to Arezzo in order to see the place where he was born; the citizens had heard of his arrival and came out to meet him, as if a king had come to visit. The fame and honor attributed to him by every city and province and by all the people throughout Italy were so great that it seemed an incredible miracle. Not only the citizens and the farmers, but also the noble and great princes and lords, sought and honored him and made extraordinary provisions for his welcome. For with Prince Galeazzo Visconti he resided some time, having been asked most graciously to deign to stay with him; similarly, he was honored by the lord of Padua; and his reputation and the respect offered him by those gentlemen was so great that there were often great disputes whether to send him along in his journey, or to send him to some place and favor him with more honors. Thus Petrarca lived honored and esteemed to the end of his life.

2   The Lombard rule of Italy ended in AD 800 with the coming of Charlemagne.

In his studies, Petrarca had one particular gift: he was very much suited to both prose and verse, and he wrote a good deal in each. His prose is graceful and elegant, his verse polished and finished and elevated in style. This gift for both the one and the other has been found in few if any but in him, for it seems that natural talent tends toward one or the other, and man usually gives himself over to that one which has the natural advantage. So it happens that Virgil, most excellent in verse, wrote or is worth nothing in prose; Cicero, grand master of prose, is worth nothing in verse. We see the same in other poets and orators, that one of the two styles has been their source of excelling praise; but I remember having read none of them in both. Petrarca alone has been excellent in the one and the other style, through his singular gift; and he composed many works in prose and in verse, which there is no reason to enumerate, for they are known.

Petrarca died in Arquà, a village in the province of Padua, where he had chosen to live in his old age, retiring to a quiet and leisurely life separated from all complications. While he lived he kept up a very close friendship with Giovanni Boccaccio, who at that time was famous for the same studies as Petrarca; so it came about that with the death of Petrarca, the Florentine Muses became the property of Boccaccio, as if by hereditary succession; and in him then resided the fame of the previously discarded studies. It was also a succession in time, since when Dante died Petrarca was seventeen years old, and when Petrarca died Boccaccio was nine years younger than he. Thus go the Muses by succession.

Part II
The Limits of Intra-Italian Statecraft

Introduction to Part II

Shortly before the Peace of Lodi (1454) established a tenuous balance of power among territorial states in the Italian peninsula, the Byzantine capital city, Constantinople, fell to the Ottoman Turks, an event suggesting the inherent limitations of purely local political solutions. In subsequent decades, the Turks advanced into eastern Europe, adding to their empire Serbia (1459), Bosnia (1463), and Herzegovina (1482). The Turkish conquest in 1480 of Otranto, a town on the seacoast of the Kingdom of Naples, brought home to the Italians the reality of the threat. Under Süleyman I "The Magnificent" (ca. 1495–1566), the Turks continued their expansion, yet repeated papal attempts failed to unite Christian princes against the threat.

In the meantime, the newly formed nation-states of western Europe emerged as a more immediate danger to Italian autonomy. Beginning with the French invasion of 1494, the peninsula became once again an object of northern European dynastic ambitions, and in the early decades of the sixteenth century France and Spain fought for control over it. By 1530, the year that Charles V (who was also king of Spain and of Naples) was officially crowned Holy Roman Emperor in Bologna, Spain had become dominant on the Italian peninsula. But when Machiavelli wrote *The Prince*, the outcome of the Italian wars was still far from clear, and he wrote in the hope that somehow the *libertà d'Italia* – the political autonomy of the Italians – could be asserted successfully in the face of foreign encroachments.

4

Pope Pius II (Aeneas Silvius Piccolomini, 1405–1464)

From a poor but noble Sienese family, Piccolomini gained distinction in the 1430s and 1440s for his service as a Latin secretary and diplomatic envoy on behalf of prominent churchmen. Starting in 1442 he worked in the chancery of the ruler of Austria, Frederick III. A polished and effective advocate of his employers' interests, he was also skilled in humanistic studies, and his writings in classical Latin genres included a widely circulated novella, *The Tale of Two Lovers* (1444). Following his appointment as bishop of Trieste in 1447, he rose rapidly in the hierarchy: after being transferred to the bishopric of Siena (1450), he was created cardinal (1456), and finally elected to succeed Pope Calixtus III (d. 1458). Like his predecessor, Pope Pius II sought above all to organize a Crusade against the Ottoman Turks, whose conquest of the Byzantine capital Constantinople in 1453 had been followed by rapid expansion into the Balkans. But none of his efforts to unite Italian and European princes in a Crusade issued in success. He died in 1464 in Ancona, where he had assembled a fleet that he himself intended to lead into battle against the Turks.

In his *Commentaries*, Pius writes of his own career and accomplishments. While obviously not an objective account, the *Commentaries* contain much important detail about mid-fifteenth-century Italian politics. In addition, they can tell us something about the goals and aspirations of Renaissance popes, including how they wished to be remembered. In the selection below, Pius, writing about himself in the third person, tells us how he formally received in Rome the relic of the head of St. Andrew (brother of St. Peter) in Holy Week of 1462.

Questions

1 Why is Pius II so eager to get the relic of Andrew's head? What is the symbolic significance of the relic? What spiritual benefits might it bestow? What political benefits?
2 How does Pius make use of the themes of exile and of a journey (or pilgrimage)?
3 For what reasons does Pius urge his listeners to make war on the Turks? How does he justify the war? How is Andrew supposed to help the cause? And, who is supposed to lead the Christian offensive?
4 Why is the magnificence of the procession route so important? What significance might there be to the fact that the procession ends at St. Peter's basilica rather than at St. John Lateran, the official center of western Christendom? Why does Cardinal Bessarion have such an important role?

Commentaries VIII

Andrew, Apostle of Jesus Christ, brother of St. Peter, after the passion of our Lord, at which he was present, and His resurrection and ascension into heaven, of which he was witness, having received together with the other disciples the Holy Ghost, crossed from Asia into Greece and betook himself to Achaia (now called Morea), a province of the Peloponnese, where it had fallen to his lot to preach. And whereas, when he left his ship and abandoned his nets for the Lord, he had received the promise that he should be a fisher of men, he was not disappointed, for he became a great preacher and teacher of the truth and with the hook of his eloquence caught countless men whom he won for Christ. Furthermore the province under his teaching accepted the holy tenets of our religion: it recognized Christ, the Son of God, together with the Father and the Holy Ghost to be one God; it worshipped the Holy Trinity. The holy Apostle himself, when already worn out with age, was crucified under the proconsul Egeus in Patras and received the same crown of martyrdom as his brother Peter and his master, Jesus Christ. Therefore, when he stood by the Cross and had greeted it most lovingly, he said, "Receive the disciple of Jesus Christ who hung on thee."

Plate 3   *Detail, Tomb of Pius II, now in the Church of Sant' Andrea della Valle, Rome, perhaps begun by Paolo Taccone and completed by a follower of Andrea Bregno (ca. 1465). Source: Alinari.*
This detail, from a marble relief on the tomb of Pope Pius II (r. 1458–64), was commissioned by his nephew, Francesco Todeschini Piccolomini (later Pope Pius III, r. 1503). At visual center is the reliquary containing the head of St. Andrew (the brother of St. Peter), which Pius II, standing just to the right of the altar, holds above it. The bearded figure immediately to the left of the altar is Cardinal Bessarion, who has just carried the relic onto the raised wooden platform that had been constructed specifically for this ceremony, which took place in a meadow just outside Rome. Afterwards, Pius would carry the reliquary at the head of a procession into the city, stopping first at the Church of Santa Maria del Popolo, just inside the city gates.

Andrew's head had great symbolic significance: here was a relic from a shrine in the Eastern (as opposed to the Roman) Church. As the Turks continued their westward expansion into Greece, the despot Thomas Paleologus (represented here at far right) fled to Italy, taking with him Andrew's head, which had been enshrined in Patras. Thus he both saved the relic from possible desecration by the Turks and helped to ensure his own soft landing in the West. Pope Pius II, sensing the potential significance of this relic for his planned Crusade against the Turks, remunerated Thomas Paleologus and arranged for its ceremonial reception in Rome. On Monday of Holy Week in 1462, the pope met the procession just outside Rome, and welcomed Andrew to the city where his brother Peter had been martyred. The following day, Pius carried the reliquary in a procession to the basilica of St. Peter (that is, the "old" St. Peter's), where he placed it upon the high altar, calling once again for a Crusade against the Turks.

Andrew was illustrious both during his life and after his death, for many miracles, which are related in his biography. His body was embalmed with spices and buried by a pious woman named Maximilla, but long afterward it was removed to Italy and buried in the city of Amalfi, which was made a metropolitan out of reverence for him. His tomb is famed for the magnificence of its workmanship and the throngs that visit it. His head however remained at Patras, where it was closely guarded with the utmost veneration till 1460, when it was transferred in the following manner.

When the Turks invaded the Peloponnese, two tyrants were ruling there. They were Thomas and Demetrius, brothers of the Greek Emperor Constantine, who had been killed shortly before in the fall of Constantinople. Demetrius, the elder, when he found he could get no adequate help from Christians, went over to the Turks and received possessions elsewhere which would afford him the means of livelihood. But Thomas, the younger, who was regarded as the heir to the throne, could not be induced to submit to those who had murdered his brother, robbed the Greeks of their empire, and defiled Christian altars. Since he realized that he was no match for the might of the Turks and saw no hope of assistance, he decided to leave the Peloponnese, a large part of which had been surrendered by Demetrius and was in the hands of the Turks. But before he left he went to Patras, which was still his, and from the sanctuary, of which he himself was the keeper, he took the most precious head of St. Andrew, the Apostle. Then with his wife and children and many Greek nobles he took refuge with the despot of Arta on the island of Santa Maura off the coast of Epirus, for he thought so precious a treasure ought not to be abandoned to the enemy (though indeed they would have trampled it like rubbish). He saw to it that God's saint should not be thrown to the dogs and he thought too that his own journey would be more prosperous if the Apostle went with him. Thus he came safely to his royal kinsman, with whom he stayed for some time, guarding the sacred head as closely as he did his wife and children.

Meantime many Christian princes, both in Italy and beyond the Alps, hearing that the Apostle's head had been taken out of Greece, sent ambassadors to Thomas to offer large sums for the holy relic. When Pope Pius heard of it he was indeed distressed to think that so sacred a head should be an exile, but now that it had actually been driven from its abode and could not easily be restored, he thought there was no more fitting asylum for it than beside the bones of its brother, St. Peter, Prince of the Apostles, and in the Apostolic See, the citadel of the Faith, the safe refuge for all who are driven from their own churches. Therefore he too sent envoys to Thomas to say that he had acted piously in removing the most precious head of the Apostle from a city that was on the point of falling into the hands of an infidel foe and thus saving it from destruction. He would however be acting impiously and cruelly if he surrendered it to any but the Pope, whose prerogative it was to decide on the honors paid the saints, and if he desired it to rest elsewhere than with the bones of its brother at Rome. He must bring it to Rome himself. Someday, God willing, it would come about that with the help of its brother it would be restored to its own throne. Thomas must not trust so sacred an object to anyone without the Pope's orders, unless he wished to incur the anger of the Apostles. He need not plead poverty as an excuse, for if he would come to live at Rome, he should be maintained in the style befitting a prince.

The despot was persuaded by the Pope's words and promised to set sail for Ancona with the sacred pledge. He kept his word and in 1461 he landed at Ancona, having escaped unhurt (with the Apostle's help, we may well believe) from the violent and terrific gales which that year more than usual lashed the Adriatic and sank innumerable ships.

Pius when he heard of Thomas's arrival, sent Alessandro, Cardinal presbyter of Santa Susanna, a man celebrated for his holiness and learning, as his legate. If he recognized the relic of the holy Apostle, he was to take it from the hands of the despot and with the ceremony and reverence due to so sacred an object carry it to Narni and deposit it in the citadel, where it was to be guarded by the commandant till it could be brought to Rome with fitting rites and honors. (This was impossible at that time because of the fierce war which the tyrants about Rome had declared on the Pope.)

Alessandro went to Ancona and after carefully examining the head and recognizing its distinguishing marks, pronounced it to be the genuine head of the Apostle and did it reverence. He then received it from the despot and after giving Thomas sufficient funds for his journey to the Curia, he carried it with a splendid escort in solemn procession with many tapers to the citadel of Narni, where he entrusted it under seal to the commandant. Here it was kept for some time in due honor with lamps always burning before it.

Several months later, when the Pope's campaign had succeeded, when peace was restored in the territory of Rome and the people round about were enjoying security and rest, when the clash of arms was no longer heard, the Pope decided to send for the sacred head. Since the more people were present the more magnificent would be its welcome, he promised plenary remission of sins to those who came to Rome for its entrance or took part in its reception. A proclamation to this effect was sent to the chief cities of Italy naming the day when the head would come. When this was at hand he chose three cardinals: Bessarion,[1] Bishop of Tusculum, a Greek at home in both languages and a man of high repute; Alessandro, mentioned above; Francesco, administrator of the church of Siena, the son of his sister Laodamia and his nephew after the flesh. These he directed to go to Narni and bring away the sacred pledge deposited there.

Meantime at Rome all the preparations were made that were thought fitting for the solemn and magnificent reception of the holy Apostle. The Pope was afraid of seeming niggardly in the honors paid to so great an

1   As Bishop of Nicaea, the Greek scholar and theologian Bessarion (1403?–1472) represented the Greek Church at the Council of Ferrara-Florence (1438–9). A strong advocate of union, he was created cardinal of the Roman Church in 1439, and after 1440 he never returned to Greece. Bessarion actively promoted the study of the philosophy and theology of the Greek east, and after 1453 he argued strongly for a Crusade against the Turks.

Apostle and thought nothing good enough. He intended to carry out to meet him the glorious heads of the Apostles Peter and Paul, which are buried in the Church of St. John in the Lateran, and with them to greet the sacred head of Andrew outside the city. This however proved to be impossible because of the mass of silver in which the heads are imbedded. It is said to weigh more than 4,000 pounds and there is besides a great quantity of iron, which could neither be broken away without great inconvenience nor carried with them. The idea of carrying out the heads was therefore abandoned and orders were given that on the afternoons of the days when the head of St. Andrew was carried through the city in the morning the heads of the Apostles should be exhibited publicly in the Lateran, a ceremony which each time was attended by large crowds.

When the cardinals sent to Narni arrived there, after having recognized the distinguishing marks, they did reverence to the sacred bones and taking them up with emotion and profoundest veneration, carried them as far as the Ponte Molle on Palm Sunday, April 12, 1462. All along the way they were greeted by countless throngs praising God and commending themselves to the Apostle Andrew. Two miles from Rome they deposited the venerable relic in the tower on the bridge for safekeeping during the night. Two archbishops, Perotti of Manfredonia and Alexis of Benevento, were left on guard.

On the same day the Pope, after celebrating according to ancient custom the feast of Palms at St. Peter's in the Apostolic palace, decided to go in the afternoon with the holy senate of cardinals and all the clergy to the church of Santa Maria del Popolo, where he planned to pass the night, that he might start out the next morning to meet the sacred head; for the church is close to the Porta Flaminia on the road that leads to the Ponte Molle across the Tiber. He was however disturbed by fear of rain, which seemed imminent. Clouds had obscured the sky, lightning flashed all around, claps of thunder were heard from every direction, and there seemed no prospect of clearing. For many days before this the weather had been wet and cloudy, but now it looked more threatening than ever and a terrible storm seemed to be brewing. Winds from all directions were driving clouds toward Rome and no one thought he could make the trip without being caught in drenching rain. But (marvelous to relate!) great Andrew kept his own fair weather and did not suffer rain to interfere with the clergy's coming to do him honor. Though it had poured for whole days and nights that month, yet during the time that the sacred head was on the way and the Pope was going to meet it not a drop of water fell on the ground where they had to pass and all that flood of gathering rain that had seemed likely to prevent the Pope's progress held off till evening, so that he walked dryshod. A rainy night however made them despair of carrying out the ceremonies planned for the next day and it was thought they would have to be postponed. But at dawn the rain ceased and the sun shining brightly on the earth seemed to invite them to proceed.

At once the three cardinals, who had left the sacred head at the Ponte Molle, went back to get it and escorted it in procession to the city.

Near the Ponte Molle on the left as you approach Rome are broad meadows, which were then covered with grass and flowers and so gay that they seemed to be laughing. In the middle of them the Pope had ordered a wooden tribune to be constructed large and strong enough to hold all the clergy present and high enough for all in the meadows to see clearly what took place upon it. In the center was set up a high altar.

Soon after the three cardinals had been sent ahead (as has been mentioned above) the Pope himself with the rest of the senate, all the clergy, the ambassadors of princes, the nobles of the city, and a great throng of the populace passed through the Porta Flaminia carrying a palm branch, as did the cardinals likewise. The other prelates carried the palms given them the day before by the Pope himself in memory of the Savior. The whole road was thronged with people; the fields and vineyards could not be seen because of the crowds that swarmed everywhere. As soon as they reached the meadows mentioned above the Pope ordered the cardinals and prelates to dismount and after putting on their sacred robes and priestly ornaments to walk the distance of a bowshot and ascend the platform with him. The robes of all the priests were white, as were their miters and all their vestments, and in the green meadow they seemed to gleam even whiter. All were spellbound by the marvelous dignity and solemnity of the procession of so many priests carrying palms in their hands and offering prayers to God as they advanced through the meadows two by two with slow steps and grave faces, the Pope in their midst and the populace standing about.

The platform was approached by two flights of easy stairs, one opposite the Ponte Molle, the other toward the city. While the Pope followed by the sacred college and all the clergy ascended the latter with tears of joy and adoration, Bessarion with two other cardinals mounted the former. He carried a reliquary containing the sacred head, which he deposited on the center of the altar while a chorus intoned hymns. Then amid profound silence the keys were brought and when the seals had been recognized, the casket was opened. Bessarion in tears, taking the sacred head of the Apostle, offered it to the weeping Pope. But the Pope himself, before touching the holy bones, knelt at the altar and with pale and downcast face and streaming eyes said in a tremulous voice:

"Thou hast come at last, most sacred and adored head of the holy Apostle. The fury of the Turks has expelled thee from thine own abode. In exile thou hast come for asylum to thy brother, Prince of the Apostles. Thy brother will not fail thee. God willing, thou shalt be restored to thy throne with glory. Some day thou shalt say, 'O happy exile where such aid was found!' Meanwhile thou shalt tarry a space with thy brother and shalt enjoy like honor with him. This city thou seest close at hand is mother Rome, hallowed by thy brother's precious blood. To this people standing here thy most loving brother, St. Peter the Apostle, and with him the chosen vessel, St. Paul, gave a new birth in Christ the Lord. The Romans are thy nephews through thy brother. They all revere, honor, and worship thee as their uncle and their father and they doubt not that they enjoy thy advocacy in the sight of Almighty God.

"O most blessed St. Andrew, preacher of the truth, great champion of the Trinity, with what joy thou dost fill us today, while we behold thy sacred and venerable head, the head of thee who was found worthy that the Holy Ghost in the guise of fire should alight upon thee on the day of Pentecost! O ye who journey to Jerusalem out of reverence for the Savior, to see the places His feet have trod, behold the abode of the Holy Ghost, the throne of divinity! Here, here the Spirit of God alighted, here the Third Person of the Trinity was made visible, here were the eyes that often beheld God in the flesh. This mouth often spoke to Christ, these cheeks surely Jesus often kissed. Behold a mighty shrine! Behold love and piety and sweetness of soul and consolation of the spirit! Who is there who is not stirred to the depth of his being, whose inmost heart is not on fire? Who does not weep for joy at the sight of these venerable and precious relics of the Apostle of Christ? We rejoice, we exult, we shout in jubilation at thy coming, most divine Apostle Andrew. For we cannot doubt that thou art with thy carnal head and with it dost enter the city. It is true that we hate the Turks as the foes of Christianity, but in this we do not hate them, that they have been the cause of thy coming. For what blessing more to be desired could befall us than to behold thy most venerated head, to inhale its supreme fragrance? Our one grief is that we do not pay thee at thy coming the honors thou dost merit and cannot receive thee as becomes thy matchless sanctity.

"But do thou accept our intention: measure the will not the deed. Graciously suffer us to touch thy bones with our polluted hands and, sinners though we are, to accompany thee within the walls. Enter the holy city and be propitious to the Roman people. May thy coming bring safety to all Christians, thy entrance bring peace. May thy stay among us be happy and auspicious. Be thou our advocate in Heaven and together with the blessed Apostles Peter and Paul preserve this city. Take loving thought for all Christendom, that by thy intercession the mercy of God may be upon us and that, if He is angry with us for our sins, which are many, His anger may be transferred to the impious Turks and the barbarian nations who dishonor Christ the Lord. Amen."

The Pope's prayer drew tears from all eyes. There was no one on the platform, clergy or laity, who did not weep and beat his breast imploring the protection of the blessed Apostle. There were some on whom the Pope's words made so profound an impression that on reaching home they wrote them down verbatim and gave them to him. Among these was Theodore,

Bishop of Feltre, a man distinguished alike for his learning and character. When the Pope had read his copy, he marveled at the man's memory and praised his ability.

While the Pope was speaking there was profound silence except for the sobs of those who beat their breasts and could not control their tears. Torches were burning all around and the throngs in the fields waited in silence for him to finish. When he ended, he kissed the sacred head and all on the platform weeping did likewise. The Pope then prayed again:

"Omnipotent and everlasting God, Who dost rule Heaven and earth, Who hast today deigned to solace us with the coming of the precious head of St. Andrew, Thy Apostle, grant, we pray, that through his merits and intercession the insolence of the faithless Turk may be crushed, all infidels may cease from troubling us, and Christians serve Thee in freedom and safety. And this we ask in the name of Christ our Lord."

When all had answered "Amen," he took the venerable relic of the Apostle in his hands and elevating it made the circuit of the tribune showing to the people the gift so much desired. There was no one who did not have a chance to see it and presently voices from the multitude were heard crying aloud and imploring God's mercy, so that all the valleys echoed the sound. After this the canticle beginning, "Te deum laudamus," which is said to have been written by the celebrated Fathers of the Church Ambrose and Augustine, was loudly intoned and after it the choir sang the following hymn in Sapphics:

"He was first to follow Jesus's call; he first like Him endured the Cross, martyr revered forever on the shores of Greece. But when the Turks were conquering the Greeks, that he might not fall a prey to ravening hounds, Pius II carried him away and received the exile into the holy city. The Pope himself came to meet him with the holy senate, while Rome was fragrant with festal flowers and priests sang songs of praise. The priest in shining robes carries the sacred relic in his hand; the people in bright array raise the chant, 'Be thou, we pray, the prop, the father of our fostering city. O thou great champion of the holy Faith, first to hear the Lord's summons, first to triumph by a death like His, protect Rome. O gracious God, bless this day to us. Sharpen Thy three-forked bolt against the Turks.'

"Andrew gives ear to the people's prayer and answers with his own: 'I pray Thee, Creator of heaven and earth, put an end to bloodshed and punishments and at last in pity for Thy people crush the Turks!'

"This is the prayer of the great and good shepherd Pius as he kneels before Thee: 'Pity the wearied; stretch out Thine arm to a world on the brink of ruin, omnipotent King of kings.' This is the suppliant prayer of the princes of our city, Paul and Peter, and Rome, leaning upon them as upon two columns, humbly offers the same petition. Grant Pius life, we all implore Thee. He alone with unfailing courage dared to cross the Alps and raise the call to arms against the Turk. He gladly offers his own life that the world may worship the name of Christ and the faithless foe be brought to see the way of our salvation. Amen."

This hymn was written at Pius's orders by Agapetus, Bishop of Ancona. a Roman citizen of whom it would be hard to say whether he was more illustrious as jurist, orator, or poet.

The Pope now descended from the tribune surrounded by lighted tapers and carrying the sacred head in his hands. He proceeded to carry it to the city, accompanied by the cardinals, bishops, and other prelates in the order of their rank bearing palms. On the road many persons were trampled in the crowd of men and horses and it was almost impossible to make a way through such a throng. At the city gate they found some of the clergy who had come out to meet the Apostle with sacred relics. After doing him reverence they returned with him into the city. The Pope, entering the church of Santa Maria, laid the head of the Apostle on the altar before the image of the glorious Virgin, mother of our Lord, which they say was painted by St. Luke the Evangelist. Then he blessed the people and appointed from the Referendarii certain bishops to keep watch during the night. He too spent the night in the church in a chamber prepared for him.

The sun had not yet set when of a sudden the wind changed and rain drove in from the south, continuing all night till dawn. The storm was so violent that there was no hope of carrying the head through the city to the basilica of St. Peter the next day as had been intended. There was universal grief that the solemn rite that had been planned should be prevented and such eager expectation on the part of the populace disappointed. Countless strangers had flocked to Rome from Germany, France, Hungary, and other Transalpine countries, not to speak of innumerable commoners of Italy and many nobles, who were eager to see the sacred head, so that not even at the jubilee celebrated under Pope Nicholas V, which is agreed to have been the greatest ever held, was a larger throng seen on a single day. All were dejected, especially those who had not been in the meadow: for many had not arrived in time.

Pope Pius too was equally distressed and apprehensive for the populace, whose dearest wish he saw was being disappointed, and he sympathized alike with citizens and strangers, who were equally heartbroken. But now the whole city began to implore God to vouchsafe clear weather on the morrow and the Divine Mercy was not deaf to their prayers. Indeed it is probable that St. Andrew was listened to as befitted his dignity and obtained calm weather for his head. For suddenly a little before sunrise Aquilo or Boreas or some other wind scattered the clouds, leaving the sky bright and clear, and the sun himself appeared in the east extraordinarily dazzling and radiant, so that many, especially the Pope himself, recalled the couplet:

It rained all night; the shows are resumed in the morning. Caesar divides his empire with Jove.

But Pius altered the verses and said to those about him,

"It rained all night; now our weather has returned. The past night was the enemy's; the day will be God's."

And he added,

"The wet weather is past; the dry has returned. The hostile night has gone; the friendly day has shone."

The Pope gave orders that the cardinals should be summoned at once and the necessary preparations for the processions be made. He himself celebrated mass in his chamber and read the Passion of our Lord according to St. Luke. When the mass was over and the full senate and all the clergy were assembled, he called the cardinals and asked what they had better do; for though it had been decided to carry the Apostle's head in procession, whether on foot or on horseback was still unsettled. Although the people on the preceding day had cleaned all the route to be traversed, the rainy night had overlaid it thick with mud and it looked as if the slippery ground would be very difficult for the priests carrying the sacred relics and clad in their ceremonial robes. Furthermore the route seemed too long for the older men, for it was about two miles through the heart of the city from Santa Maria del Popolo to the basilica of St. Peter. Therefore many thought that cardinals, bishops, and abbots should have the privilege of riding while the rest walked.

This however did not please the Pope, who did not wish to have the procession divided nor to have it look as if the priests failed in devotion or paid less reverence to the divine Apostle. He therefore ordered that all should go on foot and do honor to the sacred head by their own exertions and earn the indulgences. However if any were too old or ill to be equal to such an effort, they might go on horseback by another route to St. Peter's and there on the steps before the doors await the arrival of the procession. Those who could not walk all the way but could manage a part of it were to walk as far as they thought they could, choosing the place from which they estimated that their feet would carry them to St. Peter's.

It was a fine and impressive sight to see those aged men walking through the slippery mud with palms in their hands and miters on their white hair, robed in priestly vestments, never lifting their eyes from the ground but praying and invoking the Divine Mercy upon the people. Some who had been reared in luxury and had scarcely been able to go a hundred feet except on horseback, on that day, weighed down as they were with their sacred robes, easily accomplished two miles through mud and water.

Guillaume, Bishop of Ostia, a noble of royal blood, had hard work to support the burden of his flesh, for he was fat and old. Alain, Cardinal of Santa Prassede, a tall man with a huge paunch, also had difficulty in propelling his great bulk. Both however cheerfully finished the course. But Juan, Bishop of Porto, a Spaniard learned in civil law, who had shortly before returned from an embassy to Hungary, excited particular admiration, for though he was old and ill, nevertheless he covered the whole distance with good courage and a joyous countenance, praying as he walked. Love carried the burden and nothing was difficult for the lover. No small difficulty was experienced on the road by Alessandro, Cardinal of Santa Susanna, and Jacopo of Sant' Anastasia, one weighted down by ill health and the other by his sixty-six years. Their devotion however conquered and they did not drop out of the procession anywhere. Latino Orsini, who was frail and usually unable to endure any exertion, on that day got new strength and seemed to have no difficulty at all in walking. All the rest were young and vigorous, as for instance Pietro of San Marco, nephew of Eugenius IV; Lodovico of Santi Quattro Coronati, nephew of Calixtus III; Richard of Coutances, who had been counsellor to King Charles of France; Niccolò of Teano, who had once commanded the armies of the Church and subdued the Narsi; Jean of Arras, who had but just returned from France after the abrogation of the Pragmatic Sanction;[2] Jacopo of Pavia, a great classical scholar; Rodrigo, the Vice-Chancellor, nephew of Calixtus and an extraordinarily able man;[3] Francesco of Siena, mentioned above; Francesco of Mantua, related to the noblest families of Italy and Germany. The faces of all expressed solemnity, reverence, and devotion. There was not a single unseemly gesture and the procession of cardinals passed with such dignity that the watching crowds along the way were stirred to worship. A like impression was produced by the bishops and other prelates and all the clergy manifested a remarkable spirit of humility.

There were present the priests of all the churches of Rome carrying sacred relics; Roman citizens splendidly dressed; the conservators of the camera; the chiefs of the sections and other magistrates. There were also ambassadors of kings and princes and the nobles of the city carrying lighted tapers and marshaled according to their rank. Some of the ambassadors and nobles were stationed about the Pope, holding over the head of the Apostle a golden

2   The Pragmatic Sanction of Bourges (1438), a royal proclamation that limited the pope's authority over the Church in France, was revoked in 1461 by King Louis XI, who sought better relations with the papacy.

3   Rodrigo Borgia, the nephew of Pope Calixtus III (1455–8), went on to become Pope Alexander VI (1492–1503). His son Cesare figures prominently in Machiavelli's *Prince* (see below).

canopy (baldacchino we call it nowadays) like an umbrella to keep off the sun's rays. The rest of the clergy brought up the rear. Some say that on that day in the procession of the clergy and laity 30,000 lighted candles could be counted as they crossed Hadrian's bridge two by two, and there were so many priests carrying sacred relics that the head of the procession reached St. Peter's before the Pope started, though the marchers left no space between them and trod close on one another's heels.

When everything was ready and the procession was well started, the Pope came down from his chamber carried on men's shoulders in his golden chair, as had come to be his custom, since gout had long since deprived him of the use of his feet. He dispatched the Bishop of Ostia with two cardinals to bring him the Apostle's head from the church of Santa Maria, since he could not himself get through because of the great crowds. They received the famous relic at the altar and put it into the Pope's hands while all the people looked on and invoked God's mercy. The Pope kissed it and then carrying it before him and blessing the crowds who surged about him he began his progress.

It was already the thirteenth hour and such throngs had blocked the streets that the soldiers massed around the Pope could scarcely open a way with their cudgels, though for some distance the route led outside the buildings of the city where the streets are broader: for the Pope turned to the right toward the Tiber and proceeded along the bank of the river leaving on his left the tomb of Augustus. In this district, though at other times there are plenty of wide spaces, that day there was not a foot of empty room and the crowds were so closely packed that if you had thrown a grain of wheat it would hardly have fallen on the ground. All the way to St. Peter's they found the streets just as crowded and it was not the same crowd leaving one place and filling up another but everywhere new faces were seen.

The route followed the Tiber till they reached the closely built districts on the right. Then the procession turned left and through narrow streets between high buildings came to the Pantheon, which the heathen consecrated to all the gods, that is demons, and our ancestors to the glorious Virgin, Mother of our Lord, and to all the saints. There after crossing the great square before the church it turned to the right till it passed the chapel of San Eustachio, where it turned left again till it reached the house of Berardo Cardinal of Santa Sabina, a most virtuous man and an authority on law. Here, bearing a third time to the right, it followed the street called the Pope's to the newly erected church of Maximo, where it again turned left to the Campo dei Fiori. Crossing this on the right it reached the square of San Lorenzo in Damaso, where it took a street to the left which brought it to the Tiber bank, and finally a road to the right which brought it to Hadrian's tomb. Here it crossed the bridge and proceeded to St. Peter's by the Via Sacra, which was everywhere strewn with flowers and fragrant herbs.

In all the city wherever private houses were built close together the street was covered with canopies and branches of trees to keep off the sun and all the houses were decked with hangings and tapestries which completely hid the walls. The Romans displayed extraordinary joy and reverence and members of the Curia and strangers alike vied with one another in honoring the Apostle. All the decorations the houses possessed were lavished to adorn the streets for the sacred head. There was no precious robe that was not displayed that day. In the floors and windows matrons and maids with lighted tapers, dressed as befitted the occasion, watched the procession, praying and adoring the sacred head. At the crossroads and in all the streets altars sent clouds of smoke. Everywhere incense and branches of fragrant shrubs were burning. Whoever had in his house paintings or fine and lifelike statues displayed them outside in the portico before his door. In many places there were actors in costume; children represented angels, some singing sweetly, others playing musical instruments. There was no instrument that might not be heard and praises of the Apostle filled the air. Besides fountains of wine and diverse wonders hanging everywhere caught the attention of the marchers.

The efforts of all his inferiors and equals were surpassed by Melchior, Procurator of the Knights of Rhodes, an excellent and learned man. He had erected in front of his house an altar smoking with clouds of incense and had added various embellishments. Singers, flute players, and trumpeters honored the relic of the Apostle as it passed with varied and delightful harmony. All the cardinals who lived along the route had decorated their houses magnificently. (There was one exception whom I forbear to mention out of respect, for fear he might be thought irreligious.) The Cardinal of Spoleto, though not present himself (for he had gone to his own church to minister to his people and his sheep during Holy Week), had left stewards at his house who had covered the adjacent square with carpets and decorated the house walls most beautifully. He was outdone however by Alain, Cardinal of Santa Prassede, generally called Cardinal of Avignon. He lived in the Campo dei Fiori where they say the Genius of Pompey the Great once stood on the site of the present palace of the Orsini, which was erected at great expense in a strange land by Pope Eugenius's nephew, the Cardinal of Porto. Alain had built in the square an altar covered with a canopy of cloth of gold with many perfumes burning on it; the lofty walls of the palace he adorned with precious tapestries which he had brought to Italy from the French city of Arras.

But all were far outstripped in expense and effort and ingenuity by Rodrigo, the Vice-Chancellor. His huge towering house which he had built on the site of the ancient mint was covered with rich and wonderful tapestries, and besides this he had raised a lofty canopy from which were suspended many and various marvels. He had decorated not only his own house but those nearby, so that the square all about them seemed a kind of park full of sweet songs and sounds, or a great palace gleaming with gold such as they say Nero's palace was. Furthermore on the walls were hung many poems recently composed by great geniuses which set forth in large letters praises of the divine Apostle and eulogies of Pope Pius.

Nor did the Tuscan merchants and bankers who lived near Hadrian's bridge leave their houses without ornament, but they tried to outdo one another in lavishness and effort and originality. There was no square or street where there were dwellings that did not display something worthy of admiration.

Thus the Pope was carried through so many wonders, himself carrying the sacred head, and came finally to the great broad square before the basilica of the Prince of the Apostles, which was already filled with a crowd of strangers; for the Romans, except those in the procession, remained in their own districts, especially the women. Here arose a great noise of voices like the murmur of many waters, since at the sight of the Apostle's head all fell to beating their breasts and with groans and wailings commended themselves to it. The Pope mounted the many steps of the marble staircase before the great doors which he himself had recently built at great expense, for the old one built by Constantine had given out. On the top stair he turned to the crowd and blessed them, exhibiting to them the sacred head.

On entering the atrium the Pope turned his eyes toward the statue of St. Peter which sits before the vestibule and, fancying that the statue wept with joy at the coming of his brother, he himself burst into tears as he reflected on the meeting and embrace between two brothers who had been so long separated. Then he entered the church, which seemed one blaze of lights, for it too was full of men and women and there were very few who did not hold lighted candles or tapers in their hands. Furthermore there was the glow of innumerable lamps and candelabra and all this was made still more marvelous by the music of the organ and the singing of the clergy. They passed to the high altar with considerable difficulty through densely packed crowds who would hardly give way before swords. Under the altar lie the bodies of the two Apostles, Peter and Paul, which are objects of worship the world over. Here the precious head of St. Andrew was deposited and all the prelates and distinguished persons present kissed it.

The preceding year Isidore, Bishop of Santa Sabina, cardinal of the Holy Roman Church, a Greek from Peloponnese who had once been assigned to the Roxani who live in the far north, had had a stroke of apoplexy which had deprived him of speech but not of intelligence. He had remained at home ill, but when he beheld the sacred head passing his house, he could not be restrained from following the holy relic. He came therefore on foot to the basilica of St. Peter and entering the iron grill that encircles the Holy of Holies and guards the high altar, he approached the Pope and indicated by signs and gestures that he desired to kiss the divine head of the Apostle. On receiving permission he knelt and with sobs and tears and profound reverence satisfied his yearning and gave vent to his exultation as if he had received an answer to prayer. Then he returned home rejoicing, for he was delighted in that he had beheld the founder of his country, and the venerable old man appeared much happier when he left than when he came.

Then Cardinal Bessarion, holding the right horn of the altar, with the Apostle's head on one side and the Pope on the other, spoke as follows:

"O most blessed Peter, Prince of the Apostles, and thou, chosen vessel and teacher of the Gentiles, who, though called last to apostleship, dost share equally with St. Peter the primacy, behold your brother! Behold, I say! your Andrew, who, first to be called, showed the rest the way to the Savior. Lo! your Andrew is here, that he who is united with you in heaven and sits beside the Creator and Savior of all the human race and enjoys the sight of His glory may now be united with you in his body on earth and dwell with you after so long a time, he who has been severed from you more than 1428 years since the Ascension of our Lord. For, as you know, Achaia, which he once dedicated to God with his own blood, kept him and guarded him most faithfully far from you and from the city of Rome which had obtained you, the founders and teachers of the Faith, its holy and true shepherds.

"The reason for this his coming is assuredly not unknown to you who behold not only all things past but much that is to come. But that this fact may come to the knowledge, not of you, but of any Christians who may be ignorant of it, he says, 'Brother Peter, behold your Andrew! After I was sent first by the Savior and then by your orders to preach the Gospel, after traveling through many and diverse nations whom I dedicated to the true Faith and the name of Christ, I came at last to Achaia, a province of Peloponnese filled full of men not only noble but learned; there I sowed the truth of the Gospel so widely that I converted the entire province from the worship of idols to the religion of the true God. Wherefore at the hands of the proconsul Egeus, whose wife I had rescued from him by the sword and fire of the spirit and offered to Christ, I too met death on the most holy Cross, as did you and our Lord and Master Jesus Christ. I was buried by Maximilla, the proconsul's wife, and until now have rested there, honored by the worshippers of Christ and extolled by their fervent praise.

"But when the Mohammedans (ah, piteous and tragic tale!) following the son of Satan, the antichrist Mahomet, after seizing the rest of Greece and the Orient, finally in these latter days most impiously subjugated Achaia too and perverted it with infamous worship, then by God's aid I fled thence from the clutches of the heathen and I have come to thee, most holy brother, to thee, teacher and master, to thee appointed by God the universal shepherd of Christ's flock, as to the safest haven, that, as thy Paul (or rather ours) let down from the walls in a basket by the brethren, escaped the most cruel hands of the governor of Damascus, that he might finish his course and complete his ministry of the Gospel, so I too taking refuge with thee, may by thy power and help restore to their former liberty the sons whom I had begotten to myself, or rather to thee, nay to Christ our Lord, who are now subject to an impious and most savage enemy and not only deprived of physical freedom but in danger of losing the integrity of their faith; and that I may bring them back to the worship of the true God and present them safe and cleansed of all heathen vileness before Christ our Lord, a purpose assuredly welcome and most acceptable to thee.

"What wilt thou do now? Wilt thou be inert or slow against the impious Turks, the bitterest enemies of the most holy Cross of our salvation, through which He Who redeemed us by it gathers to Himself both thee and me against barbarians who are savagely rending asunder Christ's limbs and continually assailing Christ Himself with blasphemy and insult? Wilt thou endure such deeds? Thou hast today a successor who besides his other virtues cherishes in his heart this supreme purpose, this yearning to avenge by righteous punishment the innocent blood of Christians that has been most cruelly shed. Now plowshares must be beaten into swords, now the tunic must be sold and the sword bought, now must thy zeal blaze forth, now must thy Paul's blade be whetted, that by thy power and aid, working through the mightiest princes of the west, the faith which thou didst preach and approve, by which thou didst become the father of all, may be defended and the Church founded on the rock that is Christ may prevail against the gates of hell through the authority and testimony of our Lord, Jesus Christ Who is very truth.

"Enough then for thee. Now I call upon thy most worthy successor and the true vicar of Christ, the Pope, who has received me with the highest honors, who welcomed me yesterday with such faith and devotion, who addressed to me such words that he himself wept and moved almost all his hearers to tears – and indeed he would easily have drawn tears from hearts of stone. Thee, Pope Pius, I beg, implore, beseech that what I have asked of my brother thou who deservedly sittest in his seat, who art his most worthy successor in the pontificate, wilt pursue and consummate. Strengthen daily the purpose thou hast thus far cherished, to avenge the blood of Christians. Cease not to exhort Christian princes and despair not because they have so often been approached by thee. One day they will come to reverence Christ, one day they will reverence Peter, and calling upon thee and me, they will put on the spirit of Christians and kings. They will at last act as becomes them and by assaulting the most cruel foe will win everlasting fame to the great glory of thy name and to the salvation of Christendom. For this may God preserve thee safe and fortunate for long time to come, to steer the course of Peter's See with all temperance and seemliness and may He in His mercy grant thee grace, that thou who hast received me this day in this city with great glory may one day restore me to my country with even greater honor, as thou didst voluntarily promise yesterday with deep emotion."

Bessarion was heard with attention and favor, though the Fathers, wearied with the march, desired rest and it was already the sixteenth hour. Nevertheless when he ended they did not find it burdensome to listen to the Pope's reply, which was as follows:

"If the most holy bodies of the blessed Apostles which lie beneath the altar could speak, they would assuredly rejoice exceedingly at the coming of thy most reverend head, divine Andrew, and would express their joy in noble words and voluntarily promise the aid thou hast asked. But they lie voiceless till the day of Resurrection. Nevertheless they experience today, we think, a wondrous sweetness and an inner gladness at the presence of a head so beloved and so closely akin; and especially is this true of the bones of thy brother Peter, whose joy is enhanced by fraternal affection. But their souls are in heaven in God's kingdom, in Christ's kingdom, nor can we doubt that they are thinking of thee and invoke the divine aid to restore this head of thine to its own throne.

"As far as concerns us (since mention has been made of us too), the unworthy holder of thy brother's place, we will be brief. To thee Andrew, most worthy Apostle of Christ, whom from our youth to this day we have venerated with especial devotion and have chosen with many others among those who dwell in heaven to be our advocate and protector, we promise willingly and eagerly all the aid in our power to recover thy sheep and thy home here on earth. For nothing is closer to our heart than the defense of the Christian religion and the orthodox faith, which thine enemies and ours, the Turks, are striving to trample underfoot. But if Christian princes and people will hear our voice and follow their shepherd, all the Church will see and be glad that we have not neglected the duties of our office and that thou hast not in vain come hither to obtain thy brother's aid."

After these words and the singing of the collect, he rose and laid the famous relic on the altar, that it might be exhibited that day for all to see, and the auditors of the holy palace were set to guard it. Then while the cardinals and bishops sang praises to God with a loud voice, he went to a place where he could be seen by all and blessed the multitude, and the Cardinal of Siena, his nephew after the flesh, announced plenary indulgence. They then returned to the palace. On the following days of Holy Week the divine services assigned to each by long usage were observed and the Passion of our Lord was celebrated with profound devotion on the part of the populace.

On Saturday, April 17, after high mass, when the Pope blessed the people, he promised that the next day, in reverence for the Resurrection, he would himself celebrate mass in the church of the Prince of the Apostles and would bring thither the sacred head of Andrew so that it might be repeatedly seen.

(It had been removed from the altar of St. Peter and locked up in the palace.) This was a strange and unexpected event, for because of the illnesses and absences of the Pope it was four years since the Romans had seen their pontiff elevating the divine Host; and because Pius could not stand on his feet they contrived a way for him to celebrate practically seated.

From the time when the sacred head was brought from Narni until that Saturday it rained every day and night except while it was on the road. The pious took this for an omen, thinking that God granted that fair weather to his Apostle when he went abroad, and the superstition was increased on Easter day: for although it had rained all night, with morning it was clear again and as long as the ceremony and the sacred procession lasted the sun shone, so that the Pope said a second time, "It rained all night, but in the morning fair weather returned. Lo! the night was Satan's; the light will be God's."

So the Pope came down into the apostolic church carrying before him the sacred head. He celebrated mass, offering to God the most acceptable of all offerings, His own Son, and he administered the most holy Body of Christ with his own hand to great numbers of the clergy and the laity. At the close of the mass the Pope took the venerable head and walked in procession with the cardinals and clergy to the part of the church where holy Veronica is kept (this is what they call the miraculous likeness of Jesus Christ imprinted on the towel which the celebrated woman Veronica is said to have offered him). Then standing at a little distance he ordered the towel to be displayed. Pietro, Cardinal of San Marco, a noble Venetian, Eugenius's nephew, and archpresbyter of that church, ascended the steps and exhibited the venerable and holy face of our Lord while the people, as is the custom, thrice implored mercy. It was a marvelous and awesome thing to behold on one hand the holy face of the Savior and on the other the precious relic of His apostle and furthermore to see the Pope with the cardinals and all the clergy praying bareheaded on their knees.

After this they proceeded to the place of benediction where there was as great a throng as there had been recently at the earlier procession. Even those who had come last saw the famous head of the Apostle and those who had prepared themselves through confession and contrition received the Pope's blessing and plenary remission of their sins. The Pope then withdrew to the palace carrying with him the sacred relic of the Apostle, which he deposited in the castle of Sant'Angelo to be kept till a proper receptacle could be prepared for it.

5

Niccolò Machiavelli (1469–1527)

Machiavelli was born into one of the less distinguished families in the Florentine aristocracy. His father, a lawyer, ensured that the boy was exposed to the Latin classics, including Livy's histories of the Roman Republic, which would later provide the immediate subject of Machiavelli's *Discourses*. We know little of his life before 1498 when, in the aftermath of the execution of the controversial friar and prophet Girolamo Savonarola, Machiavelli became the Second Chancellor of the Florentine government, a secretarial post responsible for official correspondence on a regional scale. In addition, he was entrusted with diplomatic missions that brought him into contact with some of the most powerful men in Europe, including Cesare Borgia (1502 and 1503), King Louis XII of France (1505), and Pope Julius II (1506). Cesare Borgia, the impetuous illegitimate son of Pope Alexander VI, particularly impressed Machiavelli as a man of decisive and effective action, but one whose spectacular early successes gave way to ill fortune after Pope Alexander's death in 1503.

Machiavelli's own fortunes declined precipitously soon after the Medici returned to power in Florence in August of 1512. In November, against his wishes, he was removed from office. Then, in February 1513, he was implicated in a plot to overthrow the Medici. Imprisoned and tortured, he steadfastly maintained his innocence, but still received a sentence of life imprisonment. Fortunately for Machiavelli, when Giovanni de' Medici was elected pope on March 11, a celebratory general pardon was declared. Following his unexpected release, Machiavelli still had no role in the government, and he retired to his family farm in a small town outside Florence. There he soon wrote *The Prince*, which would be followed by other major compositions, including the *Discourses*, and the *Florentine Histories*, which Cardinal Giulio de' Medici (the future Pope Clement VII) had commissioned in 1520. Never again did he hold public office, and he died in June of 1527, just weeks after the Medici were once again expelled from Florence in the aftermath of the sack of Rome.

The Prince is a deceptively simple book. On one level, it is what it purports to be: a guidebook for new princes showing how to consolidate power. Yet it is also a job application of sorts, directed at the Medici in the hope that they would restore him to a role in government. Much like the Cicero revealed in the letters to Atticus that so disconcerted Petrarch, Machiavelli was a political creature whose enforced leisure frustrated his desire to be back in the fray. Thirdly, with the inclusion of the final chapter, which many scholars believe is a later addition, it becomes a guidebook for consolidating power to serve a specific purpose: the expulsion of the "barbarian" armies from Italy.

Alongside these deadly serious purposes, Machiavelli ruthlessly pokes fun at the idealism of conventional advice-books presented to new princes, which sought to inspire them to imitate distinguished examples of moral leadership. Consider the following, which Petrarch wrote to a new prince, Francesco da Carrara of Padua, advising him on how he "ought" to behave:

> I want you to look at yourself in this letter as though you were gazing in a mirror. If you see yourself in what I am describing (as no doubt you will quite often), enjoy it.... On the other hand, if sometimes you feel that it is difficult for you to meet the standards I describe, I advise you to put your hands to your face and polish the countenance of your great reputation written there, so that you might become more attractive, and certainly more illustrious, as a result of this experience.[1]

Machiavelli, in sharp contrast, often appears to hold up for imitation examples of flagrant criminality and extreme cruelty. Does he do so mainly as a rhetorical flourish to make his point more memorable? Or, might he actually mean all of what he says?

Questions

1 From what sources does Machiavelli claim to have derived his precepts? From which time periods does he draw his examples of princely success and failure?
2 To what extent is it useful to imitate examples of past rulers? What are the potential problems with doing so?
3 Earlier advice-books to princes emphasized moral behavior as a key to success. On what grounds does Machiavelli criticize that approach? What room is there for morality in rulership? What is his view of human nature, and how does it shape the advice he gives?

1 From *The Earthly Republic: Italian Humanists on Government and Society*, ed. B. G. Kohl and R. G. Witt (Philadelphia, 1978), pp. 41–2.

4 In a famous passage in chapter 18, Machiavelli wrote that "in the actions of all men, and especially of princes, where there is no court to appeal to, one looks to the end." Does this differ, in practical terms, from saying that the ends justify the means?

5 Would you recommend this book to an aspiring prince? Suppose that you did, and that your advice proved effective. Based upon your reading of *The Prince*, what reward ought you to expect for your advice? (Consider the reward Machiavelli hoped to obtain for his book, as well as the reward that Remirro de Orco received for his loyal service to Cesare Borgia.)

The Prince

Dedicatory Letter

Niccolò Machiavelli to the Magnificent Lorenzo de' Medici:

It is customary most of the time for those who desire to acquire favor with a Prince to come to meet him with things that they care most for among their own or with things that they see please him most. Thus, one sees them[1] many times being presented with horses, arms, cloth of gold, precious stones and similar ornaments worthy of their greatness. Thus, since I desire to offer myself to your Magnificence[2] with some testimony of my homage to you, I have found nothing in my belongings that I care so much for and esteem so greatly as the knowledge of the actions of great men, learned by me from long experience with modern things and a continuous reading of ancient ones. Having thought out and examined these things with great diligence for a long time, and now reduced them to one small volume. I send it to your Magnificence.

And although I judge this work undeserving of your presence, yet I have much confidence that through your humanity it may be accepted, considering that no greater gift could be made by me than to give you the capacity to be able to understand in a very short time all that I have learned and

---

1 Machiavelli switches from a singular to the plural, a device he uses frequently.

2 Lorenzo de' Medici (1492–1519), grandson of Lorenzo the Magnificent (1449–92); he became duke of Urbino in 1516. Machiavelli had at first intended to dedicate *The Prince* to Giuliano de' Medici, son of Lorenzo the Magnificent and duke of Nemours, who died in 1516. See his letter to Vettori of December 10, 1513, printed below.

Plate 4   Attrib. to Rosso Fiorentino (1494–1540), *Portrait of Niccolò Machiavelli*, Casa del Machiavelli, Sant' Andrea in Percussina. *Source*: Art Resource/Scala.

understood in so many years and with so many hardships and dangers for myself. I have not ornamented this work, nor filled it with fulsome phrases nor with pompous and magnificent words, nor with any blandishment or superfluous ornament whatever, with which it is customary for many to describe and adorn their things. For I wanted it either not to be honored for anything or to please solely for the variety of the matter and the gravity of the subject. Nor do I want it to be reputed presumption if a man from a low and mean state dares to discuss and give rules for the governments of princes. For just as those who sketch landscapes place themselves down in the plain to consider the nature of mountains and high places and to consider the nature of low places place themselves high atop mountains, similarly, to know well the nature of peoples one needs to be prince, and to know well the nature of princes one needs to be of the people.

Therefore, your Magnificence, take this small gift in the spirit with which I send it. If your Magnificence considers and reads it diligently, you will learn from it my extreme desire that you arrive at the greatness that fortune and your other qualities promise you. And if your Magnificence will at some time turn your eyes from the summit of your height to these low places, you will learn how undeservedly I endure a great and continuous malignity of fortune.

7
Of New Principalities That Are Acquired by Others' Arms and Fortune

Those who become princes from private individual solely by fortune become so with little trouble, but maintain themselves with much. They have no difficulty along the path because they fly there, but all the difficulties arise when they are in place. And such princes come to be when a state is given to someone either for money or by the favor of whoever gives it, as happened to many in Greece, in the cities of Ionia and of the Hellespont, where they were made princes by Darius so that they might hold on to those cities for his security and glory;[3] as also those emperors were made who from private individual attained the empire through corrupting the soldiers. These persons rest simply on the will and fortune of whoever has given a state to them, which are two very inconstant and unstable things. They do not know how to hold and they cannot hold that rank: they do not know how, because if one is not a man of great ingenuity and virtue,[4] it is not reasonable, that having always lived in private fortune, he should know how to command; they cannot hold that rank because they do not have forces that can be friendly and faithful to them. Then, too, states that come to be suddenly, like all other things in nature that are born and grow quickly, cannot have roots and branches, so that the first adverse weather eliminates them – unless, indeed, as was said, those who have suddenly become princes have so much virtue that they know immediately how to prepare to keep what fortune has placed in their laps; and the foundations that others have laid before becoming princes they lay afterwards.

3   Darius I (521–486 BC).
4   *Virtù*, translated "virtue" throughout this selection, can also be rendered "capacity" or "prowess."

To both of the modes mentioned of becoming prince, by virtue or by fortune, I want to bring up two examples that have occurred in days within our memory; and these are Francesco Sforza and Cesare Borgia. Francesco became duke of Milan from private individual by proper means and with a great virtue of his own; and that which he had acquired with a thousand pains he maintained with little trouble. On the other hand Cesare Borgia, called Duke Valentino by the vulgar, acquired his state through the fortune of his father and lost it through the same, notwithstanding the fact that he made use of every deed and did all those things that should be done by a prudent and virtuous man to put his roots in the states that the arms and fortune of others had given him. For, as was said above, whoever does not lay his foundations at first might be able, with great virtue, to lay them later, although they might have to be laid with hardship for the architect and with danger to the building. Thus, if one considers all the steps of the duke, one will see that he had laid for himself great foundations for future power, which I do not judge superfluous to discuss; for I do not know what better teaching I could give to a new prince than the example of his actions. And if his orders did not bring profit to him, it was not his fault, because this arose from an extraordinary and extreme malignity of fortune.

Alexander VI had very many difficulties, both present and future, when he decided to make his son the duke great. First, he did not see the path to being able to make him lord of any state that was not a state of the Church; and when he decided to take that of the Church, he knew that the duke of Milan and the Venetians would not consent to it because Faenza and Rimini had for long been under the protection of the Venetians. Besides this, he saw that the arms of Italy, and especially the arms of anyone whom he might have been able to make use of, were in the hands of those who had to fear the greatness of the pope; and so he could not trust them, as they were all with the Orsini and the Colonna and their accomplices.[5] It was thus necessary to upset those orders and to bring disorder to their states so as to be able to make himself lord securely of part of them. This was easy for him, because he found that the Venetians, moved by other causes, were engaged in getting the French to come back into Italy, which he not only did not oppose but made easier by the dissolution of the former marriage of King Louis. So the king came into Italy with the aid of the Venetians and the consent of Alexander, and he was no sooner in Milan than the pope got men from him for a campaign in Romagna, which was granted to him because of the reputation of the king. So after the duke had acquired Romagna and beaten down the Colonna, two things prevented him from maintaining that and going further ahead: one, that his arms did not appear to him to be faithful; the other, the will of

5   The Orsini and Colonna were the two principal noble families of Rome which had long fought for control of Rome and the papacy.

France: that is, the Orsini arms of which he had availed himself might fail under him, and not only prevent him from acquiring but also take away what he had acquired; and the king might also do the same to him. He had a test of the Orsini when, after the capture of Faenza, he attacked Bologna and saw them go coolly to that attack; and regarding the king, the duke knew his mind when after he had taken the duchy of Urbino, he attacked Tuscany, and the king made him desist from that campaign. Hence the duke decided to depend no longer on the arms and fortune of others. And the first thing he did was to weaken the Orsini and Colonna parties in Rome. For he gained to himself all their adherents, who were gentlemen, by making them his gentlemen and by giving them large allowances; and he honored them, according to their qualities, with commands and with government posts, so that in a few months the partisan affections in their minds were eliminated, and all affection turned toward the duke. After this he waited for an opportunity to eliminate the heads of the Orsini, since he had dispersed those of the Colonna house. A good one came to him, and he used it better; for when the Orsini became aware, late, that the greatness of the duke and of the Church was ruin for them, they held a meeting at Magione, near Perugia.[6] From that arose rebellion in Urbino, tumults in Romagna, and infinite dangers for the duke, who overcame them all with the aid of the French. And when his reputation had been restored, he trusted neither France nor other external forces, and so as not to put them to the test, he turned to deceit. He knew so well how to dissimulate his intent that the Orsini themselves, through Signor Paolo, became reconciled with him. The duke did not fail to fulfill every kind of duty to secure Signor Paolo, giving him money, garments, and horses, so that their simplicity brought them into the duke's hands at Sinigaglia. So, when these heads had been eliminated, and their partisans had been turned into his friends, the duke had laid very good foundations for his power, since he had all Romagna with the duchy of Urbino. He thought, especially, that he had acquired the friendship of Romagna, and that he had gained all those peoples to himself since they had begun to taste well-being.

And because this point is deserving of notice and of being imitated by others, I do not want to leave it out. Once the duke had taken over Romagna, he found it had been commanded by impotent lords who had been readier to despoil their subjects than to correct them, and had given their subjects matter for disunion, not for union. Since that province was quite full of robberies, quarrels, and every other kind of insolence, he judged it necessary to give it good government, if he wanted to reduce it to peace and obedience to a kingly arm. So he put there Messer Remirro de Orco, a cruel and ready man, to whom he gave the fullest power. In a short time Remirro reduced it to peace and unity, with the very greatest reputation for himself. Then the

6   October 9, 1502.

duke judged that such excessive authority was not necessary, because he feared that it might become hateful; and he set up a civil court in the middle of the province, with a most excellent president, where each city had its advocate. And because he knew that past rigors had generated some hatred for Remirro, to purge the spirits of that people and to gain them entirely to himself, he wished to show that if any cruelty had been committed, this had not come from him but from the harsh nature of his minister. And having seized this opportunity, he had him placed one morning in the piazza at Cesena in two pieces, with a piece of wood and a bloody knife beside him. The ferocity of this spectacle left the people at once satisfied and stupefied.

But let us return to where we left off. I say that when the duke found himself very powerful and secure in part against present dangers – since he had armed to suit himself and had in good part eliminated those arms which were near enough to have attacked him – there remained for him, if he wanted to proceed with acquisition, to consider the king of France. For he knew that this would not be tolerated by the king, who had been late to perceive his error. And so he began to seek out new friendships and to vacillate with France in the expedition that the French were making toward the kingdom of Naples against the Spanish who were besieging Gaeta. His intent was to secure himself against them:[7] in which he would soon have succeeded, if Alexander had lived.

And these were his arrangements as to present things. But as to the future, he had to fear, first, that a new successor in the Church might not be friendly to him and might seek to take away what Alexander had given him. He thought he might secure himself against this in four modes: first, to eliminate the bloodlines of all those lords he had despoiled, so as to take that opportunity away from the pope; second, to win over to himself all the gentlemen in Rome, as was said, so as to be able to hold the pope in check with them; third, to make the College of Cardinals as much his as he could; fourth, to acquire so much empire before the pope died that he could resist a first attack on his own. Of these four things he had accomplished three at the death of Alexander; the fourth he almost accomplished. For of the lords he had despoiled he killed as many as he could reach, and very few saved themselves; the Roman gentlemen had been won over to himself; in the College he had a very large party; and as to new acquisition, he had planned to become lord over Tuscany, he already possessed Perugia and Piombino, and he had taken Pisa under his protection. And, as soon as he did not have to pay regard to France (which he did not have to do any longer, since the French had already been stripped of the kingdom by the Spanish, so that each of them was forced of necessity to buy his friendship), he would have jumped on Pisa. After this, Lucca and Siena would have quickly yielded, in part through envy of the

7   assure himself of Spanish support, or against the French.

Florentines, in part through fear; the Florentines had no remedy. If he had succeeded in this (as he was succeeding the same year that Alexander died), he would have acquired such force and reputation that he would have stood by himself and would no longer have depended on the fortune and force of someone else, but on his own power and virtue. But Alexander died five years after he had begun to draw his sword. He left the duke with only the state of Romagna consolidated, with all the others in the air, between two very powerful enemy armies, and sick to death. And there was such ferocity and such virtue in the duke, and he knew so well how men have to be won over or lost, and so sound were the foundations that he had laid in so little time, that if he had not had these armies on his back or if he had been healthy, he would have been equal to every difficulty. And that his foundations were good one may see: Romagna waited for him for more than a month; in Rome, though he was half-alive, he remained secure; and although the Baglioni, Vitelli, and Orsini came to Rome, none followed them against him; if he could not make pope whomever he wanted, at least it would not be someone he did not want. But if at the death of Alexander the duke had been healthy, everything would have been easy for him. And he told me, on the day that Julius II was created,[8] that he had thought about what might happen when his father was dying, and had found a remedy for everything, except that he never thought that at his death he himself would also be on the point of dying.

Thus, if I summed up all the actions of the duke, I would not know how to reproach him; on the contrary, it seems to me he should be put forward, as I have done, to be imitated by all those who have risen to empire through fortune and by the arms of others. For with his great spirit and high intention, he could not have conducted himself otherwise and the only things in the way of his plans were the brevity of Alexander's life and his own sickness. So whoever judges it necessary in his new principality to secure himself against enemies, to gain friends to himself, to conquer either by force or by fraud, to make himself loved and feared by the people, and followed and revered by the soldiers, to eliminate those who can or might offend[9] you, to renew old orders through new modes, to be severe and pleasant, magnanimous and liberal, to eliminate an unfaithful military, to create a new one, to maintain friendships with kings and princes so that they must either benefit you with favor or be hesitant to offend you – can find no fresher examples than the actions of that man. One could only accuse him in the creation of Julius as pontiff, in which he made a bad choice; for, as was said, though he could not make a pope to suit himself, he could have kept

---

8 Machiavelli was in Rome at the time of the conclave that elected Julius II pope in October–December 1503.

9 *offendere* (here and below) is not merely to slight, but to harm so as to cause offense.

anyone from being pope. And for the papacy he should never have consented to those cardinals whom he had offended or who, having become pope, would have to be afraid of him. For men offend either from fear or for hatred. Those whom he had offended were, among others, San Piero ad Vincula, Colonna, San Giorgio, Ascanio;[10] all the others, if they had become pope, would have had to fear him, except Rouen and the Spaniards, the latter because of kinship and obligation, the former for his power, because he was connected to the kingdom of France.[11] Therefore the duke, before everything else, should have created a Spaniard pope, and if he could not, should have consented to Rouen, and not San Piero ad Vincula. And whoever believes that among great personages new benefits will make old injuries be forgotten deceives himself. So the duke erred in this choice and it was the cause of his ultimate ruin.

15
Of Those Things for Which Men and Especially Princes Are Praised or Blamed

It remains now to see what the modes and government of a prince should be with subjects and with friends. And because I know that many have written of this, I fear that in writing of it again, I may be held presumptuous, especially since in disputing this matter I depart from the orders of others. But since my intent is to write something useful to whoever understands it, it has appeared to me more fitting to go directly to the effectual truth of the thing than to the imagination of it. And many have imagined republics and principalities that have never been seen or known to exist in truth; for it is so far from how one lives to how one should live that he who lets go of what is done for what should be done learns his ruin rather than his preservation. For a man who wants to make a profession of good in all regards must come to ruin among so many who are not good. Hence it is necessary to a prince, if he wants to maintain himself, to learn to be able not to be good, and to use this and not use it according to necessity.

Thus, leaving out what is imagined about a prince and discussing what is true, I say that all men, whenever one speaks of them, and especially princes, since they are placed higher, are noted for some of the qualities that bring them either blame or praise. And this is why someone is considered liberal, someone mean (using a Tuscan term because *avaro* [avaricious] in our

---

10   In this irreverent listing of cardinals, Giuliano della Rovere (who became Pope Julius II) is named by his church in Rome, San Pietro in Vincoli; Giovanni Colonna; Raffaelo Riario, named for San Giorgio; Ascanio Sforza.
11   Cardinal Georges d'Amboise, bishop of Rouen.

language is still one who desires to have something by rapine, *misero* [mean] we call one who refrains too much from using what is his); someone is considered a giver, someone rapacious; someone cruel, someone merciful; the one a breaker of faith, the other faithful; the one effeminate and pusillanimous, the other fierce and spirited; the one humane, the other proud; the one lascivious, the other chaste; the one honest, the other astute; the one hard, the other agreeable; the one grave, the other light; the one religious, the other unbelieving, and the like. And I know that everyone will confess that it would be a very praiseworthy thing to find in a prince all of the above-mentioned qualities that are held good. But because he cannot have them, nor wholly[12] observe them, since human conditions do not permit it, it is necessary for him to be so prudent as to know how to avoid the infamy of those vices that would take his state from him and to be on guard against those that do not, if that is possible; but if one cannot, one can let them go on with less hesitation. And furthermore one should not care about incurring the fame[13] of those vices without which it is difficult to save one's state; for if one considers everything well, one will find something appears to be virtue, which if pursued would be one's ruin, and something else appears to be vice, which if pursued results in one's security and well-being.

17
Of Cruelty and Mercy,[14] and Whether It Is Better to Be Loved Than Feared, or the Contrary

Descending next to the other qualities cited before, I say that each prince should desire to be held merciful and not cruel; nonetheless he should take care not to use this mercy badly. Cesare Borgia was held to be cruel; nonetheless his cruelty restored the Romagna, united it, and reduced it to peace and to faith. If one considers this well, one will see that he was much more merciful than the Florentine people, who so as to escape a name for cruelty, allowed Pistoia to be destroyed.[15] A prince, therefore, so as to keep his subjects united and faithful, should not care about the infamy of cruelty, because with very few examples he will be more merciful than those who for the sake of too much mercy allow disorders to continue, from which come killings or robberies; for these customarily hurt a whole community, but the executions that come from the prince hurt one particular person. And of all

12 Or honestly.
13 Some manuscripts have *infamia*, "infamy."
14 Or piety, throughout *The Prince*.
15 From 1500 to 1502 Pistoia, a city subject to Florence, was torn by factional disputes and riots. Machiavelli was there as representative of the Florentines on several occasions in 1501.

princes, it is impossible for the new prince to escape a name for cruelty because new states are full of dangers. And Virgil says in the mouth of Dido: "The harshness of things and the newness of the kingdom compel me to contrive such things, and to keep a broad watch over the borders."[16]

Nonetheless, he should be slow to believe and to move, nor should he make himself feared, and he should proceed in a temperate mode with prudence and humanity so that too much confidence does not make him incautious and too much diffidence does not render him intolerable.

From this a dispute arises whether it is better to be loved than feared, or the reverse. The response is that one would want to be both the one and the other; but because it is difficult to put them together, it is much safer to be feared than loved, if one has to lack one of the two. For one can say this generally of men: that they are ungrateful, fickle, pretenders and dissemblers, evaders of danger, eager for gain. While you do them good, they are yours, offering you their blood, property, lives, and children, as I said above, when the need for them is far away; but, when it is close to you, they revolt. And that prince who has founded himself entirely on their words, stripped of other preparation, is ruined; for friendships that are acquired at a price and not with greatness and nobility of spirit are bought, but they are not owned and when the time comes they cannot be spent. And men have less hesitation to offend one who makes himself loved than one who makes himself feared; for love is held by a chain of obligation, which, because men are wicked, is broken at every opportunity for their own utility, but fear is held by a dread of punishment that never forsakes you.

The prince should nonetheless make himself feared in such a mode that if he does not acquire love, he escapes hatred, because being feared and not being hated can go together very well. This he will always do if he abstains from the property of his citizens and his subjects, and from their women; and if he also needs to proceed against someone's life, he must do it when there is suitable justification and manifest cause for it. But above all, he must abstain from the property of others, because men forget the death of a father more quickly than the loss of a patrimony. Furthermore, causes for taking away property are never lacking, and he who begins to live by rapine always finds cause to seize others' property; and, on the contrary, causes for taking life are rarer and disappear more quickly.

But when the prince is with his armies and has a multitude of soldiers under his government, then it is above all necessary not to care about a name for cruelty, because without this name he never holds his army united, or disposed to any action. Among the admirable actions of Hannibal is numbered this one: that when he had a very large army, mixed with infinite kinds of men, and had led it to fight in alien lands, no dissension ever arose in

16   Virgil, *Aeneid* I, 563–4.

it, neither among themselves nor against the prince, in bad as well as in his good fortune. This could not have arisen from anything other than his inhuman cruelty which, together with his infinite virtues, always made him venerable and terrible in the sight of his soldiers; and without it, his other virtues would not have sufficed to bring about this effect. And the writers, having considered little in this, on the one hand admire this action of his but on the other condemn the principal cause of it.

And to see that it is true that his other virtues would not have been enough, one can consider Scipio, who was very rare not only in his times but also in the entire memory of things known – whose armies in Spain rebelled against him. This arose from nothing but his excessive mercy, which had allowed his soldiers more license than is fitting for military discipline. Scipio's mercy was reproved in the Senate by Fabius Maximus, who called him the corruptor of the Roman military. After the Locrians had been destroyed by a legate of Scipio's, they were not avenged by him, nor was the insolence of that legate corrected – all of which arose from his agreeable nature, so that when someone in the Senate wanted to excuse him, he said that there were many men who knew better how not to err than how to correct errors. Such a nature would in time have sullied Scipio's fame and glory if he had continued with it in the empire; but while he lived under the government of the Senate, this damaging quality of his not only was hidden, but made for his glory.[17]

I conclude, then, returning to being feared and loved, that since men love at their convenience and fear at the convenience of the prince, a wise prince should found himself on what is his, not on what is someone else's; he should only contrive to avoid hatred, as was said.

18
In What Mode Faith Should Be Kept by Princes

How praiseworthy it is for a prince to keep his faith, and to live with honesty and not by astuteness, everyone understands. Nonetheless one sees by experience in our times that the princes who have done great things are those who have taken little account of faith and have known how to get around men's brains with their astuteness; and in the end they have overcome those who have founded themselves on loyalty.

Thus, you must know that there are two kinds of combat: one with laws, the other with force. The first is proper to man, the second to beasts; but because the first is often not enough, one must have recourse to the second. Therefore it is necessary for a prince to know well how to use the beast and

17   Machiavelli's source is Livy, XXIX, 19, 21.

the man. This role was taught covertly to princes by ancient writers, who wrote that Achilles, and many other ancient princes, were given to Chiron the centaur to be raised, so that he would look after them with his discipline. To have as teacher a half-beast, half-man means nothing other than that a prince needs to know how to use both natures; and the one without the other is not lasting.

Thus, since a prince is compelled of necessity to know well how to use the beast, he should pick the fox and the lion,[18] because the lion does not defend itself from snares and the fox does not defend itself from wolves. So one needs to be a fox to recognize snares and a lion to frighten the wolves. Those who stay simply with the lion do not understand this. A prudent lord, therefore, cannot observe faith, nor should he, when such observance turns against him, and the causes that made him promise have been eliminated. And if all men were good, this teaching would not be good; but because they are wicked and do not observe faith with you, you also do not have to observe it with them. Nor does a prince ever lack legitimate causes to color his failure to observe faith. One could give infinite modern examples of this, and show how many peace treaties and promises have been rendered invalid and vain through the infidelity of princes; and the one who has known best how to use the fox has come out best. But it is necessary to know well how to color this nature, and to be a great pretender and dissembler; and men are so simple and so obedient to present necessities that he who deceives will always find someone who will let himself be deceived.

I do not want to be silent about one of the recent examples. Alexander VI never did anything, nor ever thought of anything, but how to deceive men, and he always found a subject to whom he could do it. And there never was a man with greater efficacy in asserting a thing, and in affirming it with greater oaths, who observed it less; nonetheless, his deceits succeeded at his will, because he well knew this aspect of the world.

Thus, it is not necessary for a prince to have all the above-mentioned qualities in fact, but it is indeed necessary to appear to have them. Nay, I dare say this, that by having them and always observing them, they are harmful; and by appearing to have them, they are useful, as it is to appear merciful, faithful, humane, honest, and religious, and to be so; but to remain with a spirit built so that, if you need not to be those things, you are able and know how to change to the contrary. This has to be understood: that a prince, and especially a new prince, cannot observe all those things for which men are held good, since he is often under a necessity, to maintain his state, of acting against faith, against charity, against humanity, against religion. And so he needs to have a spirit disposed to change as the winds of fortune and variations

18 A possible source for this: Cicero, *De officiis*, I. 11. 34; 13.41.

of things command him, and as I said above, not depart from good, when possible, but know how to enter into evil, when forced by necessity.

A prince should thus take great care that nothing escape his mouth that is not full of the above-mentioned five qualities and that, to see him and hear him, he should appear all mercy, all faith, all honesty, all humanity, all religion. And nothing is more necessary to appear to have than this last quality. Men in general judge more by their eyes than by their hands because seeing is given to everyone, touching to few. Everyone sees how you appear, few touch what you are; and these few dare not oppose the opinion of many, who have the majesty of the state to defend them; and in the actions of all men, and especially of princes, where there is no court to appeal to, one looks to the end. So let a prince win and maintain his state: the means will always be judged honorable, and will be praised by everyone. For the vulgar are taken in by the appearance and the outcome of a thing, and in the world there is no one but the vulgar; the few have a place there[19] when the many have somewhere to lean on. A certain prince of present times, whom it is not well to name,[20] never preaches anything but peace and faith, and is very hostile to both. If he had observed both, he would have had either his reputation or his state taken from him many times.

25

How Much Fortune Can Do in Human Affairs, and in What Mode It May Be Opposed

It is not unknown to me that many have held and hold the opinion that worldly things are so governed by fortune and by God, that men cannot correct them with their prudence, indeed that they have no remedy at all; and on account of this they might judge that one need not sweat much over things but let oneself be governed by chance. This opinion has been believed more in our times because of the great variability of things which have been seen and are seen every day, beyond every human conjecture. When I have thought about this sometimes, I have been in some part inclined to their opinion. Nonetheless, so that our free will not be eliminated, I judge that it might be true that fortune is arbiter of half of our actions, but also that she leaves the other half, or close to it, for us to govern. And I liken her to one of these violent rivers which, when they become enraged, flood the plains, ruin the trees and the buildings, lift earth from this part, drop in another; each person flees before them, everyone yields to their impetus without being able

19   One manuscript says "the few have no place there . . . "; and the authorities are divided on which reading to follow.
20   Apparently Ferdinand of Aragon.

to hinder them in any regard. And although they are like this, it is not as if men, when times are quiet, could not provide for them with dikes and dams so that when they rise later, either they go by a canal or their impetus is neither so wanton nor so damaging. It happens similarly with fortune, which demonstrates her power where virtue has not been put in order[21] to resist her and therefore turns her impetus where she knows that dams and dikes have not been made to contain her. And if you consider Italy, which is the seat of these variations and that which has given them motion, you will see a country without dams and without any dike. If it had been diked by suitable virtue, like Germany, Spain, and France, either this flood would not have brought the great variations that it has, or it would not have come here.

And I wish that this may be enough to have said about opposing fortune in general. But restricting myself more to particulars, I say that one sees a given prince be happy today and come to ruin tomorrow without having seen him change his nature or any quality. This I believe arises, first, from the causes that have been discussed at length in the preceding, that is, that the prince who leans entirely on his fortune comes to ruin as it varies. I believe, further, that he is happy who adapts his mode of proceeding to the qualities of the times; and similarly, he is unhappy whose procedure is in disaccord with the times. For one sees that in the things that lead men to the end that each has before him, that is, glories and riches, they proceed variously: one with caution, the other with impetuosity; one by violence, the other with art; one with patience, the other with its contrary – and with these different modes each can attain it. One also sees two cautious persons, one attaining his plan, the other not; and similarly two persons are equally happy with two different methods, one being cautious, the other impetuous. This arises from nothing other than from the quality of the times that they conform to or not in their procedure. From this follows what I said, that two persons working differently come out with the same effect; and of two persons working identically, one is led to his end, the other not. On this also depends the variability of the good: for if one governs himself with caution and patience, and the times and affairs turn in such a way that his government is good, he comes out happy; but if the times and affairs change, he is ruined because he does not change his mode of proceeding. Nor may a man be found so prudent as to know how to accommodate himself to this, whether because he cannot deviate from what nature inclines him to or also because, when one has always flourished by walking on one path, he cannot be persuaded to depart from it. And so the cautious man, when it is time to come to impetuosity, does not know how to do it, hence comes to ruin: for if he would change his nature with the times and with affairs, his fortune would not change.

---

21 lit.: ordered.

Pope Julius II proceeded impetuously in all his affairs, and he found the times and affairs so much in conformity with his mode of proceeding that he always achieved a happy end. Consider the first enterprise that he undertook in Bologna, while Messer Giovanni Bentivoglio was still living. The Venetians were not content with it; nor was the king of Spain; with France he was holding discussions on that enterprise; and nonetheless, with his ferocity and impetuosity, he personally put that expedition into motion. This move made Spain and the Venetians stand still in suspense, the latter out of fear and the other because of the desire he had to recover the whole kingdom of Naples. From the other side he pulled the king of France after him; because when that king saw him move, and since he desired to make Julius his friend in order to bring down the Venetians, he judged he could not deny him his troops without injuring him openly. Julius thus accomplished with his impetuous move what no other pontiff, with all human prudence, would ever have accomplished, because if he had waited to depart from Rome with firm conclusions and everything in order, as any other pontiff would have done, he would never have succeeded. For the king of France would have had a thousand excuses and the others would have raised in him a thousand fears. I wish to omit all his other actions, since all have been alike and all succeeded well. And the brevity of his life did not allow him to feel the contrary, because if times had come when he had needed to proceed with caution, his ruin would have followed: he would never have deviated from those modes to which nature inclined him.

I conclude, thus, that when fortune varies and men remain obstinate in their modes, men are happy while they are in accord, and as they come into discord, unhappy. I judge this indeed, that it is better to be impetuous than cautious, because fortune is a woman; and it is necessary, if one wants to hold her down, to beat her and strike her down. And one sees that she lets herself be won more by the impetuous than by those who proceed coldly. And so always, like a woman, she is the friend of the young, because they are less cautious, more ferocious, and command her with more audacity.

26

Exhortation to Seize Italy and to Free Her from the Barbarians

Thus, having considered everything discussed above, and thinking to myself whether in Italy at present the times have been tending to the honor of a new prince, and whether there is matter to give opportunity to someone prudent and virtuous to introduce a form that would bring honor to him and good to the community of men there, it appears to me that so many things are tending to the benefit of a new prince that I do not know what time has ever been more apt for it. And if, as I said, it was necessary for anyone wanting to see the virtue of Moses that the people of Israel be enslaved in Egypt, and to learn the greatness of spirit of Cyrus, that the Persians be oppressed by the Medes, and to learn the excellence of Theseus, that the Athenians be dispersed, so at present to know the virtue of an Italian spirit it was necessary that Italy be reduced to the condition in which she is at present, which is more enslaved than the Hebrews, more servile than the Persians, more dispersed than the Athenians, without a head, without order, beaten, despoiled, torn, pillaged, and having endured ruin of every sort.

And although up to now a glimmer has shone in someone who could judge that he had been ordered by God for her redemption, yet later it was seen that in the highest course of his actions, he was repulsed by fortune. So, left as if lifeless, she awaits whoever it can be that will heal her wounds, and put an end to the sacking of Lombardy, to the taxes on the kingdom and on Tuscany, and cure her of her sores that have festered now for a long time. One may see how she prays God to send her someone to redeem her from these barbarous cruelties and insults. One may also see her ready and disposed to follow a flag, provided that there be someone to pick it up. Nor may one see at present anyone in whom she can hope more than in your illustrious house, which with its fortune and virtue, supported by God and by the Church of which it is now prince,[22] can put itself at the head of this redemption. This is not very difficult if you summon up the actions and lives of those named above. And although these men are rare and marvelous, nonetheless they were men, and each of them had less opportunity than the present; for their undertaking was not more just than this one, nor easier, nor was God more friendly to them than to you. Here there is great justice: "for war is just to whom it is necessary, and arms are pious when there is no hope but in arms."[23] Here there is very great readiness, and where there is great readiness, there cannot be great difficulty, provided that your house keeps its aim on the orders of those whom I have put forth. Besides this, here may be seen extraordinary things without example, brought about by God: the sea has opened; a cloud has escorted you along the way; the stone has poured forth water; here manna has rained;[24] everything has concurred in your greatness. The remainder you must do yourself. God does not want to do everything, so as not to take free will from us and that part of the glory that falls to us.

And it is not a marvel if none of the Italians named before has been able to do what it is hoped will be done by your illustrious house, and if in so many

22 Cardinal Giovanni de' Medici, Lorenzo's uncle, became Pope Leo X in 1513.
23 Quoted in Latin from Livy IX.1.
24 These are references to miracles that occurred as Moses led the Israelites to the promised land, just before the revelation at Mount Sinai. They are not given in the same order as in the Bible, Exodus 14:21, 13:21, 17:6, 16:4.

revolutions in Italy and in so many maneuvers of war, it always appears that military virtue has died out in her. This arises from the fact that her ancient orders were not good, and that there has not been anyone who has known how to find new ones; and nothing brings so much honor to a man rising newly as the new laws and the new orders found by him. When these things have been founded well and have greatness in them, they make him revered and admirable. And in Italy matter is not lacking for introducing every form; here there is great virtue in the limbs, if it were not lacking in the heads. Look how in duels and in encounters with few the Italians are superior in force, dexterity, and ingenuity. But when it comes to armies, they do not compare. And everything follows from the weakness at the head, because those who know are not obeyed, and each thinks he knows, since up to now no one has been able to raise himself, both by virtue and by fortune, to a point where the others will yield to him. From this it follows that in so much time, in so many wars made in the last twenty years, when there has been an army entirely Italian it has always proven to be bad. The first testimony to this is Taro, then Alessandria, Capua, Genoa, Vailà, Bologna, Mestre.[25]

Thus, if your illustrious house wants to follow those excellent men who redeemed their countries,[26] it is necessary before all other things, as the true foundation of every undertaking, to provide itself with its own arms; for one cannot have more faithful, nor truer, nor better soldiers. And although each of them may be good, all together become better when they see themselves commanded by their prince, and honored and indulged by him. It is necessary, therefore, to prepare such arms for oneself so as to be able with Italian virtue to defend oneself from foreigners. And although Swiss and Spanish infantry are esteemed to be terrifying, nonetheless there is a defect in both, by means of which a third order might not only oppose them but also be confident of overcoming them. For the Spanish cannot withstand horse, and the Swiss have to be afraid of infantry if they meet in combat any that are obstinate like themselves. Hence it has been seen, and will be seen by experience, that the Spanish cannot withstand French cavalry, and the Swiss are ruined by Spanish infantry. And although a complete experiment of this last has not been seen, yet an indication of it was seen in the battle of Ravenna,[27] when the Spanish infantry confronted the German battalions, who use the same order as the Swiss. There the Spanish, with their agile bodies and aided by their bucklers, came between and under the Germans' pikes and attacked them safely without their having any remedy for it; and if it had not been for the cavalry that charged them, they would have worn out all the Germans. Having thus learned the defects of both of these infantry,

---

25 Seven battles that were Italian defeats, from 1495 to 1513.
26 lit.: provinces.
27 April 11, 1512.

one can order a new one that would resist horse and not be afraid of infantry; this will be done by a regeneration of arms and a change in orders. And these are among those things which, when newly ordered, give reputation and greatness to a new prince.

Thus, one should not let this opportunity pass, for Italy, after so much time, to see her redeemer. I cannot express with what love he would be received in all those provinces that have suffered from these floods from outside; with what thirst for revenge, with what obstinate faith, with what piety, with what tears. What doors would be closed to him? What peoples would deny him obedience? What envy would oppose him? What Italian would deny him homage? This barbarian domination stinks to everyone. Then may your illustrious house take up this task with the spirit and hope in which just enterprises are taken up, so that under its emblem this fatherland may be ennobled and under its auspices the saying of Petrarch's may come true:

> Virtue will take up arms against fury,
> and make the battle short,
> because the ancient valor in Italian hearts
> is not yet dead.[28]

28 Petrarch, *Italia mia*, verses 93–6.

Part III

Urban Life and Values

Introduction to Part III

While Italy in the fourteenth through sixteenth centuries remained, like the rest of Europe, predominantly rural, Renaissance humanism, art, and architecture flourished particularly in urban centers. Whereas political and intellectual historians have explored possible links between new forms of civic government and the innovative ideas and cultural objects that arose, social historians have done much to elucidate the rhythms of daily life, the often unwritten codes of behavior that shaped people's interactions, and the values that guided their choices and commitments. The readings in this section offer three distinct windows onto Renaissance urban culture: a fictional account of a small-town merchant's fumbling about the Neapolitan underworld; private letters of a Florentine widow to her exiled sons concerning family matters and economic advancement; and an exchange of letters between Machiavelli, living discontentedly on his farm, and his friend Francesco Vettori, who had recently become Florentine ambassador to the court of Pope Leo X.

Plate 5 Donatello, *Judith and Holofernes* (ca. late 1450s), Sala dei Gigli, Palazzo Vecchio, Florence. *Source*: Scala/Art Resource, NY.

The Florentine sculptor Donatello (ca. 1386–1466), a favorite of the Medici, worked in a variety of media, including marble, wood, and terracotta, in addition to bronze, in which this statue is cast. The incident depicted is the act by which Judith, a beautiful and pious Israelite widow, thwarted an Assyrian army offensive by beheading its commander, Holofernes (Judith 12:10–13:11). Seeming to be receptive to his advances, she contrived to be left alone with him in his tent following a banquet. As he lay on his bed "dead drunk," she used his own sword to strike off his head. Then, secreting the head in her food bag, she returned to her people, and the following morning they displayed the head on the town wall.

Initially serving as the centerpiece of the enclosed garden in the Medici palace, the sculpture was inscribed on its base with the words, "Kingdoms fall through luxury, cities rise by virtues. Behold the neck of pride severed by the hand of humility." A few years later, probably in the aftermath of an unsuccessful challenge to the Medici regime following the death of Cosimo "The Elder" in 1464, his son Piero "The Gouty" had a second inscription added. Explicitly connecting the theme of civic virtue with the Medici family, it read: "The salvation of the state. Piero de' Medici, son of Cosimo, dedicated this statue of a woman both to liberty and to fortitude, whereby the citizens with unvanquished and constant heart might return to the republic."[1] After the expulsion of the Medici from Florence in 1494, however, the *Judith and Holofernes* was appropriated to communicate quite a different message: taken from the Palazzo Medici and placed in front of the town hall (the Palazzo della Signoria), it wore a new inscription alluding transparently to the defeat (for the time being) of Medicean rule: "The citizens positioned [this statue] in 1495 as an object-lesson of the communal welfare."[2]

---

1 The translations are those of Nicolai Rubinstein, as cited in Dale Kent, *Cosimo de' Medici and the Florentine Renaissance* (New Haven and London, 2000), p. 283. I follow Kent's interpretation of the inscriptions.

2 Translation from Latin inscription by K. Gouwens.

6

Giovanni Boccaccio (1313–1375)

Boccaccio ranks along with Dante and Petrarch as one of the most famous of all Italian writers. Born in a small town outside Florence, he spent much of his youth in Naples, where his father worked for the prestigious Bardi bank (which was based in Florence). When the bank crashed, his family returned to Florence, where he became established as an author of verse and prose, both in Latin and in Italian. Boccaccio met Petrarch in Florence in 1350, and although he was appalled when Petrarch chose to work for the Visconti in Milan rather than for the Florentine Republic, the two scholars remained close friends.

The *Decameron* (1348–51), easily his most popular and famous composition, is a collection of 100 stories. The tales are framed by the interaction of ten storytellers – seven women and three men – who have fled the Black Death then ravaging Florence for a country estate in nearby Fiesole. To pass the time, each one tells a story every day for ten days. Although Boccaccio reshaped the tales and organized them into a coherent whole, he drew extensively upon existing material, and the stories may reveal something of the assumptions and values of the culture that produced them. In the tale of Andreuccio (second day, fifth story), we follow the practical education of a naive merchant from Perugia making his first visit to the city of Naples.

Questions

1 What kinds of behavior first get Andreuccio into trouble? Why do his circumstances spiral downwards so quickly?

2   At what point(s) do his fortunes take a turn for the better, and why?
    How has he changed by the end of the story?
3   How is human nature portrayed? What do you imagine Machiavelli
    might have thought of the tale?
4   What qualities are deemed praiseworthy, and why? To what extent
    does the tale express values appropriate to a merchant society?

Decameron II, 5

Andreuccio from Perugia goes to Naples to buy horses, is caught up in three unfortunate adventures in one night, escapes from them all, and returns home with a ruby.

The precious stones found by Landolfo – said Fiammetta, whose turn it was to tell the next tale – remind me of a story no less full of dangers than the one recounted by Lauretta, but it differs from hers in that these dangers all occur within the space of a single night, as you are about to hear, whereas in her story they happened over a period of several years.

There once lived in Perugia, according to what I have been told, a young man whose name was Andreuccio di Pietro, a dealer in horses who, when he heard that in Naples horses were being sold at a low price, put five hundred gold florins in his purse and, though he had never been outside of his own town before, set out for Naples with some other merchants and arrived there on Sunday evening around vespers, and at the advice of his landlord the following morning he went to the marketplace, where he saw many horses, a good number of which he liked, but he was not able to strike a bargain no matter how hard he tried; in fact, to show that he was really ready to do business, being the crass and incautious fool that he was, more than once he pulled out his purse full of florins in front of everyone who passed by. While he was in the midst of these dealings, with his purse on full display, a young and very beautiful Sicilian lady – one who, for a small price, would be happy to please any man – passed close to him, and without being seen by him, she caught a glimpse of his purse and immediately said to herself:

"Who would be better off than I if that money were mine?" – and she walked past.

With this young lady there was an old woman, also Sicilian, who, when she saw Andreuccio, let her young companion walk ahead while she ran up to him and embraced him affectionately; when the young girl saw this, she said nothing, and waited nearby for her companion. Andreuccio turned around, recognized the old woman, and greeted her with a great deal of pleasure, and after she promised to visit him at his inn, they said no more and parted company, and Andreuccio returned to his bargaining; but he bought nothing that morning.

The young woman who had first seen Andreuccio's purse as well as his familiarity with her older companion cautiously began to ask who that man was and where he came from and what he was doing there and how her friend knew him, in order to see if she could find a way of getting that money of his – if not all of it, at least a part. The old woman told her everything about Andreuccio almost as well as he himself might have told it, for she had lived a long time in Sicily and then in Perugia with Andreuccio's father; she also told her where he was staying and why he had come. Once the young woman felt herself well enough informed about his relatives and their names, she devised a cunning trick, based on what she had learned, to satisfy her desires. As soon as she returned home, she sent the old woman on errands for the entire day so that she would not be able to return to Andreuccio; then, around vespers, she sent one of her young servant girls, whom she had well trained for such missions, to the inn where Andreuccio was staying. Arriving there, the servant girl found Andreuccio by chance alone at the door, and she asked him where Andreuccio was. When he told her he was standing right before her, drawing him aside, she said:

"Sir, a genteel lady who lives in this city would like to speak to you at your leisure."

When Andreuccio heard this, he immediately assumed, for he considered himself a handsome young man, that such a woman as that must be in love with him (as if there were no man in all of Naples as handsome as he), and he immediately replied that he was ready and asked her where and when this lady wished to speak to him. To this, the young servant girl answered:

"Sir, whenever you wish to come, she awaits you at her home."

Quickly, and without mentioning anything to anyone at the inn, Andreuccio replied:

"Let's go, then, you lead the way; I'll follow you."

Whereupon the servant girl led him to her house, which was in a district called the Malpertugio, which was as respectable a district as its very name implies.[1] But Andreuccio knew or suspected nothing, believing he was going to a most respectable place and to the house of a respectable lady, and so he calmly followed the servant girl into the house. Climbing up the stairs, the

---

1   This ill-famed district of Naples actually existed in Boccaccio's day, and its name might best be rendered into English as "Evilhole."

servant girl called to her mistress: "Here's Andreuccio!" and he saw her appear at the head of the stairs to greet him.

She was still very young, tall, with a very beautiful face, and elegantly dressed and adorned. Andreuccio started toward her, and she descended three steps to greet him with open arms, and throwing her arms around his neck, she remained in that position for a while without saying a word – as if some overpowering emotion had stolen her words – then she started crying and kissing his forehead, and in a broken voice she said:

"Oh my Andreuccio, how happy I am to see you!"

Andreuccio, amazed at such tender greetings, and completely astonished, replied:

"My lady, the pleasure is mine!"

Then she took his hand and led him through her sitting room, and from there, without saying a word, into her bedroom, which was all scented with roses, orange blossoms, and other fragrances; there he saw a very beautiful curtained bed, and many dresses hanging on pegs (as was the custom there), and other very beautiful and expensive things. And since all those lovely things were new to him, Andreuccio was convinced that she had to be nothing less than a great lady. They sat together on a chest at the foot of her bed, and she began speaking to him:

"Andreuccio, I am quite sure that you are amazed at my tears and caresses, for perhaps you do not know me or do not remember hearing of me; but you are about to hear something that will amaze you even more: I am your sister! And now that God has granted me the favor of seeing one of my brothers before I die (oh, how I wish I could see them all!), I assure you I shall pass away content. Since you know nothing about this, I shall tell you. Pietro, your father and mine, as I think you probably know, resided for a long time in Palermo, and because of his kindness and friendliness, he was dearly loved and still is loved by those who knew him; but among those who loved him very much, my mother, who was a lady of noble birth and then a widow, was the one who loved him the most, so much so that she put aside the fear of her father and brothers and her own honor and lived with him in so intimate a way that I was born, and here I am right here before your eyes. Then when Pietro had to leave Palermo and return to Perugia, he left me, a tiny child, with my mother, and as far as I know, he never thought of me or my mother again. If he were not my father, I would criticize him severely for his ingratitude toward my mother (to say nothing of the love he owed me, his daughter, not born from any servant girl or from some woman of low birth), who had put herself as well as her possessions into his hands, moved by a true love for a man she did not really know.

"But what does it matter? Things done badly in the past are more easily criticized than amended – that's how it all ended. He abandoned me as a little girl in Palermo, where, grown up almost as much as I am now, my mother, who was a rich lady, gave me as a wife to a rich man of noble birth from Agrigento who, out of his love for me and my mother, came to live in Palermo; and there, as he was an avid supporter of the Guelfs,[2] he began to carry on some kind of intrigue with our King Charles. But King Frederick discovered the plot before it could be put into effect, and this was the cause of our fleeing from Sicily – and just when I was about to become the greatest lady that island ever knew. Taking with us those few things we could (I say 'few' as compared to the many things we owned), we abandoned our lands and palaces and took refuge in this land, where we found King Charles so grateful to us that he restored in part the losses which we had suffered on his account, and he gave us property and houses; and he continues to provide my husband, your brother-in-law, with a good salary, as you can see for yourself; and so, my sweet brother, here I am, and with no thanks to you but rather through the mercy of God I have come to meet you."

And having said all this, she embraced him once more, and continuing to weep tenderly, she kissed his forehead. Hearing this fable so carefully and skillfully told by the young lady, who never hesitated over a word or fumbled in any way, Andreuccio recalled it was indeed true that his father had been in Palermo, and since he himself knew the ways of young men who easily fall in love when they are young and since he had just witnessed the piteous tears, the embraces, and the pure kisses of this young lady, he took everything she said to be the absolute truth; and when she had finished speaking, he said:

"My lady, it should not surprise you to see me amazed, for to tell the truth, either my father never spoke of you and your mother, or, if he did, I never heard a word about it, for I had no more knowledge of you than if you never existed; but I am all the more delighted to have found a sister, for I am completely alone here, and I never hoped for such a thing and, truly, I don't know of any man of whatever rank or station to whom you would not be very dear, not to mention an insignificant merchant like me. But I beg you to clarify one thing for me: how did you know I was here?"

To this she answered:

"I was told about it this morning by a poor woman whom I often see, and according to her story, she was with our father for a long time both in Palermo and in Perugia; and if it were not for the fact that it seemed to me more proper for you to come to my house than for me to visit you in a stranger's house, I would have come to see you much sooner."

Then she began to ask about all his relatives individually by name, and Andreuccio replied to all her questions about them, and her questions made him believe even more of what he should not have believed at all. They talked

2   The Guelfs, supporters of the Papacy, were opposed by the Ghibellines, the imperial party in medieval Italy. The names are derived from "Waiblingen" and "Welf," the names of two twelfth-century families heading rival parties in the Holy Roman Empire.

for a long time, and since it was so hot that day, she had Greek wine and confections served to Andreuccio; then it was suppertime, and Andreuccio got up to leave, but the lady would not hear of this, and pretending to get angry, she said as she embraced him:

"Alas, poor me! How clearly I see that you care very little for me! How is it possible? Here you are with a sister of yours that you have never seen before, and she is in her own house, where you ought to be staying, and you want to leave her, to eat at some inn? You shall certainly dine with me, and though my husband is not here (a fact which displeases me a great deal) I shall honor you as best a woman can."

Not knowing what to say to this, Andreuccio replied:

"I hold you as dear as one can hold a sister, but if I don't leave, they'll wait all evening for me to come to supper, and I'll make a bad impression."

And she said:

"God be praised! As if I did not have anyone to send to tell them not to wait for you! But you would do me an even greater courtesy by inviting all of your companions to have supper here and then, if you still wished to leave, you could all leave together."

Andreuccio replied that he did not want to be with his companions that evening, and that he would stay as she wished. Then she pretended to send someone to notify the inn that he should not be expected for supper; and, after much conversation, they finally sat down and were served a number of splendid courses, and she cleverly prolonged the supper until night came; then, when they got up from the table and Andreuccio decided it was time to leave, she said that under no circumstances would she permit it, for Naples was not the kind of town in which to wander around at night, especially if you were a stranger, and furthermore, she said that when she had sent the message telling them not to expect him for supper, she had also told them not to expect him back that night. Since he believed everything she said and enjoyed being with her, because of his false belief, he decided to stay with her. After supper, and not without her reasons, she kept him engaged in a lengthy conversation; and when a good part of the night had passed, she left Andreuccio in her bedroom in the company of a young boy who would assist him if he wanted anything, and she withdrew into another bedroom with her chambermaids.

The heat of the night was intense, and because of this and since he was alone, Andreuccio quickly stripped to his waist and took off his pants, placing them at the head of the bed; and then the natural need of having to deposit the superfluous load in his stomach beckoned him, so he asked the boy servant where he should do it, and the boy pointed to a place in one corner of the bedroom and said: "Go in there."

Andreuccio innocently entered the place and as he did, by chance he happened to step on a plank which was not nailed to the beam it rested on;

this overturned the plank, and he with the plank plunged down through the floor. But by the love of God he was spared from hurting himself in the fall, in spite of the height from which he fell; he was, however, completely covered by the filth that filled the place. In order for you to understand better just what took place and what was going to take place, I shall now describe to you the kind of place it was. Andreuccio was in a narrow alley like the kind we often see between two houses; some planks had been nailed on two beams placed between one house and the other, and there was a place to sit down; and the plank which plunged with him to the bottom was precisely one of these two supporting planks.

Andreuccio, finding himself down there in the alley, to his great discomfort, began calling the boy, but as soon as the boy heard Andreuccio fall, he ran to tell the lady, and she rushed to Andreuccio's bedroom and quickly checked to see if his clothes were still there. She found his clothes and in them his money, which he stupidly always carried with him, for he did not trust anyone; and when this woman of Palermo, pretending to be the sister of a Perugian, had gotten what she had set her trap for, she quickly locked the exit he had gone through when he fell, and she no longer was concerned about him.

When the boy did not answer, Andreuccio began to call him more loudly, but that did not help either; then he became suspicious, and began to realize (only too late) that he had been tricked. He climbed over a small wall which closed that alley from the street and ran to the door of the house, which he recognized all to well, and there he shouted and shook and pounded on the door for a long time, but all in vain. Then, as one who sees clearly his misfortune, he began to sob, saying:

"Alas, poor me! I have lost five hundred florins and a sister, and in so short a time!"

And after many such laments, he began all over again to beat on the door and to scream; and he kept this up for so long that many of the neighbors were awakened and forced out of bed by the disturbance; one of the lady's servants, pretending to be sleepy, came to the window and said in a complaining tone of voice: "Who's that knocking down there?"

"Oh," said Andreuccio, "don't you recognize me? I am Andreuccio, brother to Madam Fiordaliso."

To this the servant replied:

"My good man, if you've drunk too much, go sleep it off and come back in the morning; I don't know what Andreuccio you are talking about or any other nonsense. Off with you, and let us sleep, if you please!"

"What," said Andreuccio, "you don't know what I'm talking about? You've got to know; but if this is what it is like to be related in Sicily – that you forget your ties so quickly – then at least give me back the clothes I left up there, and in God's name I'll gladly be off!"

To this, in a laughing voice the woman replied:

"You must be dreaming, my good man!"

No sooner had she said this than she shut the window. Andreuccio, now most certain of his loss, was so vexed that his anger was turning to rage, and he decided to get back by force what he could not get back with words: he picked up a large stone and began all over again – but with harder blows this time – to beat furiously at the door, and many of the neighbors who had been aroused from their beds not long before thought that he was some sort of pest who had invented all this to bother that good lady, and so they took offense at the racket he was making. They appeared at their windows, and began to shout in a way not unlike all the dogs in a neighborhood who bark at a stray:

"It's an outrage to come at this hour to a decent lady's house and shout such foul things. In God's name leave, good man; let us sleep, if you don't mind; if you have any business with her, come back tomorrow and don't bother us anymore tonight."

The good woman's pimp, who was inside the house and whom Andreuccio had neither seen nor heard, taking courage from his neighbors' words, exclaimed in a horrible, ferocious, roaring voice:

"Who's down there?"

Andreuccio raised his head at the sound of that voice and saw someone who, as far as he could tell, looked like some sort of big shot; he had a thick black beard and was yawning and rubbing his eyes as if he had just been awakened from a sound sleep. Andreuccio, not without fear, replied:

"I am the brother of the lady who lives here ... "

But the man did not wait for Andreuccio to finish what he had to say; with a voice more menacing than the first time, he howled:

"I don't know what's keeping me from coming down there and beating the shit out of you, you dumb ass, you drunken sot – you're not going to let anybody get any sleep tonight, are you?"

He turned inside and banged the window shut. Some of the neighbors, who knew this man for what he was, said to Andreuccio in a kindly way:

"For God's sake, man, get out of here quick before you witness your own murder tonight! For your own good, leave!"

Frightened by the voice and face of the man at the window and persuaded by the advice of the neighbors, who seemed kindly disposed toward him, Andreuccio, as sorrowful as anyone ever could be and despairing over the loss of his money, and not knowing which way to go, started moving in the direction that the servant girl had led him that day, as he tried to find his way back to the inn. Even *he* found the stench he was giving off disgusting; so, turning to the left, he took a street called Catalan Street and headed for the sea in order to wash himself off; but he was heading toward the upper part of town, and in so doing, he happened to see two men with lanterns in their hands coming in his direction, and fearing that they might be the police or other men who could do him harm, he cautiously took shelter in a hut he saw nearby. But the two men were headed for the very same spot and they, too, entered the hut; once inside, one of them put down the iron tools he was carrying and began examining them and discussing them with the other. All of a sudden, one of them remarked:

"What's going on here? That's the worst stink I've ever smelled!"

As he said this, he tilted his lantern up a bit and saw Andreuccio, the poor devil. Amazed, he asked:

"Who's there?"

Andreuccio did not utter a word; the two men drew closer with the light, and one of them asked him how he had gotten so filthy; Andreuccio told them everything that had happened to him. Having guessed where all this must have taken place, they said to each other:

"This guy really knows the head of the Mafia – he's been to Spitfire's place!"[3]

Turning to Andreuccio, one of them said:

"My good man, you might have lost your money, but you still have God to thank for not going back into the house after you fell; if you had not fallen, you can be sure that before you fell asleep, you would have been murdered and, along with your money, you would have lost your life. You have as much chance of getting a penny of your money back as you do of plucking a star from the sky! You could even get killed if that guy finds out you ever said a word about it!"

After telling him this, he consulted with his companion for a while, then said:

"Look, we've taken pity on you, so if you want to come with us and do what we plan to do, we're sure that your share of what we all get will be more than what you've lost."

Andreuccio was so desperate that he said he was willing to go along. That day an Archbishop of Naples named Messer Filippo Minutolo had been buried, and with him the richest of vestments and a ruby on his finger which was worth more than five hundred gold florins; this is what they were out to get, and they let Andreuccio in on their plan. More avaricious than wise, he set off with them, and as they made their way toward the cathedral, Andreuccio stank so badly that one of them said:

"Can't we find some way for this guy to wash up a little, so that he doesn't stink so bad?"

The other answered:

3   Spitfire (*Buttafuoco*) is called a *scarabone* by the two men in the original Italian, meaning an important figure in the local criminal underworld – what is known today as the Camorra, a Neapolitan equivalent of the Sicilian Mafia.

"All right. We're near a well that should have a pulley and a large bucket; let's go give him a quick washing up."

When they reached the well, they discovered that the rope was there but the bucket had been removed, so they decided between themselves that they would tie Andreuccio to the rope and lower him into the well, and he could wash himself down there; then, when he was washed, he could tug on the rope and they would pull him up. And this is what they did. It happened that no sooner had they lowered him into the well than some police watchmen, who had been chasing someone else and were thirsty because of the heat, came to the well for a drink; when the two men saw the police heading for the well, they quickly fled without being seen.

Andreuccio, who had just cleaned himself up at the bottom of the well, gave a pull on the rope. The thirsty night watchmen had just laid down their shields, arms, and other gear and were beginning to pull up the rope, thinking that a bucket full of water was at the other end. When Andreuccio saw himself nearing the rim of the well, he dropped the rope and grabbed the edge with his two hands; when the night watchmen saw him, they were terrified, and dropping the rope without wasting a word, they began to run away as fast as they could. Andreuccio was very surprised at all this, and if he had not held on tightly, he would have fallen back to the bottom of the well and perhaps have hurt himself seriously or even killed himself; when he climbed out and discovered the weapons, which he knew his companions had not brought with them, he became even more puzzled. Afraid, not understanding a thing, and lamenting his misfortune, he decided to leave that spot without touching a thing; and off he went, not knowing where he was going.

But on his way, he ran into his two companions, who were on their way back to pull him out of the well, and when they saw him, they were amazed and asked him who had pulled him out of the well. Andreuccio replied that he did not know, and then he told them exactly what had happened and what he had discovered near the well. They then realized what had actually taken place and, laughing, they told him why they had run away and who the people were who had pulled him up. Without any further conversation (for it was already midnight), they went to the cathedral and managed to get in without any trouble at all; they went up to the tomb, which was very large and made of marble; with their iron bars, they raised up the heavy cover just as much as was necessary for a man to get inside, and then they propped it up. And when this was done, one of them said:

"Who'll go inside?"

To this, the other replied:

"Not me!"

"Not me either," answered the other. "You go, Andreuccio."

"Not me," said Andreuccio.

Both of them turned toward Andreuccio and said:

"What do you mean, you won't go in? By God, if you don't, we'll beat your head in with one of these iron bars till you drop dead!"

This frightened Andreuccio, so he climbed in, and as he entered the tomb, he thought to himself:

"These guys are making me go into the tomb to cheat me: as soon as I give them everything that's inside and I am trying to get out of the tomb, they will take off with the goods and leave me with nothing!"

And so he thought about protecting his own share from the start: he remembered the two men had talked about an expensive ring, so as soon as he had climbed into the tomb, he took the ring from the Archbishop's finger and placed it on his own; then he handed out the Archbishop's staff, his miter, and his gloves, and stripping him down to his shirt, he handed over everything to them, announcing, finally, that there was nothing left, but they insisted that the ring must be there and told him to look all over for it; but Andreuccio answered that he could not find it, and he kept them waiting there for some time while he pretended to search for it. The other two, on the other hand, were just as tricky as Andreuccio was trying to be, and at the right moment they pulled away the prop that held up the cover and fled, leaving Andreuccio trapped inside the tomb.

When Andreuccio heard this, you can imagine how he felt. He tried time and again, with both his head and his shoulders, to raise the cover, but he labored in vain; overcome with despair, he fainted and fell upon the dead body of the Archbishop; and anyone seeing the two of them there together would have had a hard time telling which one of them was really dead: he or the Archbishop. Regaining consciousness, he began to sob bitterly, realizing that being where he was, without any doubt one of two kinds of death awaited him: either he would die in the tomb from hunger and from the stench of the maggots on the dead body (that is, if no one came to open the tomb); or, if someone came and found him in the tomb, he would be hanged as a thief.

With this terrible thought in his head, and filled with grief, he heard people walking and talking in the church; they were people, it seemed to him, who had come to do what he and his companions had already done – this terrified him all the more! As soon as these people raised the cover of the tomb and propped it up, they began arguing about who should go in, and no one wanted to do so; then, after a long discussion, a priest said:

"Why are you afraid? Do you think he is going to eat you? The dead don't eat the living! I'll go inside myself."

After saying this, he leaned his chest against the rim of the tomb, then swung around and put his legs inside, and he was about to climb down when Andreuccio saw him and rose to his feet, grabbing the priest by one of his legs and pretending to pull him down. When the priest felt this, he let out a terrible scream and instantly jumped out of the tomb. This terrified all the others, who, leaving the tomb open, began to flee as if a hundred thousand devils were chasing them.

Andreuccio, happy beyond his wildest dreams, jumped out of the tomb and left the church by the way he had come in. It was almost dawn, and he started wandering about with the ring on his finger until finally he reached the waterfront and stumbled upon his inn, where he found that the innkeeper and his companions had been up all night worried about him.

He told them the story of what had happened to him, and the innkeeper advised him to leave Naples immediately; he did so at once and returned to Perugia, having invested his money in a ring when he had set out to buy horses.

7

Alessandra Macinghi Strozzi (1407–1471)

Alessandra Strozzi wrote numerous letters to her children that can help us to understand the centrality of the family to politics and values in Renaissance Florence. In 1422 she married Matteo di Simone Strozzi (he was ten years her senior), a wool merchant from a distinguished family in the governing class. In 1433, Matteo's political position was particularly strong: he was an advocate of the oligarchical government that sent its chief rival, Cosimo de' Medici ("The Elder") into exile. But in 1434, fortune's wheel turned 180 degrees: in the September elections, Medici partisans gained key government posts, and they managed to arrange for the Medici to be invited back to the city. Cosimo moved quickly to consolidate power: in November the government banished around 100 of his political enemies, including Matteo Strozzi, who betook himself and his family to Pesaro. The following year, things got still worse for them: a plague ravaged Pesaro, and its victims included Alessandra's husband and three of their children. Twenty-eight years old and once again pregnant, she returned to Florence with their surviving children – Filippo, Caterina, Lorenzo, and Alessandra – and there she gave birth to Matteo, named in memory of his father.

While men controlled economic life in Florence, in times of need women were allowed to act as their husbands' substitutes in financial affairs. Thus, when Matteo was exiled, Alessandra became joint executor of his property. Following his death, she had to take charge arranging suitable marriages for their children: that is, matches that would enhance the honor and reputation of the family as well as bringing profit to them. In addition, she had to keep the household afloat financially, and she sought through family connections to get her sons established in business. The family's exclusion from political power in Florence made these tasks far more difficult.

Of the seven letters that follow, four (letters 2, 3, 5, and 6) were already abridged in the collection from which this book draws them. The omitted passages are briefly summarized in italics (see, for example, the start of letter 2 below). No further abridgements have been made.

Questions

1 What factors does Alessandra consider in arranging for her children's marriages? How do those factors rank in importance for her? How do dowries work into her calculations?
2 Religious concerns figure large in the letters, especially where the subject of death occurs. To what extent does religion affect Alessandra's behavior?
3 What sorts of day-to-day expenses does Alessandra deal with? What can we learn of everyday life in Florence from her letters?
4 What do her letters tell us about the role of women in Florentine society? To what extent was she, personally, able to exercise power and influence? What constraints did being a woman place upon her?

Selected letters

I

This is the earliest surviving letter of Alessandra Strozzi. It was written to her eldest son, Filippo, to tell him about the marriage she had arranged for his sister Caterina, who was to be married to a young man called Marco Parenti, a silk merchant. The letter also deals with taxes, the education of Alessandra's youngest son, Matteo, and the need for Filippo to be suitably grateful to Niccolò Strozzi, his father's cousin, who had taken him into his business in Naples.

In the name of God. 24 August 1447.

Dearest son, in the last few days I have received your letter of the 16th of July, which I will answer in this one.

And first I must tell you how by the grace of God we have arranged a marriage for our Caterina to the son of Parente di Piero Parenti. He is a young man of good birth and abilities and an only son, rich and twenty-five years of age, and he has a silk manufacturing business. And they take a small part in the government, as a little while ago his father was [an officeholder] in the College.[1] And so I am giving him one thousand florins of dowry, that is, five hundred florins that she is due in May 1448 from the Fund,[2] and the other five hundred I have to give him, made up of cash and trousseau, when she goes to her husband's house, which I believe will be in November, God willing. And this money will be partly yours and partly mine. If I hadn't taken this decision she wouldn't have been married this year, because he who marries is looking for cash and I couldn't find anyone who was willing to wait for the dowry until 1448, and part in 1450. So as I'm giving him this five hundred made up of cash and trousseau, the 1450 [money] will be mine if she lives until then.[3] We've taken this decision for the best because she was sixteen and we didn't want to wait any longer to arrange a marriage. And we found that to place her in a nobler family with greater political status would have needed fourteen hundred or fifteen hundred florins, which would have ruined both of us. And I'm not sure it would have made the girl any happier, because outside the regime[4] there's not a great choice, and this is a big problem for us. Everything considered, I decided to settle the girl well and not to take such things into account. I'm sure she'll be as well placed as any girl in Florence, because she'll have a mother- and father-in-law who are only happy making her happy. Oh and I haven't told you about Marco yet, [Caterina's] husband, he's always saying to her "If you want anything ask me for it." When she was betrothed he ordered a gown of crimson velvet for her made of silk and a surcoat of the same fabric, which is the most beautiful cloth in Florence. He had it made in his workshop. And he had a garland of feathers and pearls made [for her] which cost eighty florins, the headdress underneath has two strings of pearls costing sixty florins or more. When she goes out she'll have more than four hundred florins on her back. And he ordered some crimson velvet to be made up into long sleeves lined with marten, for [her to wear] when she goes to her husband's house. And he's having a rose-colored gown made, embroidered with pearls. He feels he can't do enough having things made, because she's beautiful and he wants her to look even more so. There isn't a girl in Florence to compare with her and

---

1   He had held office in one of the two magistracies which constituted the "Colleges" of the Signoria, or Priorate, which assisted and advised the priors: the "Twelve Goodmen" and the "Sixteen Gonfaloniers of Companies," popularly known as the Twelve and the Sixteen.
2   The Dowry Fund was established in 1425, allowing parents of some means to deposit a sum on their infant daughters' behalf, to mature after a set term. This was paid to her husband after the marriage had been consummated or after the term of the investment was completed, if that was a later date.
3   If a girl died before her marriage, or after it but before a Dowry Fund investment matured, only the deposit was returned to her relatives.
4   The elite group who held high office and enjoyed real political power.

she's beautiful in every way, or so many people think. May God give them his grace and good health for a long time, as I wish.

About sending Matteo away,[5] I wouldn't want to do so for the present because although he's so little he keeps me company and I'd be in a bad way without him, at least at the present time while Caterina's getting ready to go and live with her husband. After that it seems to me I'll be on my own too much. For the present I'm not inclined to send him away. If he wants to be good I'll keep him here. He can't be taxed[6] until he's sixteen and he was only eleven in March. I've taken him away from learning arithmetic and he's learning to write.[7] I'll put him at the writing desk and he can stay there this winter. After that we'll see what he wants to do. May God give him those abilities which he's going to need.

So far as the Commune[8] is concerned, I must tell you that I owe them two hundred and forty florins and that I've been persecuted by no less than four Offices[9] trying to recover [money] for the Commune. For the last six months I've done nothing but go to one Office after another. Now by the grace of God I've reached an agreement to pay them all, up until February, nine florins a month or thereabouts. They say the new tax may be imposed for all of October. If they do the right thing by me as they say they will, not imposing the assessment on widows and orphans, I won't have two florins [to pay], so perhaps I won't have so many debts. And since the Duke of Milan is dead[10] they think we won't have to pay so much [tax], if the King of Aragon[11] doesn't give us trouble, which he's already begun [to do] close to Monte-varchi[12] at a castle called Cennina. It was said when they took it that it could be retaken in a day because they wouldn't be able to stay there. They've already been there for three weeks and look like [they're] staying because it's in such [good] countryside. It's said there was so much grain and goods they could live off it for a year. It's said that before they [the Florentines] retake it they will have spent more than forty thousand florins. May God provide for our needs.

Caterina says you should arrange it so she can get some of that soap and if there's any good water or anything else [in Naples] to make [her] beautiful

---

5   Filippo had raised the question of whether Matteo, who was eleven, should leave Florence to begin learning merchant practice in one of the branches (in Naples, Bruges, and Barcelona) of the bank of Niccolò, Filippo, and Jacopo di Lionardo Strozzi. They were first cousins of Alessandra's husband, Matteo.

6   The head tax.

7   That is, he was learning to write business letters, and also to write a clearer script.

8   The Florentine state or government.

9   Branches or divisions of the Florentine government, in charge of its various fiscal functions.

10   Filippo Maria Visconti, Duke of Milan (died 13 August 1447), had spent much of the previous three decades at war with Florence.

11   Alfonso I of Naples (Alfonso V of Aragon), ruled 1443–58.

12   In the Val d'Arno, about 45 kilometers to the southeast of Florence.

she begs you to send it quickly and by a trustworthy person, because otherwise he [the carrier] might do something mischievous with it.

Don't be surprised if I don't write often, because I'm very busy arranging everything for Caterina. You'll be paid back when Matteo has learned to write, but don't expect letters from me. Do write by every messenger though, if only to say that you're well and that Niccolò is.[13] I don't know how you're going with your tasks or whether you're keen to do them. God knows the disappointment I suffered when you couldn't come to Florence while you were at Livorno, because you can say things in person which you can't put in a letter. May it please God to let me see you again safe and well before I die. In the past year you've made me very unhappy with your bad behavior.[14] Above all my son, you must behave better and give me comfort instead. You should consider your position and think what Niccolò has done for you and be worthy to kiss the ground the walks on. And I say this out of love for you, because you have a greater obligation to him than to your father or mother, when I think of all he's done for you, which no one else would have done. So do be aware of this and don't be ungrateful for the kindness he has shown to you and yours, and that you constantly receive from him. I don't want to say any more. You should understand because you're no longer a boy: you were nineteen in July, which is [old] enough. Above all, do be careful with money; you must, because you're in a worse position than you realize. Nothing more for now. May God keep you from harm. I haven't written to Niccolò about Caterina because I know he's heard all about it from Giovanni and Antonio.[15] Remember us to him, and if you're the cashier, act in a way that does you credit and keep a strict tally so I don't have any more grief than I've had already.[16]

2

The plague was raging in Florence and the subject of death clearly occupied Alessandra's mind as she wrote to Filippo. Niccolò's brother, Filippo di Lionardo Strozzi, had died in Barcelona some months earlier, and several other relations had recently died of the plague in Florence. Alessandra was also concerned that Caterina (who was expecting her first child the following February) might die in childbirth, and the final installment of her dowry might thus be lost. She discusses whether they should insure against this possibility.

13   Niccolò di Lionardo Strozzi, for whom Filippo worked in Naples at this time.
14   Her remark at the end of this paragraph suggests that this misdemeanor involved carelessness with money.
15   Giovanni della Luna and Antonio di Benedetto Strozzi. Antonio had been only a distant relation of Matteo Strozzi, but was one of Alessandra's closest friends and advisers at this time.
16   Alessandra forgot to sign this letter.

In the name of God. 26 December 1449.

Two paragraphs: she had had many letters from Filippo which she had not answered; she had been ill, and had gone to stay with Marco and Caterina and then with her brother, Zanobi Macinghi, at Antella.[1]

I heard from you and first from Soldo degli Strozzi and Matteo di Giorgio Brandolini[2] of the death of our Filippo, which has made me very sad and still does, considering the harm it will do to us first and then to the whole family.[3] He was such a good man, he gave a good reputation to [us] all. There's nothing we can do about his death; we must endure whatever God wills. F[rancesco] della Luna[4] has also died, which has been a great loss. And Antonangiolo Macinghi has died and [so have] many other Strozzi relations. Margherita di Pippo Manetti died today[5] and two of her children, so this time our immediate family has been hit. May God in his mercy bring it to an end. About the death of Filippo, I've [heard from] your letters and from Jacopo's how he [Jacopo] and Niccolò met in Barcelona.[6] May God give them a good journey. You tell me I should honor Niccolò, who will be staying with us, and how he will be taking Matteo with him to Barcelona and that I should get everything organized. I've done so and I'm looking forward to his arrival because I'm eager to see him. I'll try to do him as much honor as I can. I know I can't do him all the honor he deserves because I don't know how to. He'll have to excuse me when I do whatever I can and do it willingly. May God bring him here safely. Yesterday I heard he was in Rome; I imagine he'll leave there after the [Christmas] festival and we'll expect him here on the 4th or 5th of January.

Three paragraphs: cloth for shirts and flax; a list of their debtors in Pesaro; another discussion about the neighboring house belonging to Donato Rucellai.

I gather you've heard from Marco that Caterina is pregnant and expecting the child in the middle of February. As that's the case I think we should take out some insurance so we won't lose the five hundred florins they're owed from the [Dowry] Fund,[7] as we could lose her and the money at the same time. We could lose it if God has other plans for her. I've discussed it with

1   A village to the southeast of Florence.
2   Formerly a business partner of Alessandra's husband, he now worked for Niccolò Strozzi and his brothers.
3   The Strozzi lineage.
4   Husband of Alessandra di Messer Filippo Strozzi, who was an aunt of the Filippo Strozzi whose death has just been mentioned.
5   A first cousin of Alessandra's husband.
6   To discuss the administration of their brother's estate.
7   This money belonged to Alessandra because she had paid Marco 500 florins of her own money at the time of the marriage.

Antonio degli Strozzi and he thinks we should spend the 12 florins, which is what it would cost for insurance for these three months, that is for January, February and March. I'll wait for Niccolò, who'll be here soon, and do as he advises me. Marco thinks we shouldn't do it; he says that as she's keeping so well in herself we shouldn't throw away these few florins. It seems to me better to throw them away and be sure. For that reason [I won't] write to him about it, so he won't take it badly, because it's our business. I pray God will bring her through it at the proper time and healthy in body and soul, as I wish.

I'm thinking of going to Rome, God willing, later on in April for the Holy Indulgence.[8] If by any chance you could come too, so that I could see you again before I die, it would be a great comfort to me. You see there's nothing else I care about in this world except you, my three sons, and I've sent you away one after the other for your own good and not considering my own happiness. Now I am so sad at sending away this last one. I don't know how I can live without him, because I feel so unhappy and love him too much because he is just like his father. And he's become such a beautiful boy while he's been in the country; if you'd seen him before and saw him now you wouldn't know he was the same boy. May God let him be a comfort to me. And because I'm so sad I beg you to give me a little comfort from this trip to Rome. May God let me live long enough to see you all again, as I wish.

I've had a letter from Lorenzo which he wrote in October. He says he's well. Do write to him often because it will be good for him. I received the power of attorney you sent me and I'll let you know if I need anything else. Nothing more for now; may God keep you from harm. From your Alessandra[9] in Florence.

3

The Medici regime had now moved to enforce by law the exile of Alessandra's sons from Florence, and she begins this letter to Lorenzo by discussing this development. She then describes the marriage arranged for Isabella, Jacopo Strozzi's illegitimate daughter, who had been sent to Florence so that a suitable husband could be found for her.

In the name of God. 19 February 1459.

My last letter to you was on the 20th of last month, and since then I've had yours of the 19th of December. It's been a comfort to me, seeing you've

---

8 Pilgrims to Rome could obtain a plenary or full indulgence which remitted all temporal punishment for their sins up to that time.
9 Here and in the letters below, the spelling of "Alessandra" has been standardized.

taken what has happened[1] as well as you possibly could. You've made the right decision, because there's nothing we can do about it. Since then they have brought the limits closer, to 50 miles, and we have been given permission to write letters without showing them to the Eight,[2] either yours or mine. And Bat[t]ista[3] and the others have also been given permission to write [to those exiled], except about political matters, which is what a man wants.

Two paragraphs about money, property, and a power of attorney which Lorenzo should send.

I must tell you how on the 9th we married Isabella to Marco di Giovanni di Marco, a silk weaver and mercer and a silk merchant in a small way. His father has no other sons, but seven girls, one married and six still at home; five of them have dowries in the Fund. People say they're well off and good people and God-fearing, which is the main thing. We've had the wedding and from what I saw of them I think she's been lucky. Considering her status[4] and that she's longsighted, as you know, we weren't looking to put her in a wealthy household so much as one where she'll be loved and well looked after. That's what she needs, as we saw it. The young man is twenty-one, and Pierotto, who will carry this letter, will tell you what he looks like because last night he saw him at supper at Francesco Strozzi's[5] house. He was treated with more honor there, out of love for Jacopo, than he was in mine, but I'll do the same in future. I know Bat[t]ista will tell Jacopo all about it and about the money he sent me and how much I used for the things she needed, because if she looks like a girl from a good family they're more likely to think of her that way.[6] I don't have time to write to Jacopo but I know the others will tell him all about it.

I'll send you the jar of aromatic [herbs], but the best medicine for your stomach is to watch what you put in your mouth. Do write often as we're allowed to, and [let me know] how you are in yourself; that will make me happy. Nothing more [for now]; remember me to Jacopo. May God keep you from all harm. From your Alessandra in Florence.

1   During the second half of 1458 the Medici regime sought to strengthen its position (among other measures) by renewing the sentences of exile imposed on their enemies in 1434. In the case of some families, including the Strozzi, the sentence was also extended to the male descendants of the original exiles. Initially those affected were obliged to stay 100 miles from the city, but this was then reduced to 50 miles.
2   The Eight of Watch (or Guard), a committee of state security.
3   Battista di Francesco Strozzi.
4   Her illegitimacy.
5   Probably Francesco di Benedetto Strozzi, a business associate of Jacopo.
6   Although it is not mentioned here, Isabella would also have received a dowry from her father.

4

Matteo died in Naples in August 1459 at the age of twenty-three, and his death grieved Alessandra deeply. In this letter to Filippo she emphasizes how important it was to her that Matteo had had time to receive all the last rites of the Church, rather than dying suddenly.

In the name of God. 6 September 1459.

My sweet son, on the 11th of last month I had your letter of the 29th of July, saying how my dear and beloved son Matteo had fallen ill. And as you didn't say what he was suffering from I was extremely upset and worried a great deal about him. I sent for Francesco[1] and for Matteo di Giorgio[2] and heard from both of them that he was suffering from tertian fever,[3] which was a great comfort because with tertian fevers you don't die unless you get something else as well. After that you let me know how he was getting better, so although I was still worried my heart was a bit lighter. But since then I've heard how on the 23rd [of August] it pleased Him who gave him to me to take him back. [He was] fully aware and in a state of grace and with all the sacraments a good and faithful Christian needs. Being deprived of my son has given me the greatest grief and while I've lost a son's love it seems as if I've suffered an even greater loss through his death; and you as well, my other two sons, who are now reduced to such a small number. I praise and thank our Lord for everything which is His will, because I'm sure God took him when He saw his soul was healthy. I see from what you've written that you've resigned yourself to this trial and this hard and bitter death. I've heard this too from letters other people have had from there. And although the pain in my heart is like nothing I ever felt before, I've taken comfort from two things. First, he was with you so I'm certain he had doctors and medicines and everything was done for his well-being, and any remedies which could be used were used and nothing was neglected to keep him alive, but that nothing was any help to him and it was the will of God that it should be so. The other thing which has comforted me is that Our Lord gave him the opportunity while he was dying to free himself of sin, to ask for confession and communion and extreme unction, and all of this, I gather, he did with piety. We can hope from these signs that God has prepared a good place for him. And knowing we must all take this journey and not knowing how and not being sure of doing so in the way my beautiful son Matteo has (having

1   Francesco di Piero Strozzi.
2   Matteo di Giorgio Brandolini.
3   Malaria; later Alessandra believed that Matteo had died of the plague, although the description given does not seem to support this conclusion.

achieved a state of grace) gives me peace, keeping in mind that God could have done far worse to me, because those who die suddenly, who are cut to pieces (and this happens to many of the dead), they lose their body and soul together.[4] And if by His grace and mercy He leaves me both of you my sons, he won't give me any more suffering. Now my only thought is to hear that you've taken what has happened in the right way, because I know you're grieving, but make sure it's not in a way which does you harm, so we don't throw the handle out after the axe blade. Nothing was lacking in the care he received, on the contrary it was God's will that he escape the cares of this world, which is so full of troubles. From your letter of the 26th I saw how you're suffering in mind and body and this has upset me greatly and will until I hear that you've consoled yourself. I hope God doesn't let me live long enough to go through this again. I've been thinking that what with sleepless nights, the grief caused by death, and other things, you're probably not too well yourself. I've been worrying about this day and night and I can't get any rest. I wish I hadn't taken anyone's advice and had done what seemed right to me instead, what I wanted to do, because then I would have got there in time to see and touch my sweet living son, and that would have comforted me and him and you. I want to believe everything is for the best. I want to ask you, if my prayers can persuade you and I hope they can, to resign yourself to this for my sake and look after yourself and put your business affairs to one side for a little while. You should purge yourself a little with something mild, by one means or another. And then you should get some fresh air if you can manage it, remembering to look after yourself better than your property, because in the end you leave it all behind. And what would I, your grieving mother, do without you? I gather you're making a lot of money and letting your body waste away while you do so, with all your cares and discomforts. I'm sorry I'm not there with you so I could help share your load, which is what you need. You should have told me the first day Matteo was sick and I could have jumped on a horse and been there in a few days. But I know you didn't do it because you were afraid I'd make myself sick or suffer discomfort, and so I've suffered in mind instead of body. Now God be praised for everything, because I'm taking it all for the best.

About the honors you gave my son when you buried him, I believe you honored yourself as well as him. You've done all the better in honoring him there because it isn't the custom here to do anything for those who die in your circumstances,[5] so I'm glad you've done so. I'm here with these two unhappy girls who are wearing mourning for their brother. And because I hadn't cut out the cloth to make myself a cloak, I've had it done now and I'll pay for it myself. There are thirteen *braccia* of cloth in [each] one of them,

4 Because they had no time to confess and receive the last rites.
5 As legal exiles.

which costs in ready money four florins and a quarter the rod;[6] in all there are six and a half rods. I'll pay this through Matteo di Giorgio [Brandolini] and he'll let you know about it.

I've seen the copy of his will and I'd like you to act as quickly as possible to carry out those parts which are for the good of his soul. The rest can be dealt with at greater leisure. I ask you to do this and let me know if there's anything I can do here. Your boy[7] has a sister here who's married but can't go to live with her husband because she's so poor. I suggested you help her in other letters, but you've never replied. Now given what's happened I'd like to help her;[8] it's a matter of fifteen florins in all and it's something we shouldn't fail to do. If there isn't enough of his money to do what he asked I'd like to do it with my money or yours, which is all the same thing. So I'm letting you know about it. You should let me know how things stand and what we can do.

Messer Giannozzo[9] has kindly sent me a letter which has been a great comfort, seeing how fond he is of you and how he's tried so kindly to persuade me to resign myself, with so many good examples.[10] May God hold this in his favor. And as I don't have the knowledge or ability to write an answer to a man like him, I'll delay and you can thank him on my behalf as well as you can. Do let me know as often as you can how you're feeling. May God grant me what I want, because although I've been used to troubles in the past I'm feeling this more. You should also thank Bernardo de' Medici[11] by letter; I can't tell you how much love he's shown, coming to see me and comfort me, and how he's sympathized with us in what has happened and how we've suffered. I won't say anything else for now so as not to try your patience, but only that I'm waiting for your letters [to hear] you've consoled yourself and that you're well. May blessed Jesus give you grace, as I wish. From your poor little mother in Florence.

5

This is one of a number of letters written by Alessandra to Filippo which are dominated by the topic of finding him a wife, and it gives some examples of the detailed calculations which the choice of a wife could entail.

---

6   A rod was a linear measurement of varying length.

7   A boy who worked for Filippo.

8   Matteo had left a sum in his will to be used for good works, and Alessandra felt that this young woman would be a suitable recipient of the intended charity.

9   Messer Giannozzo Manetti, a humanist scholar and formerly a wealthy Florentine merchant, who was living in Naples.

10   Probably drawn from classical or Christian literature.

11   Also called Bernardetto, he was a personal friend of Alessandra and was connected to the Strozzi by marriage.

In the name of God. 20 April 1465.

My last letter was on the 13th. Since then I've had yours of the 7th, which I'll answer as I need to.

I see that Lorenzo has told you that he thinks I still really want to come and live with you both, and [you say] nothing could give you more comfort, and that there is only the matter of the wife left to be settled. To which I say, for my part, that it's always been my dearest wish to be with you, but you saw how long it took to sell my property here, and once it was sold there was some hope of you coming back here, and the delay in getting you married came from that. And because of my age I became discouraged and lost any hope of ever having any comfort from you, except through letters. But after seeing Lorenzo and hearing that you want to get married and that you've made up your mind to do it, I think it's reasonable and my duty to stay here until it's all arranged. Then we'll have to see. I must say that [even] if it weren't for this business of finding you a wife I wouldn't have much hope of ever going to live with you, because there's always been something to stop me from having the comfort of living with you. And if it would be a big comfort to you, it would be a much bigger one to me, because in the natural course of things I love you and feel much more tenderness for you than you do for me. And the reason is because I can only do badly without you, but you can do everything without me. So you can certainly believe that I told Lorenzo the truth about what I want. Now I pray God to bring us whatever will be for the best.

One paragraph: the Florentine ambassadors will have arrived in Naples, and Filippo will have talked to them and perhaps heard something useful.

About finding you a wife, it seems to us and also to Tommaso Davizzi[1] that if Francesco di Messer Guglielmino Tanagli were willing to give you his daughter, it would be a good match for all seasons, and that out of those which are available, this has the most to recommend it. I liked the da Vernia match, but from what I've heard she is clumsy and looks like a peasant. Now I will talk about it with Marco, about whether there are any others who would be better, and if there aren't, about finding out whether he [Francesco] wants to give her to you; we have only discussed it among ourselves. Francesco is well thought of and he takes part in the government, though not in the more important positions. Still, he has held offices. And if you ask "but why would he give her to an exile?" there are many reasons why he might do so. First, there's a shortage of young men of good family who have both money and abilities. Second, she has only a small dowry, I think it's a

---

1 A cousin of her husband, and also a relation of Tommaso Ginori.

thousand florins, which is an artisan's dowry; the Manfredi gave their girl two thousand florins to marry her into the Pitti family, and she is only fifteen, whereas she [the Tanagli girl] is seventeen.[2] So you see how it is. The third reason why I think he'll give her to us is that he has a big family and needs help to get them settled. This is the main reason why I think he'll agree. I'll find out more about it and if he doesn't want to, we'll find someone else. We will let you know.

I hear that you sent 80 pounds of flax to Mona Ginevra di Gino.[3] I am glad, as it will really seem as if you value the favor she did for you here.

I see that Mona Lucrezia di Piero[4] has sent you a fine letter for love of the flax you sent her. She would do well to reward you with something she doesn't have to spend anything on, apart from words, by speaking to Piero on your behalf, [to the effect] that he should return you to your family. I always thank God for everything, because he gives us our prosperity, and adversity to punish us for our sins. We should be thankful for everything, and I pray He may give us the grace to know the good things we receive from Him.

Three short paragraphs: Alessandra is glad to hear that Filippo and Lorenzo are getting on well together; she is pleased that Piero [de' Medici] knows of the honor Filippo has shown to Messer Carlo for his sake; Niccolò Ardinghelli is taking his wife to his home tomorrow.

Don Federigo arrived on Wednesday, and I hear he has been treated with great honor. On Thursday two gentlemen[5] came to visit me who said they lived near you, and they praised you greatly and told me wonderful things about you. I thanked them for coming, and then I offered them our hospitality and offered to do anything we could for them and asked them to consider your property as their own, and said some other fine things as they occurred to me, and they did the same, and then they left. I am letting you know so that you can thank them when you have the opportunity. Nothing else occurs to me for now; may God keep you from all harm. From your Alessandra Strozzi, Florence.

Postscript: Lessandra and Giovanni have come to stay for a month; Alessandra has given Maestro Lodovico[6] cloth worth four florins and twelve soldi to mark the birth of his daughter, because of the number of times he has treated her without payment.

2   Patrician girls were married at sixteen or even younger, if possible.
3   Probably the wife of Gino di Neri Capponi.
4   Lucrezia Tornabuoni, wife of Piero de' Medici.
5   Rinaldo and Carlo Mormino, members of Don Federigo's retinue.
6   Her doctor.

6

The somber mood continues here, in a letter which ranges over a discussion of unsatisfactory domestic slaves, political gossip, the poor agricultural season, and the plague. Alessandra ends on an equally dark note by telling Filippo of the despair felt by Pandolfo Pandolfini's widow.

In the name of God. 2 November 1465.

One paragraph: her last letter was on the 26th of October, she is writing now to tell Filippo that Niccolò Soderini is the new Gonfalonier of Justice, and to discuss marriage prospects.

You told me in your letter of the 28th of September that there was a slave there who used to belong to Lionardo Vernacci, and that you would have bought her if it hadn't been for the old one you have in your house. To that I say that she wouldn't be what you need, as I see it; Lionardo's wife had her for four, or really five, years, and because her appearance was dubious and she had bad blood – so that you wondered whether she'd do harm to herself or someone else – they got her out of the house. She was immoral as well. They sold her to Antonio della Luna, but she only stayed there for a little while because they didn't want her and they sent her back; so she was sent there [to Naples]. Lionardo's wife used her for the sewing, but she didn't have the brains for it. If she'd been a good servant she would have kept her for herself. You say you have one [slave] in the house, who used to belong to Filippo degli Albizzi. They thought she knew a lot, but they sold her because the wine was starting to do her harm and she was always tipsy, and she was immoral as well, and the wives had their daughters to think of, so they didn't want her in the house. They praised her as trustworthy and knowledgeable. Do what you think is best; I've told you all I know. I didn't remember to tell you [about this] in my other letter, but writing now about 33[1] reminded me, as the need for it came to mind. 32[2] and 56[3] are getting even worse, so that it's thought that it will do them harm; Lionardo Ginori's relation, who on other occasions has told 56 what he was, and then cooled down, well, now, because he has made this marriage alliance that I told you about in my last letter, he has told him heatedly that he should crow less. And you shouldn't ask about the blows he dealt 56. They say he is disheartened, and they are waiting to see what 18,[4] who is his enemy, will do. May God let them choose the best path.

1 Matrimonial negotiations.
2 Piero de' Medici.
3 Antonio Pucci.
4 Niccolò Soderini.

Payment of the 47th *catasto*[5] is due on the 6th of this month, as they have extended the due date until now. Those who have *Monte* shares paid it several months ago, and so they have to pay the 46th for December, which will be lost.[6] And I believe that from these [taxes] onward we will pay eight of these, which have been imposed for three years. May it please God to put a stop to us having to pay so much. They say that Niccolò[7] will raise one of these taxes, so for the moment I'll take the money for them out of the bank, which will be 9 and 10 gold florins. I'll also take out 5 florins, to have masses said and give alms on behalf of the souls of your father and my son, and the other departed members of our family – because for a time I didn't do it, as I used to – on this All Souls' Day.[8] I must tell you that I harvested 27 and a half bushels of grain and nine barrels of wine[9] at Pazzolatico, some white and some red, and nine at Quaracchi, so altogether I have 18 barrels. If it weren't for the shortage of bread, wine would be worth one large florin a barrel, but as it is it's only worth something over 3 lire. It's been a hard year for poor men, and there's plague as well; several people have died of it in the last few days. A son of Meo Pecori, twenty-eight years old, [died of it] in two days, and one of Saracino Pucci's, who was fourteen. In Rinieri da Ricasoli's house his mother died of it, and then a slave and an illegitimate daughter. Now it's in two houses close to here and it's leaving few survivors. So it is beginning, and it is winter. God help us.

I must tell you that Pandolfo's wife is nearly in despair, something which I can't possibly agree with, and so as not to spare her anything, Priore[10] and the others have returned [from Naples] and told her that he died very unwillingly and was doubly desperate,[11] which has increased her despair. May God, who has the power to do so, comfort her. She was so happy when she gave birth to a boy, but it has so soon turned to bitterness. All our hopes in this world come to little, and we can only hope in God, who shows us this in many ways. We must think about our end, so that God may let us make it a good one. No more for now; may God keep you from harm.

Tell Lorenzo that I have his letter of the 17th of last month and that because I was out late at Mass I don't have time to answer it now. God willing I will do so at the first opportunity. From your Alessandra Strozzi, Florence.

---

5 During the period in which a certain tax measure was current (which could be a number of years), each occasion on which it was levied was numbered.

6 A direct tax, not yielding shares in the *Monte*.

7 Niccolò Soderini, who had just become Gonfalonier of Justice.

8 All Souls' Day, November 2, when prayers were said and offerings made for the souls of dead relatives presumed to be still in Purgatory.

9 A barrel of wine was of standard capacity, holding about 45 liters.

10 Pandolfo Pandolfini's brother.

11 It was believed that the only appropriate attitude for the devout Christian, when faced with death, was resignation and faith in God and the Church; to despair was considered a sin.

7

This is Alessandra's last surviving letter, written to Filippo about ten months before her death. Lorenzo had given up his ambition to marry Marietta Strozzi, either in obedience to Filippo's wishes or because he had not reached an agreement with her family, and was betrothed to Antonia Baroncelli in June 1470.

In the name of God. 14 April 1470.

In the past few days I've had several letters from you, in which you told me how you were leaving there, and according to what you told me in your last letter, of the 30th of last month, that may be in the middle of this month, and [you say] you will go to Rome; may God go with you. And I've also had the inventory for a bale of cloth and flax, and *greco* wine,[1] that you are sending via Pisa. They haven't turned up yet and I don't think it's a good idea to send them to Lari[2] because it would be too much trouble. Because it's not new there's not too much duty to pay on the cloth; we will pay for the *greco* in any case, and there's little duty on the flax. We have received what you sent with Biagio, as described on the inventory, and it's in good order. We did what you asked us to do with it.

You say you're thinking about taking the slave's position and style [of living] away [from her]; I'd be pleased by that.

If Lorenzo is provided with the things he is going to need, he will have done well.

About the fodder, that is the spelt,[3] I've bought 18 bushels at 9 soldi the bushel, and one thousand two hundred sheaves of barley straw. It's dear here, worth more than 10 soldi the hundred, because the price of grain has gone up to 20 soldi the bushel. That's our luck, we're always having to buy things once they get dear. We'll have to do the same with the wine for the summer, as we'll have to buy several barrels for our own use. Because it's been so cold and still is, the grapevines aren't setting fruit and they say it's very dry for them, so they've got dearer. (These are among our other supplies.) God give us grace that things may still turn out well. If you haven't sent that powder for cleaning silver I won't be needing it, because I'm sure you'll have as much here as I need. I've had a trough and a hayrack made in that house at the back,[4] [which is finished] as far as the cleaning up; it will be wide enough for three horses. So you're coming [home] to your place; let

1 Made in Tuscany from what were called *greco*, or Greek, grapes.
2 A small town to the southeast of Florence, near Livorno.
3 Two-row barley, which was apparently used as horse feed.
4 A separate small house near their main residence, converted for use as a stable.

us know exactly when you expect to be here so we can get things ready for you.

Alfonso is well, and so are the rest of us.

You will have heard about the revolt which took place here.[5] To begin with they broke out of the Stinche twice, the prison that is;[6] the first time they broke the windows and got out into the courtyard. They were retaken and pardoned. The second time they burned down the doors of the prison and broke down the wall where it was broken down when Matteo di Giorgio got out,[7] but they didn't succeed because they were heard and some of the guards who live in the Piazza[8] ran there and shot one of them with their crossbows while he was trying to get out through the holes. Then they were taken, and three of them were beheaded and the others were put back inside. And later, on the sixth of this month, at 8 o'clock in the morning, we heard that one of the Nardi[9] had entered Prato[10] with a good two hundred soldiers and that Prato was lost. Oh, don't ask about the confusion that reigned in this land: for two hours there was complete confusion, with people running about the streets, and particularly around Lorenzo di Piero's house,[11] and they carried all the bread they could find between Lorenzo's house and the Palazzo,[12] so there was neither bread nor flour to be found;[13] I thought things were looking bad, because I had no grain. Later, by the grace of God, news came that this Nardi had been taken with all his men; they say there were about sixty of them. And he was imprisoned the same day, and later, the next day, on the 7th, 15 of them came [to Florence], all tied to a rope, and on Monday the 9th Nardi was beheaded. And the same day three more men were captured, but from Prato, and they say the Podestà[14] has hanged fourteen of them there. This morning four of them have been hanged, and they say seven more will go this coming Friday. I don't know what they'll do with the rest. All the people have been terrified, and it seems a very dreadful thing, with so many people dead and tortured. And apart from this great

---

5   Piero de' Medici had died on December 2, 1469, and the events described here showed continuing discontent with Medici rule in some quarters.

6   Alessandra connects this escape attempt with the more obviously political episodes which followed it.

7   Matteo di Giorgio Brandolini.

8   Probably Piazza Santa Croce.

9   Bernardo Nardi was one of the anti-Medicean exiles of 1466 and had also been condemned as a rebel.

10   A town about 16 kilometers to the northwest of Florence, which had been part of the Florentine territorial state since the mid-fourteenth century.

11   The Medici palace in the Via Cavour.

12   The Palazzo della Signoria.

13   At times of open opposition to their rule, it seems to have been a Medici tactic to secure the support of the poor by monopolizing all supplies of bread and flour in the city.

14   The Florentine official who governed Prato.

trouble, there's been an earthquake: the very morning that poor man entered Prato, there was a very big earthquake. Between one fear and the other I seem to have been half beside myself; I thought we were close to the end of the world. So it's good to put your soul in order and be ready. May God keep us from further troubles. I also hear there's been I don't know what [happening] in Pistoia,[15] and they say the Panciatichi[16] have all left in fear. May it please God to bring it to an end. No more for now; may God keep you from harm. From your Alessandra Strozzi in Florence.

15   A town about 34 kilometers to the northwest of Florence, which had come under permanent Florentine rule from 1341 onward.
16   The leading family of Pistoia.

8

Francesco Vettori (1474–1539)

A longtime friend and correspondent of Niccolò Machiavelli, Francesco Vettori came from an aristocratic Florentine family linked by marriage with the Medici, as well as with other powerful lineages including the Capponi, the Guicciardini, and the Rucellai. In the years preceding the return of the Medici in 1512, while Machiavelli served as Second Chancellor of the Florentine Republic over which Piero Soderini was presiding, the better-born and better-connected Vettori held office intermittently on several of the ruling councils.

Following the return of the Medici, the two friends' fortunes diverged more sharply. Whereas in November 1512 Machiavelli lost his job, the following month Vettori – who had been instrumental in smoothing the transfer of power back into the hands of the Medici – was rewarded by the new government with his appointment as Florentine ambassador to Pope Julius II (r. 1503–13). When Giovanni de' Medici was elevated as Pope Leo X (March 1513), Machiavelli was freed from prison, but having no political opportunities, he retired to his family's farm. Meanwhile, Vettori – whose family connections helped him to secure the favor of the Medici, and whose affiliation with Soderini had been shorter – found himself an honored member of the new regime.

In the two letters below, exchanged in late 1513, the friends describe their daily routines. The second, in which Machiavelli tells Vettori about his composition of The Prince (here called De principatibus), is crucially important for understanding the context in which the book was written. Try reading that letter first, and then go back and read the two letters sequentially.

Questions

1 How would you characterize Machiavelli's daily routine, as he portrays it?
2 Consider the rituals surrounding his evening work in his study. What does this passage tell us about the way he reads the great authors of antiquity, and seeks to interact with them?
3 Now consider Vettori's letter, with its description of his daily routine in Rome. What is the tone of the letter? How might its news have been received by Machiavelli?
4 Consider the "conversation" between the two correspondents in these letters. To what extent is Machiavelli's letter a response to Vettori's, or perhaps even a parody of it? If you were to read only Machiavelli's letter, what aspects of it might you be likely to miss?
5 Note that Machiavelli addresses Vettori as his "Patron and Benefactor." What patronage does he seek? Based upon your reading of Vettori's letter, how effective a patron is he likely to be to Machiavelli?

Two letters between Machiavelli and Vettori

Francesco Vettori to Niccolò Machiavelli
Rome, 23 November 1513

To the Notable Niccolò di Messer Bernardo Machiavelli.
In Florence.

My dear *compare*. As Cristofano Sernigi says, I have treated you so sparingly with my pen that I cannot recollect where I was. I do seem to recall that the last letter I had from you began with the story of the lion and the fox; I have looked around for it among my letters, and not finding it right away, I decided not to search any more. For in truth I did not reply back then because I was afraid that what has sometimes happened to me and Panzano would happen to you and me: we would begin playing with dirty old cards and send for new ones, and when the messenger came back with them, one of the two of us had already lost money. And so we were talking about bringing the princes together, and they went right on playing, so I was afraid that while we were wasting our letters bringing them together, some of them would have lost money. And since we last wrote, several events have occurred. Even though the party is not over, still it seems to have quieted down somewhat; and I believe it is a good idea not to talk of it until it has started up again.

So in this letter I have decided to describe to you what my life in Rome is like. It seems fitting for me to let you know, first of all, where I am living, since I have moved and I am no longer near as many courtesans as I was last summer. My residence is called San Michele in Borgo, and it is quite near the palace and Saint Peter's square; but it is in a somewhat secluded place, because it is toward the hill the ancients called the Janiculum. The house is very nice and has many rooms, though small ones; and it faces toward the north wind, so that the air is just right.

From the house you enter the church, which, what with my being as religious as you know, comes in very handy for me. It is true that the church is used more for walking in than it is for anything else, since neither mass nor any other holy service is ever said there, except once in an entire year. From the church you enter a garden, which formerly was clean and pretty but is now largely abandoned; still, it gets tidied up regularly. From the garden you go up the Janiculum, where you can walk at leisure through lanes and vineyards without being seen by anyone; according to the ancients, this was the site of Nero's gardens, vestiges of which are still visible. I am staying in this house with nine servants and, in addition to them, Brancacci, a chaplain, a scribe, and seven horses; I easily spend all the salary I get. When I first came here, I began by trying to live lavishly and elegantly, inviting out-of-town guests, serving three or four courses, eating out of silver dishes, and so forth. Then I realized that I was spending too much and that I was not at all better off for it; so I decided to stop inviting people and to live at a good, normal level. I returned the silver plates to those who had lent them to me, both so that I would not have to watch over them and also because they would often request me to speak to O[ur] L[ordship] about some need of theirs. I would do it and they would not be helped; so I determined to rid myself of this chore and not to annoy or to burden anyone else, so that I would not be annoyed or burdened by them.

Mornings, these days, I get up at ten o'clock, and after dressing, I go over to the palace; not every morning, however, but once out of every two or three. There, on occasion, I speak twenty words with the pope, ten with

Cardinal de' Medici,[1] six with Giuliano the Magnificent;[2] and if I cannot speak with him, I speak with Piero Ardinghelli, then with whatever ambassadors happen to be in those chambers; and I hear a thing or two, though little of any moment. Having done that, I go back home; except that sometimes I dine with Cardinal de' Medici. When I get home, I eat with my household and sometimes a guest or two who come to see them, such as Ser Sano and that Ser Tommaso who was in Trent, Giovanni Rucellai, or Giovanni Girolami. After eating, I would play cards if I had someone to do it with; but since I do not, I walk through the church and the garden. Then, when the weather is fine, I go for a short horseback ride outside of Rome. At nightfall I return home; and I have arranged to get quite a few histories, especially of the Romans: for instance, Livy with the epitome of Lucius Florus, Sallust, Plutarch, Appianus Alexandrinus, Cornelius Tacitus, Suetonius, Lampridius, and Spartianus, and those others who write about the emperors – Herodian, Ammianus Marcellinus, and Procopius. And with them I pass the time; and I consider the emperors that this poor Rome, which once made the world tremble, has put up with, and so it is no wonder if it has also put up with two pontiffs[3] of the kind that the last have been. Once every four days, I write a letter to Their Lordships of the Ten, and I relate some tired and irrelevant news, since I have nothing else to write for reasons that you yourself can understand. Then I go off to sleep, after I have had supper and exchanged some bits of news with Brancacci and with M. Giovan Battista Nasi, who often stays with me. On holidays I hear mass; I do not do as you, who sometimes do not bother. If you asked me whether or not I have any courtesans, I would tell you that when I first came here I did have a few, as I wrote you; then, frightened by the summer air, I abstained. Nevertheless, I had accustomed one so that she often comes here on her own; she is reasonably pretty and pleasant in speech. Even though this place is secluded, I also have a neighbor whom you would not find unattractive; and although she is of noble family, she does carry on some business.

Niccolò my friend, this is the life I invite you to; and if you come, you will give me pleasure, and then we shall go back up there together. Here you will have no other business than seeing the sights and then coming back home to joke and to laugh. And I do not want you to think that I live like an ambassador, because I have always insisted on being free. Sometimes I dress

---

1 Giulio de' Medici (1478–1534), Leo X's cousin, who went on to be elected Pope Clement VII in 1523.
2 Giuliano de' Medici (1479–1516), Pope Leo's younger brother, whom Machiavelli had known before the Medici were exiled in 1494, and to whom he first intended to dedicate *The Prince.*
3 A reference to Pope Alexander VI (r. 1492–1503) and Pope Julius II (r. 1503–13). Pope Pius III (1503), whose pontificate was very brief, is presumably not intended here.

up, and sometimes I do not; I go riding by myself, with my servants on foot, and sometimes with them on horseback. I never go to the cardinals', because I have no one to visit except Medici and sometimes Bibbiena,[4] when he is well. And let anyone say what he will, if I do not satisfy them, let them recall me. For in conclusion, I intend to go home at the end of a year and to have held on to my capital, once my clothes and horses have been sold off; I would prefer not to be out of pocket if I can help it. I want you to believe one thing, which I say without any flattery: although I have gone to no great trouble, nonetheless the throng is so great that one cannot help meeting a great number of people. In point of fact, few of them satisfy me, and I have not found any man of better judgment than you. *Sed fatis trahimur.*[5] For when I speak at length to some, when I read their letters, I find myself astonished that they have attained any rank whatsoever, since they are nothing but ceremony, lies, and tales, and there are very few of them who are at all out of the ordinary. Bernardo da Bibbiena, who is now a cardinal, has a well-bred mind, in truth, and he is a witty and discerning man and has done his share of labor in his day. Nonetheless, he is ill now, and he has been so for three months; I do not know if he will ever again be as he was wont to be. And thus we often labor to find rest, and it does not turn out. So let us be merry, come what may. And remember that I am at your service and that I send my regards to you, to Filippo and Giovanni Machiavelli, to Donato, and to Messer Ciaio. Nothing more. Christ watch over you.

Francesco Vettori, ambassador
23 November 1513, in Rome.

Niccolò Machiavelli to Francesco Vettori
Florence, 10 December 1513

To the Magnificent Francesco Vettori, His Patron and Benefactor,
Florentine Ambassador to the Supreme Pontiff.
In Rome.

Magnificent Ambassador. "Divine favors were never late." I say this because it seemed to me that I had lost – no, rather, strayed from – your favor; it has

4   Cardinal Bernardo Dovizi, known as "Bibbiena," served as vice-chancellor of the Church under Pope Leo X.
5   "But we are dragged by the fates." This is a variation on a saying by the Roman Stoic philosopher Seneca (4 BC–AD 65), "The fates lead the willing, and drag the unwilling."

been a long time since you wrote me, and I was unclear about what the reason might be. And I paid little attention to all those reasons that came to mind except for one: I was afraid that you might have ceased writing to me because someone had written you that I was not a good steward of your letters. I knew that, except for Filippo and Paolo, no one else had seen them through my doing. I am reassured by your recent letter of the 23rd of last month, from which I am extremely pleased to see how methodically and calmly you fulfill your public duties. I exhort you to continue in this manner, because whoever forgoes his own interests for those of others sacrifices his own and gets no gratitude from them. And since Fortune is eager to shape everything, she wants people to let her do so, to be still, not to trouble her, and to await the moment when she will let men do something. That will be the moment for you to persevere more unfailingly, to be more alert about matters, and for me to leave my farm and announce, "Here I am." Since I want to repay you in the same coin, therefore, I can tell you nothing else in this letter except what my life is like. If you decide you would like to swap it for yours, I shall be happy to make the exchange.

I am living on my farm, and since my latest disasters, I have not spent a total of twenty days in Florence. Until now, I have been catching thrushes with my own hands. I would get up before daybreak, prepare the birdlime, and go out with such a bundle of birdcages on my back that I looked like Geta when he came back from the harbor with Amphitryon's books.[6] I would catch at least two, at most six, thrushes. And thus I passed the entire month of November. Eventually this diversion, albeit contemptible and foreign to me, petered out – to my regret. I shall tell you about my life. I get up in the morning with the sun and go into one of my woods that I am having cut down; there I spend a couple of hours inspecting the work of the previous day and kill some time with the woodsmen who always have some dispute on their hands either among themselves or with their neighbors. I could tell you a thousand good stories about these woods and my experiences with them, and about Frosino da Panzano and other men who wanted some of this firewood. In particular, Frosino sent for some loads of wood without saying a word to me; when it came time to settle, he wanted to withhold ten lire that he said he had won off me four years ago when he had beaten me at *cricca* at Antonio Guicciardini's house. I started to raise hell; I was going to call the wagoner who had come for the wood a thief, but Giovanni Machiavelli eventually stepped in and got us to agree. Once the north wind started blowing, Battista Guicciardini, Filippo Ginori, Tommaso del Bene, and some other citizens all ordered a load from me. I promised some to each one; I sent

6   An allusion to a popular novella, "Geta and Birria," in which Geta, a servant, returns from Greece carrying his master's books. His fellow-servant, Birria, hides, hoping to avoid having to help shoulder the burden.

Tommaso a load, which turned into half a load in Florence because he, his wife, his children, and the servants were all there to stack it – they looked like Gaburra on Thursdays when he and his crew flay an ox. Consequently, once I realized who was profiting, I told the others that I had no more wood; all of them were angry about it, especially Battista, who includes this among the other calamities of Prato.[7]

Upon leaving the woods, I go to a spring; from there, to one of the places where I hang my birdnets. I have a book under my arm: Dante, Petrarch, or one of the minor poets like Tibullus, Ovid, or some such. I read about their amorous passions and their loves, remember my own, and these reflections make me happy for a while. Then I make my way along the road toward the inn, I chat with passersby, I ask news of their regions, I learn about various matters, I observe mankind: the variety of its tastes, the diversity of its fancies. By then it is time to eat; with my household I eat what food this poor farm and my minuscule patrimony yield. When I have finished eating, I return to the inn, where there usually are the innkeeper, a butcher, a miller, and a couple of kilnworkers. I slum around with them for the rest of the day playing *cricca* and backgammon: these games lead to thousands of squabbles and endless abuses and vituperations. More often than not we are wrangling over a penny; be that as it may, people can hear us yelling even in San Casciano. Thus, having been cooped up among these lice, I get the mold out of my brain and let out the malice of my fate, content to be ridden over roughshod in this fashion if only to discover whether or not my fate is ashamed of treating me so.

When evening comes, I return home and enter my study; on the threshold I take off my workday clothes, covered with mud and dirt, and put on the garments of court and palace. Fitted out appropriately, I step inside the venerable courts of the ancients, where, solicitously received by them, I nourish myself on that food that *alone* is mine and for which I was born; where I am unashamed to converse with them and to question them about the motives for their actions, and they, out of their human kindness, answer me. And for four hours at a time I feel no boredom, I forget all my troubles, I do not dread poverty, and I am not terrified by death. I absorb myself into them completely. And because Dante says that no one understands anything unless he retains what he has understood, I have jotted down what I have profited from in their conversation and composed a short study, *De principatibus*, in which I delve as deeply as I can into the ideas concerning this topic, discussing the definition of a princedom, the categories of princedoms, how they are acquired, how they are retained, and why they are lost. And if ever

7   This refers primarily to the sack of Prato by Spanish troops in 1512, an event that led directly to the fall of the Soderini government in Florence and the restoration to power there of the Medici.

any whimsy of mine has given you pleasure, this one should not displease you. It ought to be welcomed by a prince, and especially by a new prince; therefore I am dedicating it to His Magnificence Giuliano.[8] Filippo da Casavecchia has seen it. He will be able to give you some account of both the work itself and the discussions I have had with him about it, although I am continually fattening and currying it.

Magnificent Ambassador, you would like me to abandon this life and come and enjoy yours with you. I shall do so in any case, but I am kept here by certain commitments that I shall attend to within six weeks. What makes me hesitate is that those Soderinis are in Rome; were I to come there, I would be obliged to visit and to talk with them. I am afraid upon my return that I might not count on dismounting at home but rather that I should dismount at the Bargello.[9] For although this regime has extremely strong foundations and great security, it is still new and, consequently, suspicious. There are plenty of rogues like Paolo Bertini who, in order to be impressive, would order a meal for others and leave the tab for me to pick up. I beg you to make this fear evaporate, and then, come what may, I shall come and see you in any case at the time mentioned.

I have discussed this little study of mine with Filippo and whether or not it would be a good idea to present it [to Giuliano], and if it were a good idea, whether I should take it myself or should send it to you. Against presenting it would be my suspicion that he might not even read it and that that person Ardinghelli might take the credit for this most recent of my endeavors. In favor of presenting it would be the necessity that hounds me, because I am wasting away and cannot continue on like this much longer without becoming contemptible because of my poverty. Besides, there is my desire that these Medici princes should begin to engage my services, even if they should start out by having me roll along a stone.[10] For then, if I could not win them over, I should have only myself to blame. And through this study of mine, were it to be read, it would be evident that during the fifteen years I have been studying the art of the state I have neither slept nor fooled around, and anybody ought to be happy to utilize someone who has had so much experience at the expense of others. There should be no doubt about my word; for, since I have always kept it, I should not start learning how to break it now. Whoever has been honest and faithful for forty-three years, as I have, is unable to change his nature; my poverty is a witness to my loyalty and honesty.

8   i.e., Giuliano de' Medici (see note 2 above).
9   The Bargello is a prison in Florence.
10   An allusion to Sisyphus, a mythical figure condemned to spend his afterlife repeatedly pushing a boulder up a hill, only to have it roll down again.

So I should like you, too, to write me what your opinion is about all this. I commend myself to you. *Be happy.*

10 December 1513.
Niccolò Machiavelli, in Florence.

Part IV

Gender and Society

Introduction to Part IV

Over a generation ago, the historian Joan Kelly influentially asked whether there had in fact been a Renaissance for women.[1] Her own answer was overwhelmingly negative: denied access to political and economic power, and even to much of public life, women actually were losing ground rather than gaining it. Subsequent scholarship has demonstrated that, despite the constraints placed upon them, women in the Renaissance often had significant influence upon political and economic life, above all through their role in maintaining and advancing family interests, which were an integral part of civic life. While by no means equal to men either in theory or in practice, they thus had considerably more agency than historians a generation ago tended to credit them with having. This agency, certainly evident in Alessandra Strozzi's letters above, may best be understood in the context of social expectations of men and women, above all with respect to their roles in the family. In the selections that follow, consider the portrayal of men's and women's gender roles, and how behavioral expectations shaped and limited their opportunities for political influence and for self-expression.

1 Joan Kelly, "Did Women Have a Renaissance?" in *Becoming Visible: Women in European History*, ed. Renate Bridenthal and Claudia Koonz (Boston, 1977).

Plate 6   Sofonisba Anguissola, *A Game of Chess, involving the painter's three sisters and a servant* (1555), Muzeum Narodowe, Poznan, Poland. *Source:* Erich Lessing/Art Resource, NY.

Born in Cremona in northwestern Italy, Sofonisba Anguissola (1532–1625) received a humanist education, as did her five younger sisters (three of whom also became artists). This painting, in the northern Italian genre of narrative group portraits, tells a story about the interaction of the Anguissola sisters. Lucia and Minerva have just reached a critical moment in their chess game. Lucia's left hand caresses two pieces she has taken, and her right hand has not yet released the piece she has just moved. Minerva raises her right hand, evidently resigning the game, while a serving-woman looks on from behind her. The youngest of the three girls, Europa, gazes smilingly at Minerva, drawing our attention to the gesture that ends the game. Lucia, meanwhile, looks directly outward, thus engaging the viewer in the story. Of course, the initial spectator who implicitly participates in the narrative is the artist herself. While her sisters are positioned on three sides of the table, Sofonisba looks on from its fourth side, thus completing the symmetry.

No male artist of the time painted a scene like this one, in which girls are engaged in a game that both requires and signifies intellectual prowess. To be sure, the choice of subject matter is in part a function of the limitations imposed upon women in the Renaissance: the public sphere was predominantly a male domain; as an unwed woman (she did not marry until 1573), Sofonisba was not even allowed to be alone in a room with a male sitter. This particular domestic scene is remarkable, however, in that it shows two girls playing a competitive game that demands intelligence and finesse, while the third is evidently learning from their example. Significantly, Sofonisba depicts all three of her sisters with broad, high foreheads, a physical characteristic believed at the time to indicate a capacious mind (note, by contrast, the less elevated forehead of the serving-woman). Thus the painting not only commemorates the dynamics among the sisters, it also celebrates their intellectual vitality in a way that transcends conventions for representing women in the Renaissance.

9

Boccaccio

In Boccaccio's *Decameron*, the final story is that of patient Griselda, a peasant girl whom Gualtieri, the Marquis of Saluzzo, marries, and then proceeds to mistreat severely in the name of testing her loyalty and endurance. Here Boccaccio has taken a traditional story that involved a monster rather than a marquis, and he has rewritten it in light of customs and rituals in fourteenth-century Tuscany. Notably, in Florentine tradition, the fiancé was expected to "dress" his betrothed, thus making a gift that served as a "counter-dowry" of sorts. By Boccaccio's time, this dressing of the fiancée had lost its financial significance: in fact, sometimes the husband merely borrowed or rented the clothing and jewels, returning them after the wedding festivities had ended. Still, the ritual retained symbolic importance.[1]

Petrarch so delighted in this story that he translated it into Latin, which, as he noted, would increase its circulation, and he sent the translation to Boccaccio in 1373. In Petrarch's view, the dutifulness that Griselda showed to her husband would be nearly impossible to imitate, but he expressed his hope that the story would instead inspire women to emulate Griselda's constancy in their submission of themselves to God.

---

1   I draw these observations from an essay by Christiane Klapisch-Zuber, "The Griselda Complex: Dowry and Marriage Gifts in the Quattrocento," in her book *Women, Family, and Ritual in Renaissance Italy*, trans. Lydia G. Cochrane (Chicago and London, 1985), pp. 213–46.

Questions

1 By placing this story last in the *Decameron*, Boccaccio gave it particular emphasis. Why do you suppose he did so?
2 Although the story has a "happy" ending, it also includes graphic details of Gualtieri's cruel treatment of Griselda. Are these elements necessary for the tale to be effective? Do you find the ending satisfying? If not, why not?
3 What do you imagine Alessandra Strozzi might have thought of the story? How about Machiavelli?
4 For all his ridicule of corrupt priests and monks, Boccaccio was in fact devoutly Christian. Those familiar with the Book of Job in the Hebrew Scriptures (i.e., the Old Testament) will doubtless see parallels in this story to Job's endurance of utter ruin that has been visited upon him for no other reason than to test his faith in and obedience to God. What repercussions are there (whether intended or not) to having Gualtieri rather than God doing the testing in Boccaccio's story? What are its possible implications for husbands and wives?

Plate 7 Pesellino (1422–57), *Story of Griselda* (detail), Accademia Carrara, Bergamo. *Source*: Erich Lessing/Art Resource, NY.

Decameron X, 10

The Marquis of Sanluzzo is urged by the requests of his vassals to take a wife, and in order to have his own way in the matter, he chooses the daughter of a peasant and by her he has two children, whom he pretends to have put to death. Then, under the pretense that she has displeased him, he pretends to have taken another wife, and has their own daughter brought into the house as if she were his new wife, having driven out his real wife in nothing more than her shift. Having found that she has patiently endured all this, he brings her back home, more beloved than ever, shows their grown children to her, honors her, and has others honor her, as the Marchioness.

. . . Realizing that he alone remained to speak, Dioneo began:

Gentle ladies of mine, it seems to me this day has been devoted to kings, sultans, and people like that; therefore, in order not to stray too far from your path, I should like to tell you about a marquis and not about a generous act of his but, rather, about his insane cruelty, which, while good did result from it in the end, I would never advise anyone to follow as an example, for I consider it a great shame that he derived any benefit from it at all.

A long time ago, there succeeded to the Marquisate of Sanluzzo the first-born son of the family, a young man named Gualtieri, who, having no wife or children, spent his time doing nothing but hawking and hunting, never thinking of taking a wife or of having children – a very wise thing to do on his part. This did not please his vassals, and they begged him on many an occasion to take a wife so that he would not be without an heir and they without a master; they offered to find him a wife born of the kind of mother and father that might give him good expectations of her and make him happy. To this Gualtieri answered:

"My friends, you are urging me to do something that I was determined never to do, for you know how difficult it is to find a woman with a suitable character, and how plentiful is the opposite kind of woman, and what a wretched life a man would lead married to a wife that was not suitable to him. And to say that you can judge daughters by examining the characters of their fathers and mothers (which is the basis of your argument that you can find a wife to please me) is ridiculous, for I do not believe that you can come to know all the secrets of the father or mother; and even if you did, a daughter is often unlike her father and mother. But since it is your wish to tie me up with these chains, I shall do as you request; and so that I shall have only myself to blame if things turn out badly, I want to be the one who chooses her, and I tell you now that if she is not honored by you as your lady – no matter whom I choose – you will learn to your great displeasure how serious a matter it was to compel me with your requests to take a wife against my will." His worthy men replied that they would be happy if only he would choose a wife.

For some time Gualtieri had been impressed by the manners of a poor young girl who lived in a village near his home, and since she seemed very beautiful to him, he thought that life with her could be quite pleasant; so, without looking any further, he decided to marry her, and he sent for her father, who was extremely poor, and made arrangements with him to take her as his wife. After this was done, Gualtieri called all his friends in the area together and said to them:

"My friends, you wished and continue to wish for me to take a wife, and I am ready to do this, but I do so more to please you than to satisfy any desire of mine to have a wife. You know what you promised me: to honor happily anyone I chose for your lady; therefore, the time has come for me to keep my promise to you, and for you to do the same for me. I have found a young girl after my own heart, very near here, whom I intend to take as my wife and bring home in a few days. So, make sure that the wedding celebrations are splendid and that you receive her honorably, so that I may consider myself as happy with your promise as you are with mine."

The good men all happily replied that this pleased them very much and that, whoever she was, they would treat her as their lady and honor her in every way they could; and soon after this, they all set about preparing for a big, beautiful, and happy celebration, and Gualtieri did the same. He had an enormous and sumptuous wedding feast prepared, and he invited his friends and relatives and the great lords and many others from the surrounding countryside. And besides this, he had beautiful and expensive dresses cut out and tailored to fit a young girl whom he felt was about the same size as the young girl he had decided to marry; he also saw to it that girdles and rings were purchased and a rich and beautiful crown and everything else a new bride might require. When the day set for the wedding arrived, Gualtieri mounted his horse at about the middle of tierce, and all those who had come to honor him did the same; when all was arranged, he said:

"My lords, it is time to fetch the new bride."

Then he with his entire company set out, and eventually they arrived at the little village; they came to the house of the girl's father and found her returning from the well in great haste in order to be in time to go and see the arrival of Gualtieri's bride with the other women; when Gualtieri saw her, he called her by name – that is, Griselda – and asked her where her father was; to this she replied bashfully:

"My lord, he is in the house."

Then Gualtieri dismounted and ordered all his men to wait for him; alone, he entered that poor, little house, and there he found Griselda's father, who was called Giannucole, and he said to him:

"I have come to marry Griselda, but before I do, I should like to ask her some things in your presence."

And he asked her, if he were to marry her, would she always try to please him, and would she never become angry over anything he said or did, and if she would always be obedient, and many other similar questions – to all of these she replied that she would. Then Gualtieri took her by the hand, led her outside, and in the presence of his entire company and all others present, he had her stripped naked and the garments he had prepared for her brought forward; then he immediately had her dress and put on her shoes, and upon her hair, disheveled as it was, he had a crown placed; then, while everyone was marveling at the sight, he announced:

"My lords, this is the lady I intend to be my wife, if she will have me as her husband."

And then, turning to Griselda, who was standing there blushing and perplexed, he asked her:

"Griselda, do you take me for your husband?"

To this she answered: "Yes, my lord."

And he replied: "And I take you for my wife."

In the presence of them all he married her; then he had her set upon a palfrey and he led her with an honorable company to his home. The wedding feast was great and sumptuous, and the celebration was no different from what it might have been if he had married the daughter of the King of France. The young bride seemed to have changed her soul and manners along with her clothes: she was, as we have already said, beautiful in body and face, and as she was beautiful before, she became even more pleasing, attractive, and well mannered, so that she seemed to be not the shepherdess daughter of Giannucole but, rather, the daughter of some noble lord, a fact that amazed everyone who had known her before. Moreover, she was so obedient and indulgent to her husband that he considered himself the happiest and the most satisfied man on earth. And she was also so gracious and kind toward her husband's subjects that there was no one who was more beloved or gladly honored than she was; in fact, everyone prayed for her welfare, her prosperity, and her further success. Whereas everyone used to say that Gualtieri had acted unwisely in taking her as his wife, they now declared that he was the wisest and the cleverest man in the world, for none other than he could have ever recognized the noble character hidden under her poor clothes and peasant dress.

In short, she knew how to comport herself in such a manner that before long, not only in her husband's marquisate but everywhere else, her virtue and her good deeds became the topic of discussion, and for anything that had been said against her husband when he married her, she now caused the opposite to be said. Not long after she had come to live with Gualtieri, she became pregnant, and in the course of time she gave birth to a daughter, which gave Gualtieri much cause for rejoicing. But shortly afterward, a new thought entered his mind: he wished to test her patience with a long trial and intolerable proofs. First, he offended her with harsh words, pretending to be angry and saying that his vassals were very unhappy with her because of her low birth and especially now that they saw her bear children; they were most unhappy about the daughter that had been born, and they did nothing but mutter about it. When the lady heard these words, without changing her expression or intentions in any way, she answered:

"My lord, do with me what you think best for your honor and your happiness, and no matter what, I shall be happy, for I realize that I am of lower birth than they and am not worthy of this honor which your courtesy has bestowed upon me."

This reply was very gratifying to Gualtieri, for he realized that she had not become in any way haughty because of the respect which he or others had paid her. A short time later, having told his wife in vague terms that his subjects could not tolerate the daughter to whom she had given birth, he spoke to one of her servants and then sent him to her, and he, with a very sad look on his face, said to her:

"My lady, since I do not wish to die, I must do what my lord commands. He had commanded me to take this daughter of yours and to . . ." And he could say no more.

When the lady heard these words and saw her servant's face, she remembered what her husband had said to her and understood that her servant had been ordered to murder the child; so she quickly took the girl from the cradle, kissed her and blessed her, and although she felt great pain in her heart, showing no emotion, she placed her in her servant's arms and said to him:

"There, do exactly what your lord and mine has ordered you to do, but do not leave her body to be devoured by the beasts and birds unless he has ordered you to do so."

The servant took the child and told Gualtieri what the lady had said, and he was amazed at her perseverance; then he sent the servant with his daughter to one of his relatives in Bologna, requesting that she raise and educate the girl carefully but without ever telling whose daughter she was. Shortly after this, the lady became pregnant again, and in time she gave birth to a male child, which pleased Gualtieri very much; but what he had already done to his lady was not enough to satisfy him, and he wounded the lady with even a greater blow by telling her one day in a fit of feigned anger:

"Lady, since you bore me this male child, I have not been able to live with my vassals, for they bitterly complain about a grandson of Giannucolo's having to be their lord after I am gone. Because of this, I am very much afraid that unless I want to be driven out, I must do what I did the other time, and then, finally, I shall have to leave you and take another wife."

The lady listened to him patiently and made no other reply than this:

"My lord, think only of making yourself happy and of satisfying your desires and do not worry about me at all, for nothing pleases me more than to see you happy."

After a few days, Gualtieri sent for his son in the same way he had sent for his daughter, and, again pretending to have the child killed, he sent him to be raised in Bologna as he had his daughter; and the lady's face and words were no different from what they were when her daughter had been taken, and Gualtieri was greatly amazed at this and remarked to himself that no other woman could do what she had done. If he had not seen for himself how extremely fond she was of her children as long as they found favor in his sight, he might have thought that she acted as she did in order to get rid of them, but he realized that she was doing it out of obedience.

His subjects, believing he had killed his children, criticized him bitterly and regarded him as a cruel man, and they had the greatest compassion for the lady; but she never said anything to the women with whom she mourned the deaths of her children. Then, not many years after the birth of their daughter, Gualtieri felt it was time to put his wife's patience to the ultimate test: he told many of his vassals that he could no longer bear having married Griselda and that he realized he had acted badly and impetuously when he took her for his wife, and that he was going to do everything possible to procure a dispensation from the Pope so that he could marry another woman and abandon Griselda; he was reprimanded for this by many of his good men, but the only answer he gave them was that this was the way it had to be.

When the lady heard about these matters and it appeared to her that she would be returning to her father's house (perhaps even to guard the sheep as she had previously done) and that she would have to bear witness to another woman possessing the man she loved, she grieved most bitterly; but yet, as with the other injuries of Fortune which she had suffered, she was determined to bear this one, too, with firm countenance. Not long afterward, Gualtieri had forged letters sent from Rome, and he showed them to his subjects, pretending that in these letters the Pope had granted him the dispensation to take another wife and to abandon Griselda; and so, having his wife brought before him, in the presence of many people he said to her:

"Lady, because of a dispensation which I have received from the Pope, I am able to take another wife and to abandon you; and because my ancestors were great noblemen and lords of these regions while yours have always been peasants, I wish you to be my wife no longer and to return to Giannu-colo's home with the dowry that you brought me, and I shall then bring home another more suitable wife, whom I have already found."

When the lady heard these words, she managed to hold back her tears only with the greatest of effort (something quite unnatural for a woman), and she replied:

"My lord, I have always known that my lowly origins were in no way suitable to your nobility, and the position I have held with you I always recognized as having come from God and yourself; I never made it mine or considered it given to me – I always kept it as if it were a loan. If you wish to have it back again, it must please me, which it does, to return it to you: here is your ring with which you married me; take it. You order me to take back with me the dowry I brought you, and to do this no accounting on your part, nor any purse or beast of burden, will be necessary, for I have not forgotten that you received me naked; and if you judge it proper that this body which bore your children should be seen by everyone, I shall leave naked; but I beg you, in the name of my virginity which I brought here and which I cannot take with me, that you at least allow me to take away with me just one shift in addition to my dowry."

Gualtieri, who felt closer to tears than anyone else there, stood, nevertheless, with a stern face and said:

"You may take a shift."

Many of those present begged him to give her a dress, so that this woman who had been his wife for more than thirteen years would not be seen leaving his home so impoverished and in such disgrace as to leave clad only in a shift; but their entreaties were in vain, and in her shift, without shoes or anything on her head, the lady commended him to God, left his house, and returned to her father, accompanied by the tears and the weeping of all those who witnessed her departure.

Giannucolo, who had never believed that Gualtieri would keep his daughter as his wife, and who had been expecting this to happen any day, had kept the clothes that she had taken off that morning when Gualtieri married her; he gave them back to her, and she put them on and began doing the menial tasks in her father's house as she had once been accustomed to doing, suffering with brave spirit the savage assaults of a hostile Fortune.

Once Gualtieri had done this, he then led his vassals to believe that he had chosen a daughter of one of the Counts of Panago for his new wife; and while great preparations were being made for the wedding, he sent for Griselda to come to him, and when she arrived he said to her:

"I am bringing home the lady I have recently chosen as my wife, and I want to give her an honorable welcome when she first arrives; you know that I have no women in my home who know how to prepare the bedrooms or do the many chores that are required by such a grand celebration, and since you understand these matters better than anyone else in the house, I want you to make all the arrangements: invite those ladies whom you think should be invited, and receive them as if you were the lady of the house; then when the wedding is over, you can return to your home."

These words were like a dagger in Griselda's heart, for she had not yet been able to put aside the love she felt for him as she had learned to live without her good fortune, and she answered:

"My lord, I am ready and prepared."

And so in a coarse peasant dress she entered that house which she had left a short time before dressed only in a shift, and she began to clean and arrange the bedrooms, to put out hangings and ornamental tapestries on the walls, to make ready the kitchen, and to put her hands to everything, just as if she were a little servant girl in the house; and she never rested until she had organized and arranged everything as it should be. After this, she had invitations sent in Gualtieri's name to all the ladies of the region and then waited for the celebration; when the day of the wedding came, though the clothes she wore were poor, with the courtesy and graciousness of a lady, she cheerfully welcomed all the women who arrived for the celebration.

Gualtieri had seen to it that his children were raised with care in Bologna by one of his relatives who had married into the family of the Counts of Panago. His daughter was already twelve years old and the most beautiful thing ever seen; the boy was six. He sent a message to his relative in Bologna, requesting him to be so kind as to come to Sanluzzo with his daughter and his son, and to see to it that a fine and honorable retinue accompany them, and not to reveal her identity to anyone but to tell them only that he was bringing the girl as Gualtieri's bride.

The nobleman did what the Marquis had asked him: he set out, and after several days he arrived at Sanluzzo at about suppertime with the young girl, her brother, and a noble following, and there he found all the peasants and many other people from the surrounding area waiting to see Gualtieri's new bride. She was received by the ladies and then taken to the hall where the tables were set, and there Griselda, dressed as she was, cheerfully met her and said to her:

"Welcome, my lady!"

The ladies, many of whom had begged Gualtieri (but in vain) either to allow Griselda to stay in another room or that some of the clothing that had once been hers be lent to her so that she would not have to meet his guests in such condition, sat down at the table and were served. Everyone looked at the young girl and agreed that Gualtieri had made a good exchange; but it was Griselda above all who praised her as well as her little brother.

Gualtieri, who felt that he now had enough evidence of his wife's patience, having seen that these unusual circumstances had not changed Griselda one bit, and certain that her attitude was not due to stupidity, for he knew her to be very wise, felt that it was time to remove her from the bitterness he knew to be hidden behind her impassive face, and so he had her brought to him, and in the presence of everyone, he said to her with a smile:

"What do you think of my new bride?"

"My lord," replied Griselda, "she seems very beautiful to me; and if she is as wise as she is beautiful, which I believe she is, I have no doubt that living with her will make you the happiest man in the world. But I beg you with all my heart not to inflict those wounds upon her which you inflicted upon that other woman who was once your wife, for I believe that she could scarcely endure them, not only because she is younger but also because she was reared in a more refined way, whereas that other woman lived in continuous hardship from the time she was a little girl."

When Gualtieri saw that she firmly believed the girl was to be his wife, and in spite of this said nothing but good about her, he made her sit beside him, and he said:

"Griselda, it is time now for you to reap the fruit of your long patience, and it is time for those who have considered me cruel, unjust, and bestial to realize that what I have done was directed toward a preestablished goal, for I wanted to teach you how to be a wife, to show these people how to know such a wife and how to choose and keep one, and to acquire for myself lasting tranquillity for as long as I lived with you. When I decided to marry, I greatly feared that the tranquillity I cherished would be lost, and so, to test you, I submitted you to the pains and trials you have known. But since I have never known you to depart from my wishes in either word or deed, and since I now believe I shall receive from you that happiness which I always desired, I intend to return to you now what I took from you for a long time and with the greatest of delight to soothe the wounds that I inflicted upon you. And so, with a happy heart receive this girl, whom you suppose to be my bride, and her brother as your very own children and mine; they are the ones you and many others have long thought I had brutally murdered; and I am your husband, who loves you more than all else, for I believe I can boast that no other man exists who could be as happy with his wife as I am."

After he said this, he embraced and kissed her, and she was weeping for joy; they arose and together went over to their daughter, who was listening in amazement to these new developments; both of them tenderly embraced first the girl and then her brother, thus dispelling their confusion as well as that of many others who were present. The ladies, who were most delighted, arose from the tables, and they went with Griselda to her room, and with a more auspicious view of her future, they took off her old clothes and dressed her in one of her noble garments, and then they led her back into the hall as the lady of the house, which she, nonetheless, appeared to be even when she wore rags.

Everyone was very happy with the way everything had turned out, and Griselda with her husband and children celebrated in great style, with the joy and feasting increasing over a period of several days; and Gualtieri was judged to be the wisest of men (although the tests to which he had subjected his wife were regarded as harsh and intolerable), and Griselda the wisest of them all.

The Count of Panago returned to Bologna several days later, and Gualtieri took Giannucolo from his labor, setting him up in a way befitting his father-in-law so that he lived the rest of his days with honor and great comfort. After giving their daughter in marriage to a nobleman, Gualtieri lived a long and happy life with Griselda, always honoring her to the best of his ability.

What more can be said here, except that godlike spirits do sometimes rain down from heaven into poor homes, just as those more suited to governing pigs than to ruling over men make their appearances in royal palaces. Who besides Griselda could have endured the severe and unheard-of trials that Gualtieri imposed upon her and remain with a not only tearless but a happy face? It might have served Gualtieri right if he had run into the kind of woman who, once driven out of her home in nothing but a shift, would have allowed another man to warm her wool in order to get herself a nice-looking dress out of the affair!

10

Francesco Barbaro (1390–1454)

Francesco Barbaro was a Venetian noble who, in addition to having a prominent political career, put his humanist education to use in his voluminous Latin correspondence, which circulated in manuscript and later in printed form. His two-part treatise *On Wifely Duties* (1416), written in the form of a letter, was dedicated to Lorenzo de' Medici (the brother of Cosimo "The Elder") upon the occasion of Lorenzo's marriage to Ginevra Cavalcanti. A gift intended to confer distinction both on the recipient and on the giver, *On Wifely Duties* treats the family as the fundamental unit of the political and social order. Thus the moral advice it dispenses can be taken as important not only for a happy and fruitful marriage, but also for the well-being of the city-republic as a whole. While Barbaro explicitly models the treatise on the ideas of his friend and fellow Venetian Zaccaria Trevisan, he bolsters his argument with numerous examples from the moral literature of antiquity, including writings of Aristotle, Augustine, Homer, Xenophon, and especially Plutarch. The chapters below, selected from the preface and book II of the treatise, detail a woman's duties toward her husband, as well as the care and instruction of their children: a responsibility that Barbaro identifies as "the most serious of a wife's duties."

Questions

1   While saying that a wife must obey her husband, Barbaro also empha-
    sizes that she must love and support him. How is she to respond to his
    changing moods? In what contexts and in what ways is it permissible
    for her to express *her own* feelings?

2　Consider the advice on moderation in behavior, speech, and dress. What effects might following it have on a woman's socialization? To what extent is she allowed to develop an identity apart from her husband's?

3　What sorts of values is a wife to instill in her children? Why is she uniquely qualified to teach them? What aspects of the advice strike you as unusual, and why?

4　Why does Barbaro cite so many examples from antiquity? Do these enhance the argument by supporting it, or do they simply decorate it? Are there cases in which the ancient examples do not seem at all helpful or appropriate?

5　Based upon your reading of On Wifely Duties, what comments do you imagine Barbaro might have made concerning Boccaccio's story of Griselda?

On Wifely Duties

Preface

Our ancestors, my dear Lorenzo, were accustomed to making gifts on the occasion of the marriages of their friends or relatives as a token of the obligations that they felt or the love they bore toward the couple. Now this custom (as has happened to many others instituted by our ancestors) is no longer observed among us. For it happens that many people, for a variety of reasons, often borrowed money so that they could give the finest presents to those who were usually very rich. And in sowing these gifts (if I may speak in this way), they seem to me to be imitating those Babylonian peasants for whom (as the father of history, Herodotus, writes) fertile fields were expected to return two-hundredfold, and often even three-hundredfold.[1] I would call these fields anything but fertile and fruitful; but even though they were very poor, these people sent presents to the very rich while they themselves lacked everything and the wealthy had plenty. For this reason, driven on by hope for gain or for money, they lent their property

---

Translation of the preface and book two of Francesco Barbaro, "De re uxoria," ed. A. Gnesotto Atti e Memorie della R. Accademia di scienze, lettere ed arti di Padova, n.s. 32 (1915): 23–7, 62–100

1　Herodotus, Historia 1.193.

at high interest. But I think they deserve to be deluded in their hoped-for riches because they were trying to gain reward by means of a deceitful liberality and were striving for many and great advantages. But I find myself very different from these people, especially when I am dealing with you who has so many riches and such great wealth and has enjoyed so much good fortune in all your affairs that I do not see what could be the use of gifts. So I refrain from talking about the necessities of life since you have a great many precious clothes and elegant and rich furnishings in several places. Besides, when I recall the many pleasant discussions we have had, it seems to me that it would be more pleasant and welcome for you if you could be given something not from my fortune but from your friend Francesco.[2] Therefore, I have decided to write in dedication to you some brief comments on wifely virtues that I judge may be very useful on the occasion of your marriage, and perhaps not completely useless in the future. And if you will find what follows to be different from the usual precepts; it is on account of the mediocrity of my intellect that these precepts are not expressed in a more ornate style or explained at greater length. I have, for the most part, followed the ideas expressed by Zaccaria Trevisan, that very distinguished Venetian and learned man of our age, who is endowed with wisdom, justice, great experience in public affairs, and great learning, and who is closely bound to me by ties of friendship. When sometimes we had discussions on these matters, he elegantly summarized what the ancients had said on this matter.

Nor indeed do I undertake the composition of this tract just in order to instruct you yourself, but I am also attempting to teach several others of our age through you. Although I hope to instruct them in what they ought to be doing, you who have already followed these precepts, are now following them, and will continue to follow them in the future can see them more clearly in yourself for others. Really, how can I instruct you who have by nature been endowed with dignity, laud, and honor and have had such fine models at home? The very path to glory is clearly open to you who are filled with such instruction joined to nature. Indeed, you have imitated that outstanding man, your father Giovanni, and your most distinguished brother, Cosimo, and you have been abundantly fortified with their authority, wisdom, and advice.[3] In addition to these, you know several fine and very learned men with whom you have often spoken. Indeed, when I was with you I observed the great care and diligence with which you treated and

2   An allusion to Barbaro's trip to Florence in the summer of 1415 when he formed his close friendship with Lorenzo de' Medici.
3   Stressing the distinction of the Medici family, Barbaro names Lorenzo's father, Giovanni Bicci de' Medici (1360–1429), and his older brother Cosimo "The Elder" (1389–1464), who in 1434 was to gain political control over Florence.

esteemed that very learned man Roberto Rossi, from whose side you were almost never – and rightly – absent. Moreover, add to this your familiarity with that most eloquent man Leonardo Bruni, as well as with our very learned scholar, Niccoli.[4] From these men, I trust, you have heard and learned carefully a great deal on our theme as well as on many other topics. Even though you have already discussed the nature of marriage, yet I do not think it would be contrary to my love toward you if you understood just what I think on the same topic, for I have considered that it would be very pleasing for you to have something written on the subject in my own words. When Xenocrates refused to accept fifty talents of gold received from Alexander as a gift, as if the philosopher did not need royal presents, Alexander said: "Even if it is not right for Xenocrates to use the gifts of Alexander, still it is proper for Alexander to seem to be generous to Xenocrates."[5] Thus, although you have been so well instructed that you perhaps don't consider my advice especially necessary for you, writing this treatise still seemed to me a valuable thing to do, both in instructing young men and in honor of our close friendship.

Now, although all aspects of philosophy are both fruitful and profitable, and no part of it ought to be left uncultivated and undiscussed, still there is a field of it that is especially rich and fertile.[6] Thus marriage, from which all domestic duties follow, should be begun, practiced, and ended honorably, truly, and wisely, according to the best customs and the most sacred teaching. Indeed, for this reason you can easily see the bond of our will and the depth of our friendship. Indeed, I shall consider that I have won a great prize and singular reward if this, my small effort, is for you, to whom I owe everything, somewhat pleasant and profitable. My happiness will be doubled if the youth of our age will find good instruction in these brief comments. And so these precepts, which we have produced in our leisure, might be advantageous to those concerned with this matter, and those skilled in matters connected with marriage can take pleasure in seeing their views confirmed by learned men, or if they are unskilled in such affairs, they can be properly warned. Now if you find some of this treatment perhaps less than totally acceptable to you, still it is my desire and wish that you will be able to approve of the work on the whole. In like fashion at dinner parties, even though we sometimes avoid taking one of the many courses, still we are accustomed to praise the whole meal. Indeed, those few things that the stomach refuses to accept do not reduce the pleasure that the vast majority of the courses affords us. Therefore, I shall begin by talking about taking a wife, and I shall discuss this as briefly as possible. These are the same matters

---

4   The list is of Lorenzo's intellectual friends and mentors in Florence, whom Barbaro came to know in 1415: Roberto Rossi (ca. 1353–ca. 1420), who was Lorenzo's tutor, Leonardo Bruni, and Niccolò Niccoli.
5   Plutarch, *Regum et imperatorum Apophthegmata, Alexander* 30; *Moralia* 181E.
6   Cf. Cicero, *De officiis* 3.2.5.

that, as I have said, I discovered to be especially important from that fine friend of mine Zaccaria and from many other outstanding men. Now I shall do what I have proposed. I know that you will listen to me carefully and favorably, and whatever sort of work it turns out to be, I know that you will accept it as evidence of our goodwill, representing the kind of outstanding present that you ought to receive on the occasion of your wedding.

Book II

I   On the Faculty of Obedience

This is now the remaining part to be done here, in which if wives follow me, either of their own free will or by the commands of their husbands, no one will be so unfair as to think that I have not so established the duties of the wife that youth can enjoy peace and quiet the whole life long. Therefore, there are three things that, if they are diligently observed by a wife, will make a marriage praiseworthy and admirable: love for her husband, modesty of life, and diligent and complete care in domestic matters. We shall discuss the first of these, but before this I want to say something about the faculty of obedience, which is her master and companion, because nothing more important, nothing greater can be demanded of a wife than this. The import-ance of this faculty did not escape the ancient wise men who instituted the custom that when a sacrifice was made to Juno, who was called by the name Gamelia because of her governance of marriage, the gall was removed from the victim. They were wisely warning by this custom that it was proper to banish all gall and rancor from married life.[7] For this reason the Spartan woman's response has usually been approved by many learned men. When she was provoked by the slanderous reproaches of some mad old woman against her husband, she said: "Get out of here with such slanderous talk! When I was still a girl, I learned to obey the dictates of my parents, and now I realize that it is best to follow the wishes of my husband if I want to be what I ought to be."[8] Therefore, let the husband give the orders, and let the wife carry them out with an even temper. For this reason that woman called Gorgo is surely not to be censured when she gave this reply to the question of whether she made advances to the husband: "No, I have not, but he comes to me."[9] Cyrus, that great man and emperor, used to tell his troops that if the enemy advanced making a great noise, they should withstand the assault in

---

7   Cf. Plutarch, *Coniugalia praecepta* 27; *Moralia* 141F.
8   Cf. Plutarch, *Lacaenarum incertarum Apophthegmata* 23; *Moralia* 242B.
9   Cf. Plutarch, *Lacaenarum incertarum Apophthegmata* 25; *Moralia* 242C; *Coniugalia praecepta* 37; *Moralia* 143C.

silence, but if the enemy approached silently, then his men should go into battle with great noise and clamor. I would give the same advice to wives. If a husband, excited to anger, should scold you more than your ears are accustomed to hear, tolerate his wrath silently. But if he has been struck silent by a fit of depression, you should address him with sweet and suitable words, encourage, console, amuse, and humor him.[10] Those who work with elephants do not wear white clothes, and those who work with wild bulls are right not to wear red; for those beasts are made ever more ferocious by those colors. Many authors report that tigers are angered by drums and made violent by them. Wives ought to observe the same thing; if, indeed, a particular dress is offensive to a husband, then we advise them not to wear it, so that they do not give affront to their husbands, with whom they ought to live peacefully and pleasantly.[11] I think that ear guards (for so they are called because they protect the ear) are far more necessary for wives than for wrestlers, for the ears of the latter are only subject to blows, but indeed the former are subject to bills of repudiation accompanied by deep humiliation.[12] Hence, wives must take great care that they do not entertain suspicions, jealousy, or anger on account of what they hear with their ears. Indeed, wives can often prevent such errors if they will only follow the prudent example of King Alexander, who, when someone was accused and brought before him for trial, would always stop up one of his ears so that he might later open it to the accused who might want to defend himself.[13] Indeed, it seems that Hermione was speaking the truth when she testified that she was brought to ruin by wicked women with whom she had been on familiar terms. Therefore, if wives should at some time become suspicious, let them stay away from slanderous women, stop up their ears, and suppress their mutterings, so that (as the proverb has it) fire is not added to fire. Let wives learn to follow that saying of Philip, that most outstanding king. This man was urged once by his courtiers to be harsher toward the Greeks who, though they had received many benefits from him, still criticized and slandered him. But he said: "What would they do if they were ever to receive bad treatment from us?"[14] In the same way, when troublesome women say, "Your husband esteems you, who are so obedient and affectionate, only very little," then wives should answer, "What if I willingly and actively lost my modesty with my shame and my great desire for him along with my love?" A certain master found his runaway slave in a workhouse, and because the slave had been punished enough the master said: "Would that I had found you somewhere else than in this place." The wife who is angry

10 Cf. Plutarch, *Coniugalia praecepta* 37; *Moralia* 143C.
11 Cf. Plutarch, *Coniugalia praecepta* 45; *Moralia* 144E.
12 Cf. Plutarch, *De recta ratione audiendi* 2; *Moralia* 38B.
13 Cf. Plutarch, *Vitae Parallelae, Alexander* 42.2.
14 Cf. Plutarch, *Coniugalia praecepta* 40; *Moralia* 143F.

with her husband because of jealousy and is considering a separation should ask herself this question: If I put myself in a workhouse because I hate a whore, what could make her far happier and more fortunate than this? She would see me almost shipwrecked, while at the same time she was sailing with favorable winds and securely casting her anchor into my marriage bed?[15] Euripides, in his usual manner, greatly criticized those who were accustomed to listening to the harp while they were at dinner, for such music was better fitted to soothing anger or sadness than to relaxing those already immersed in pleasure.[16] In similar fashion I would criticize wives who when they are happy and contented sleep with their husbands but when they are angry sleep apart and reject their husbands' affections, which through pleasantness and pleasure easily bring about reconciliation. The word Juno in Homer means "overseer of the nuptial ties," and if I remember correctly, when she spoke of Tethys and Oceanus, she declared that she would compose their differences and bring them together in love-making and nocturnal embraces.[17] At Rome when there arose any differences between husband and wife, they entered the temple of the appeasing goddess where, after the spectators had been ushered out, they discussed everything frankly, and, finally, they returned home reconciled.[18]

It was considered very good for domestic peace and harmony if a wife kept her husband's love with total diligence. At the olympic games that were dedicated to the great god Jupiter and attended by all of Greece, Gorgias used his eloquence to urge a union of all the Greeks. Melanthus said: Our patron attempts to persuade us that we should all join together in a league, but he cannot bring himself and his wife and her maid – who are only three people – to a mutual agreement (for the wife was very jealous because Gorgias was wildly enamoured of her maid).[19] Likewise, Philip was for a long time displeased with the queen Olympias and Alexander. And when Demaratus of Corinth returned from Greece, Philip eagerly and closely questioned him about the union of the Greeks. Demaratus said to him: "Philip, I consider it a very bad thing that you are spending all your energy in bringing peace and concord to all of Greece when you are not yet reconciled with your own wife and son."[20] Therefore, if any woman wants to govern her children and servants, she should make sure that she is, first of all, at peace with her husband. Otherwise, it will seem that she wants to imitate the very things that she is trying to correct in them. In order that a wife does her duty and brings peace and harmony to her household, she must agree to the first

15 Cf. Plutarch, *Coniugalia praecepta* 41; *Moralia* 144A.
16 Cf. Euripides, *Medea* 190ff.
17 Cf. Homer, *Iliad* 14.205, 209.
18 Cf. Valerius Maximus, *Factorum ac dictorum memorabilium libri IX* 2.1.6.
19 Cf. Plutarch, *Coniugalia praecepta* 43; *Moralia* 144BC.
20 Cf. Plutarch, *Regum et imperatorum Apophthegmata, Philippus* 30; *Moralia* 179C.

principle that she does not disagree with her husband on any point. But of this enough has been said.

3 On Moderation

The next part is concerning moderation, from which very often an enduring love between man and wife is begun, always nurtured and preserved. This quality is not only pleasing to the husband but also seems very noble to all those who hear about it. Moderation in a wife is believed to consist especially in controlling her demeanor, behavior, speech, dress, eating, and lovemaking. We shall discuss briefly these things that we have perceived either by our natural powers, learning, or experience; and since the first two qualities mentioned above amount to the same thing, we shall discuss them together.

Now demeanor, which is above all the most certain expression of the personality and is found in no living creature except man, demonstrates signs of an honest, respectful, and abstemious character. In demeanor the habits that nature might otherwise have hidden completely are detected. One's demeanor declares and manifests many things without the use of words. From the face and its movement the disposition of an individual may be known. Even in dumb animals we discern anger, pleasure, and other such emotions from the movement of the body and from the eyes, which testify and make clear what kind of emotions there are inside. Wherefore many who trust in facial characteristics maintain that one can learn many things about an individual's nature in this way. But I digress too much.

I therefore would like wives to evidence modesty at all times and in all places. They can do this if they will preserve an evenness and restraint in the movements of the eyes, in their walking, and in the movement of their bodies; for the wandering of the eyes, a hasty gait, and excessive movement of the hands and other parts of the body cannot be done without loss of dignity, and such actions are always joined to vanity and are signs of frivolity. Therefore, wives should take care that their faces, countenances, and gestures (by which we can penetrate by careful observation into the most guarded thoughts) be applied to the observance of decency. If they are observant in these matters, they will merit dignity and honor; but if they are negligent they will not be able to avoid censure and criticism. Still, I am not asking that a wife's face be unpleasant, with a sour expression, but, rather, it should be pleasant. And her demeanor should not be clumsy but gracefully dignified. Moreover, I earnestly beg that wives observe the precept of avoiding immoderate laughter. This is a habit that is indecent in all persons, but it is especially hateful in a woman. On the other hand, women should not be censured if they laugh a little at a good joke and thus lapse somewhat from their serious demeanor.[21] Demosthenes used to rehearse his legal speeches at home in front of a mirror so that with his own eyes he could judge what he should do and what he should avoid in delivering his speeches at court.[22] We may well apply this practice to wifely behavior.

I wish that wives would daily think and consider what the dignity, the status of being a wife requires, so that they will not be lacking in dignified comportment. We know that Spartan wives used to go about with their faces covered, while Spartan virgins went about with their faces uncovered. When the Spartan Charillus was asked about this practice he answered: Our ancestors permitted this liberty to young virgins so that they might find husbands; but they prohibited it in married women so that they might understand that it was not their place to seek husbands but to care for and keep those they already had.[23] Indeed, our Cretan subjects permit a similar custom. They allow their young girls to stand in their doorways and sing and joke and play games with their suitors. But when their women are married they have to stay at home, just as do those women who are dedicated to the rite of Vesta; and they can scarcely even go out, as if it would be unlawful for them even to see strange men. Who would not agree that they took this custom from Xenophon? One can easily learn from the following anecdote how much Xenophon would control the gaze of women. For when Tigranes returned home from service under King Cyrus with his kinsmen and his beloved wife Armenia, many men praised the king's manners, the size of his body, and his gracefulness. Tigranes asked Armenia what she thought of Cyrus's beauty, but Armenia, swearing before the immortal gods, answered: "I never turned my eyes away from you. Therefore, I am quite ignorant of what Cyrus's size or shape may be."[24] That story is consistent with the principles of Gorgias, who wanted women to be shut up at home so that nothing could be known about them except their reputation. But Thucydides did not think that they merited such treatment, for he declared he had the best wife, about whom there was not the least word praising or censuring her.[25]

We who follow a middle way should establish some rather liberal rules for our wives. They should not be shut up in their bedrooms as in a prison but should be permitted to go out, and this privilege should be taken as evidence of their virtue and propriety. Still, wives should not act with their husbands as the moon does with the sun; for when the moon is near the sun it is never visible, but when it is distant it stands resplendent by itself. Therefore, I would

---

21 These strictures on propriety are taken from Cicero, *De legibus* 1.9.27, and *De officiis* 1.34–6.125–39.
22 Cf. Plutarch, *Vitae Parallelae, Demosthenes* 11.
23 Cf. Plutarch, *Apophthegmata Laconia, Charillus* 2; *Moralia* 232C.
24 Cf. Xenophon, *Cyropaedia* 3.1.41.
25 Cf. Plutarch, *Mulierum virtutes, Proemio; Moralia* 242EF.

have wives be seen in public with their husbands, but when their husbands are away wives should stay at home.[26] By maintaining an honest gaze in their eyes, they can communicate most significantly as in painting, which is called silent poetry.[27] They also should maintain dignity in the motion of their heads and the other movements of their bodies. [Having] spoken about demeanor and behavior, I shall now speak of speech.

4   On Speech and Silence

Isocrates warns men to speak on those matters that they know well and [those] about which they cannot, on account of their dignity, remain silent.[28] We commend women to concede the former as the property of men, but they should consider the latter to be appropriate to themselves as well as to men. Loquacity cannot be sufficiently reproached in women, as many very learned and wise men have stated, nor can silence be sufficiently applauded. For this reason women were prohibited by the laws of the Romans from pleading either criminal or civil law cases. And when Maesia, Afrania, and Hortensia deviated from these laws, their actions were reproved, criticized, and censured in the histories of the Romans. When Marcus Cato the Elder observed that Roman women, contrary to nature's law and the condition of the female sex, sometimes frequented the forum, sought a favorable decision, and spoke with strangers, he inveighed against, criticized, and restrained them as was required by that great citizen's honor and the dignity of his state.[29] We know that the Pythagoreans were ordered to be silent for at least two years after beginning their studies. In this way they were not able to lie, to be deceived, or to be in error – all of which are very shameful acts – and, moreover, they could not stubbornly defend those opinions that they had not yet sufficiently investigated.[30] But we require that wives be perpetually silent whenever there is an opportunity for frivolity, dishonesty, and impudence. When addressed, wives should reply very modestly to familiar friends and return their greetings, and they should very briefly treat those matters that the time and place offer them. In this way they will always seem to be provoked into conversation rather than to provoke it. They should also take pains to be praised for the dignified brevity of their speech rather than for its glittering prolixity. When a certain young man saw the noble woman Theano stretch her arm out of her mantle that had been drawn back, he said to his companions: "How handsome is her arm." To this

26   Cf. Plutarch, *Coniugalia praecepta* 9; *Moralia* 139C.
27   Plutarch, *Quomodo adulator ab amico internoscatur* 15; *Moralia* 58B.
28   Isocrates, *Ad Demonicum* 41.
29   Cf. Livy, *Ab urbe condita* 34.2–4; Valerius Maximus, *Memorabilia* 8.3.1–3.
30   Cf. Aulus Gellius, *Noctes Atticae* 1.9.3–4.

she replied: "It is not a public one." It is proper, however, that not only arms but indeed also the speech of women never be made public; for the speech of a noble woman can be no less dangerous than the nakedness of her limbs.[31] For this reason women ought to avoid conversations with strangers since manners and feelings often draw notice easily in these situations.

Silence is also often praised in the finest men. Pindar heaped praise on that outstanding Greek ruler Epaminondas because, though he knew much, he said little. In this matter, as in many others, Epaminondas followed the excellent teachings of nature, the mistress of life, who has clearly made known her thoughts on silence. She has with good reason furnished us with two ears but only one tongue, and this she has guarded with the double defense of lips and teeth.[32] Now Theophrastus and many other men say that nature has made us with this opening so that the virtue planted in us may enjoy the most pleasant and best results. As for the other senses that nature has bestowed upon us as scouts and messengers, they sometimes are sources of reliable knowledge but are very often only the conveyers of ignorance.[33] Yet a certain Venetian citizen, whom I don't think it is necessary to name at present, praises silence only in those who cannot gain approval by their genius, authority by their wisdom, or renown by their well-wrought speeches. To this man I usually answer that the principal consideration in every matter refers to the person and to the place as well as to the time. Even if I were to concede, following his opinion, that it is usually appropriate for men to speak, still I consider such speechmaking to be, in the main, repugnant to the modesty, constancy, and dignity of a wife. For this reason the author Sophocles, who is certainly no worse than the Venetian I am discussing – and most men consider him better – has termed silence the most outstanding ornament of women.[34] Therefore, women should believe they have achieved glory of eloquence if they will honor themselves with the outstanding ornament of silence. Neither the applause of a declamatory play nor the glory and adoration of an assembly is required of them, but all that is desired of them is eloquent, well-considered, and dignified silence. But what am I doing? I must be very careful, especially since I am treating silence, that I do not perhaps seem to you too talkative.

5   On Dress and Other Adornments

This is the point at which to discuss dress and other adornments of the body, which when they are not properly observed, lead not only to the ruin of a

31   Cf. Plutarch, *Coniugalia praecepta* 31; *Moralia* 142D.
32   Cf. Plutarch, *De recta ratione audiendi* 3; *Moralia* 39B.
33   Cf. Plutarch, *De recta ratione audiendi* 2; *Moralia* 38AB.
34   Sophocles, *Aiax* 293.

marriage but often to the squandering of a patrimony as well. All authorities who have studied these matters bear witness to this fact. If indeed one is pleased by the always praiseworthy rule of moderation, women will be recognized for modesty, and care will be taken for personal wealth and, at the same time, for the city as a whole. Here this fine precept should be followed: wives ought to care more to avoid censure than to win applause in their splendid style of dress. If they are of noble birth, they should not wear mean and despicable clothes if their wealth permits otherwise. Attention must be given, we believe, to the condition of the matter, the place, the person, and the time; for who cannot, without laughing, look upon a priest who is dressed in a soldier's mantel or someone else girdled with a states-man's purple at a literary gathering or wearing a toga at a horse race. Hence, we approve neither someone who is too finely dressed nor someone who is too negligent in her attire, but, rather, we approve someone who has preserved decency in her dress.[35] Excessive indulgence in clothes is a good sign of great vanity. Moreover, experience and authorities have shown that such wives are apt to turn from their own husbands to other lovers. King Cyrus ought to be an example to our women that they should not strive too much to have expensive clothes, for Cyrus seems to be equal to his great name, which in the Persian tongue means "sun," both in his admirable wisdom and in his splendid moderation. When ambassadors came from the king of India to make peace with the Assyrians in the city of his uncle Cyaxares, the uncle wanted the choicest part of his army to appear before them. He sent orders to his general Cyrus to appear as soon as possible with all his troops in the courtyard of the royal palace and the large market square. Cyrus carried out these orders and came with order, dignity, and unbelievable speed, wearing only a thin garment, even though Cyaxares had sent him a purple robe, a precious necklace, and other Persian ornaments to wear so that his nephew, the general of his army, might seem all the more splendid and well-dressed. But Cyrus despised all these things greatly, and it seemed to others and to himself the highest decoration to be seen arriving ready to fight with the well-trained army almost before the royal messenger had returned to Cyaxares.[36] A similar disdain for fine apparel would bring great honor to our wives.

Dionysius, the tyrant of Sicily, gave two very precious garments to Lysan-der so that his daughters might be more finely dressed. But Lysander refused the gifts and ordered the garments returned to Dionysius, saying that his daughters would be even more finely attired without the garments.[37]

---

35 Barbaro takes this idea from the *De ingenuis moribus et liberalibus adulescentiae studiis* (1402–3) by another prominent Italian humanist, Pier Paolo Vergerio the Elder (1370–1444).
36 Cf. Xenophon, *Cyropaedia* 2.4.1–6.
37 Cf. Plutarch, *Coniugalia praecepta* 26; *Moralia* 141E.

Julia, the daughter of Caesar Augustus, imagined that her fine attire was sometimes offensive to her father, so one day she put on a plain dress and went to pay him a visit. When Caesar greatly approved of her new attire, she acknowledged that she was now wearing clothes that would please her father while before she had been dressing to please her husband Agrippa.[38]

One may believe whatever he wishes. But still I think that wives wear and esteem all those fine garments so that men other than their own husbands will be impressed and pleased. For wives always neglect such adornments at home, but in the market square "this consumer of wealth"[39] cannot be sufficiently decked out or adorned. Indeed, a great variety of clothes is rarely useful and often harmful to husbands, while this same variety is always pleasing to paramours for whom such things were invented. I am wont to compare these men who are properly called "uxorious" to those who are so pleased with splendid exteriors on their houses while they are forced to do without necessary things inside. Hence, they present a golden facade to give pleasure to neighbors and the passers-by. Such husbands are also similar to unskilled but rich barbers whom middle-aged men frequent only if they wish to have their hair arranged. Their ivory tools and elaborate mirrors are no source of wealth to them, but rather of grief, when they see the most noble young men going, to their great sorrow, to the neighboring barbershops. Moreover, sumptuous attire, magnificent clothes, and luxurious apparel give pleasure to those who frequent porticos, open courts, and sidewalks or very often promenade through the whole city. Hence, it was wisely forbidden to the women of Egypt to wear ornate shoes so that they might be prevented from wandering about too freely. Indeed, if we were to deprive most women of their sumptuous clothes, they would gladly and willingly stay at home.[40]

Yet I think we ought to follow the custom – for good mores have so decayed, – that our wives adorn themselves with gold, jewels, and pearls, if we can afford it. For such adornments are the sign of a wealthy, not a lascivious, woman and are taken as evidence of the wealth of the husband more than as a desire to impress wanton eyes. I will not dwell on the fact that this sort of wealth is more durable, and less likely to entail poverty than money put into rich clothing. Moreover, jewels and gold may often easily be of great use in business and public affairs. Who does not know how useful this sort of wealth was at a certain time to the ancient Romans, who in the time of peril during the Punic War raised money – which the ancients called the "sinews of war" – for their city, following the Oppian Law.[41] Still I think that wives ought to display their jewels even less than the present

38 Cf. Macrobius, *Saturnalia* 2.5.5.
39 Terence, *Eunuchus* 79.
40 Plutarch, *Coniugalia praecepta* 30; *Moralia* 141E.
41 The story of the use of the Oppian Law to confiscate jewels for the Roman treasury during the Second Punic War is recorded in Valerius Maximus, *Memorabilia* 9.1.3.

sumptuary laws permit. Therefore, I would like them to abstain from wearing very licentious apparel and other bodily adornments, not out of necessity but because they desire to win praise by showing that "they can do without those things that they are legally allowed."[42] But you have heard enough about attire.

9   On the Education of Children

It remains to speak about the education of children, which is surely a rewarding and certainly the most serious of a wife's duties. Diligence in accumulation of money for the family is really worth nothing (as ancient Crates used to say) unless a great deal of care and really extraordinary amount of energy is expended on the upbringing and instruction of the children to whom the wealth is to be left.[43] For this care children, who owe everything to their parents, are especially obligated. But if parents do not perform the task of caring for and instructing children, the children must really and truly seem deserted and abandoned. If, indeed, we acknowledge that all things are due to the authors of our life, which all mortals naturally cherish and hold on to with good reason, what should we do if to a noble upbringing we add training in living well? On this account, if you reflect upon all the aspects of the matter, you will find that unless mothers totally repudiate the rules of nature, the duty of educating their children is so incumbent upon them that they cannot refuse this duty without great harm. For nature assigns to them an overwhelming love for their children, which they simply cannot overlook.[44] So that this fact may be amply demonstrated, I will speak of the procreation of children before they see the light of day; but time does not allow me to digress for long, and Nature has so hidden and secluded those parts of the body that what cannot be viewed without embarrassment can hardly be discussed by us without loss of dignity. However, we shall treat those matters that we absolutely cannot omit.

In pregnancy the same blood of which women otherwise are cleansed in their monthly effusions is held back. This time, following the laws of nature, the fetus is nourished by this blood until the time of birth arrives. Then, as in all animals who give birth, the nourishment of milk is supplied. For this, Nature has made breasts, which, like bountiful fountains, nourish the young child and help it to grow gradually in all its parts. Moreover, women have been given two breasts so that if they have twins they may easily suckle and nourish them together.[45] All these things have been thus provided with great

42   The phrase is from St. Augustine, *De bono coniugali* 3.
43   Cf. Plutarch, *De liberis educandis* 7; *Moralia* 4E.
44   Cf. Plutarch, *De amore prolis* 3; *Moralia* 495.
45   Cf. Plutarch, *De liberis educandis* 5; *Moralia* 3D.

wisdom, but they still might seem to have been done in vain except that Nature has also instilled in women an incredible love and affection for their offspring.[46] Here the special care and diligence of Nature can be observed, for while she has placed the nipples of other animals under their stomachs, in women she has affixed them on their breasts so that they may feed their children milk and fondle them with embraces at the same time, kiss them easily and comfortably, and, as they say, receive them to their bosoms.

Thus Nature has assigned to women the duty of bearing and rearing children not only by necessity but also with her singular goodwill and love.[47] Moreover, we can see a good argument in favor of a mother exercising great care for her newborn babies if women will but follow the habits of the terrible she-bear and other beasts. After bears have given birth to their unformed cub, they form and clean the cub with their tongues, as if the tongue were a kind of tool, so they can be justly called not just the mother of the cub but even its artificer.[48] But why should we dwell on these small matters? Surely Nature has bestowed such good feeling toward newborn infants that we can see some animals who are timid become very brave on account of their offspring, others who are lazy become diligent, and others still who are slave to the stomach and gluttony become very abstemious. Did not even the Homeric bird endure hunger in order to provide for her young ones, and did she not cheat her own stomach to keep them fed?[49] Therefore, mothers merit the severest censure if they neglect the care of their children and live carelessly. I would have them avoid no hardship in order to ensure that they make their children the best companions, comforters, and helpers in their old age. Therefore, if mothers would be free from reproach they should not neglect their offspring, but they should provide for both the bodies and souls of their children, and they should nourish and suckle them at their breasts. And the ones they nourished with their blood while still unknown mothers now will raise, since they are now born and have become human beings and are known and dear, since they require greatly not simply the care of a nurse but that of a mother as well.[50] The wife of Marcus Cato the Censor fed her infant with her own milk, and this custom continues among Roman women down to the present age.[51] In fact, because the fellowship of food and nourishment always increases friendship and love,[52] in order to make the infants of her servants more loving to her own infants, a wife

46   Cf. Plutarch, *De amore prolis* 3; *Moralia* 496A.
47   Cf. Plutarch, *De amore prolis* 3; *Moralia* 496C.
48   Cf. Plutarch, *De amore prolis* 2; *Moralia* 494C.
49   Cf. Plutarch, *De amore prolis* 2; *Moralia* 494D.
50   Cf. Aulus Gellius, *Noctes Atticae* 12.1.6.
51   Cf. Plutarch, *Vitae Parallelae, Cato major* 20.
52   An echo of Plutarch, *De liberis educandis* 5; *Moralia* 3D.

should sometimes feed them at her own breasts.[53] We beg and exhort the most noble women to follow this example of feeding her infant her own milk, for it is very important that an infant should be nourished by the same mother in whose womb and by whose blood he was conceived. No nourishment seems more proper, none more wholesome than that same nourishment of body that glowed with greatest life and heat in the womb and should thus be given as known and familiar food to newborn infants. The power of the mother's food most effectively lends itself to shaping the properties of body and mind to the character of the seed. That may be discerned quite clearly in many instances; for example, when young goats are suckled with sheep's milk their hair becomes much softer, and when lambs are fed on goats' milk, it is evident that their fleeces become much coarser. In trees it is certain that they are much more dependent on the qualities of both sap and soil than on the quality of the seed;[54] thus, if they are transplanted to other ground when flourishing and well leafed, you will find them changed enormously by the sap from the less fertile ground. Therefore, noble women should always try to feed their own offspring so that they will not degenerate from being fed on poorer, foreign milk. But if, as often happens, mothers cannot for compelling reasons suckle their own children, they ought to place them with good nurses, not with slaves, strangers, or drunken and unchaste women. They ought to give their infants to the care of those who are freeborn, well mannered, and especially those endowed with dignified speech. In this way the young infant will not imbibe corrupt habits and words and will not receive, with his milk, baseness, faults, and impure infirmities and thus be infected with a dangerous degenerative disease in mind and body.[55] For just as the limbs of an infant can be properly and precisely formed and strengthened, so can his manners be exactly and properly shaped from birth. Therefore, mothers ought to be especially careful in their choice of nurses for infants; at this tender age a child's unformed character is very susceptible to being molded, and, as we impress a seal in soft wax, so the disposition and faults of a nurse can be sealed upon an infant. That very wise poet Virgil showed how important a nurse's inclinations and nature are when he described how Dido called Aeneas harsh and unyielding. Thus he has her say: "The Hircanian tigers fed you at their breasts."[56] Likewise, that most pleasant poet Theocritus said that he detested cruel Cupid, not because he was born of his mother Venus "but because he suckled the breast of a lioness."[57]

53 Cf. Plutarch, *Vitae Parallelae, Cato major* 20.
54 Cf. Aulus Gellius, *Noctes Atticae* 12.1.11–16.
55 Cf. Plutarch, *De liberis educandis* 5; *Moralia* 3DF.
56 Aulus Gellius, *Noctes Atticae* 12.1.20, quoting Virgil, *Aeneid* 4.366–7.
57 Theocritus, *Idyllion* 3.15–16.

Therefore, women ought to consider it best, very honorable, and commendable to suckle their own children, whom they should nourish with great love, fidelity, and diligence; or they may commit this part of their duty to well-trained nurses who will esteem and care for the infants, not with a pretended enthusiasm nor out of mercenary consideration. After their offspring have passed their infancy, mothers should use all their skill, care, and effort to ensure that their children are endowed with excellent qualities of mind and body. First they should instruct them in their duty toward Immortal God, their country, and their parents, so that they will be instilled from their earliest years with those qualities that are the foundation of all other virtues. Only those children who fear God, obey the laws, honor their parents, respect their superiors, are pleasant with their equals and courteous to their inferiors, will exhibit much hope for themselves. Children should meet all people with a civil demeanor, pleasant countenance, and friendly words. But they should be on the most familiar terms with only the best people. Thus they will learn moderation in food and drink so that they may lay, as it were, the foundation of temperance for their future lives. They should be taught to avoid these pleasures that are dishonorable, and they should apply their efforts and thoughts to those matters that are the most becoming and will be useful and pleasant when they become older. If mothers are able to instruct their children in these matters, their offspring will much more easily and better receive the benefit of education. Very often we see that the commands and gifts of rulers are welcomed by their subjects, yet when these same things are bestowed by private persons they hardly even seem acceptable. Who can be unaware of what great authority the mildest and shortest reproach of a parent has on his children? Whence that wise man, Cato the Elder, instructed his offspring diligently in many subjects, including literature, so he would not be lacking in his duties as a father.[58] Even the barbarous Eurydice ought to be judged worthy of great praise, for when she was advanced in years she applied herself to the study of literature, that monument of virtue and learning, so that, having done this, she would not only be considered the source of life to her children but could also instill in them through the bountiful condiments of the humanities the art of living well and happily.[59] Mothers should often warn their children to abstain from excessive laughter and to avoid words that denote a rash character. That is the mark of stupidity, the evidence of passion. Moreover, children should be warned not ever to speak on those matters that are base in the act. Therefore, mothers should restrain them from vulgar or cutting words. If their children should say anything that is obscene or licentious, mothers should not greet it with a laugh or a kiss, but with a whip.

58   Plutarch, *Vitae Parallelae, Cato major* 20.
59   Cf. Plutarch, *De liberis educandis* 20; *Moralia* 14BC.

Moreover, they should teach their children not to criticize anyone because of his poverty or the low birth of his lineage or other misfortunes, for they are sure to make bitter enemies from such actions or develop an attitude of arrogance. Mothers should teach their children sports in which they so willingly learn to exert themselves that, if the occasion arises, they can easily bear even more difficult hardships. I would have mothers sharply criticized for displays of anger, greed, or sexual desire in the presence of their offspring, for these vices weaken virtue. If mothers act appropriately, their children will learn from infancy to condemn, avoid, and hate these most filthy mistresses and they will take care to revere the names of God and will be afraid to take them in vain. For whoever has been taught at an early age to despise the Divinity, will they not as adults surely curse Him? Therefore, it is of great importance to train children from infancy so that they never swear. Indeed, those who swear readily because of some misfortune are not deserving of trust, and those who readily swear very often unwittingly betray themselves. Mothers ought to teach their children to speak the truth. This was well established among the Persians, and for that reason they decreed that there would be no market squares in their cities since they believed that such places were only fit for lying, or telling falsehoods, or for swearing falsely.[60] Mothers should teach their children to say little at all times, and especially at banquets, unless they are ordered to speak, so that children do not become impudent or talkative – qualities that ought to be especially avoided in the young. It will be an impediment to proper education if children try to explain impudently what they themselves have not yet sufficiently understood.[61] Therefore, you should recall that saying of Cato who, when he was a youth blamed for his silence, said: "Then I shall not harm myself at all, until I shall say those things that are [ought better to be] left unsaid."[62] If children will learn such percepts from their mothers as soon as their tender years permit, they will more happily and easily obtain the dignity and learning of their parents.

There are many other matters that I shall omit at present because they are peculiar to fathers, and I do so readily because I see that some people consider this subject of wifely duties to be so vast and infinite that the subject of fatherly duties can scarcely be sufficiently treated here. I can say nothing truer than that I never intended to discuss what might be done, but, rather, I have tried to describe what ought to be done. Therefore, who is such an unjust critic that if he will approve of a marriage done for the best reasons (just as you have done) and will, in his choice of a wife, take a

60 Cf. Aulus Gellius, *Noctes Atticae* 11.11.1–2, for this distinction between telling falsehoods and lying.
61 Cf. Vergerio, *De ingenuis moribus.*
62 Cf. Plutarch, *Vitae Parallelae, Cato minor* 4.

woman outstanding in her morals, suitable in her age, family, beauty, and wealth, loving to her husband, and modest and very skillful in domestic matters – who, I say, would be so pessimistic in these matters that he cannot wish for all these great qualities or imagine that wives so endowed ought not to perform all these important precepts? Therefore, my Lorenzo, your compatriots ought to be stirred by your example and follow you with great enthusiasm, for in Ginevra you have taken a wife who is a virgin well endowed with virtue, charm, a noble lineage, and great wealth. What more outstanding, more worthy model could I propose than yours? What more shining, more worthy example than yours, since in this outstanding city of Florence you are most eminently connected through your father, grandfather, and ancestors? You have taken a wife whose great wealth the entire world indeed admires but whose chastity, constancy, and prudence all men of goodwill esteem highly. They consider that you are blessed and happy to have her as a wife, as she is to have you as a husband. Since you have contracted such an outstanding and fine marriage, these same men ask God Immortal that you will have the best children who will become very honored citizens in your state. These matters might perhaps seem negligible since I am treating them, but indeed they are, in their own fashion, borne out in your marriage. Thus, surely young men who follow your example will profit more than only by following my precepts; just as laws are much more likely to be observed in a city when they are obeyed by its ruler, so, since your own choice of a wife is consistent with my teachings, we may hope that these precepts will be followed by the youth.

But, Lorenzo, as my treatise begins with you, so shall it end. You now have, instead of a present, my opinion on wifely duties, and I hope that whatever has been said by me, not to admonish you (as I made clear from the beginning) but to declare our mutual goodwill, will in large measure be kindly accepted by many others. I am certain that it will be well received by you, in whose name I undertook this endeavor. If when you are reading our little commentary you find anything that perhaps seems to be well or wisely stated, attribute it to that excellent man Zaccaria Trevisan, who is worthy of every sort of praise and whose memory I gladly cherish, and to my study of Greek literature.[63] From the latter I have culled some things that pertain to our subject and inserted them here. Although I have been occupied with this treatise for only a few months, I still am happy to think that it will bear abundant and pleasant fruit. For I have profited so much from the learning and talent of that fine and very erudite man, Guarino da Verona, who was my tutor and my closest friend from among all my acquaintances. He was a guide to me and to several other first-rate people, in understanding

63 A reference to Barbaro's debt to his Venetian model, Zaccaria Trevisan, and to his Greek teacher, Guarino da Verona.

and advancing our study of the humanities. And he was such a fine guide that, with his help, these divine studies, to which I have devoted myself from boyhood, have become very enjoyable and profitable to me. Therefore, please accept gladly from me this wife's necklace (as I wish to call it), given on the occasion of your marriage. I know that you will esteem it greatly both because it is the sort of necklace that cannot be broken or destroyed by use (as others can) and because it is the product of my sincere friendship and of a mind that is entirely devoted to you.

Part V

The Power of Knowledge

Introduction to Part V

For Renaissance humanists, the study of the languages and literature of classical antiquity was more than simply a pleasant diversion or a way to earn a living: it was, they believed, a means to self-improvement and a guide for the revitalization of their own world. The remarkable accomplishments of the classical Romans – whether in statecraft, conquest, philosophy, architecture, or literature – provided models that inspired emulation. Just as Renaissance architects studied the remnants of ancient buildings and learned from them, so too humanists sought to imitate models of exemplary behavior as well as of literary style.

This imitation was fraught with tension, since the values of the classical past at times differed sharply from the Christian beliefs that permeated Renaissance society (see the discussion accompanying plate 1 above). Yet the tension could itself be a stimulus to creativity, for the distinct culture of antiquity gave Renaissance humanists a useful perspective for critiquing their own shared assumptions and advocating change. Meanwhile, the techniques of textual criticism that they developed – their methods of assessing the reliability of ancient manuscripts and of determining the precise meanings of the words and ideas they contained – could themselves be tools of advocacy, as well as weapons for demolishing claims made by one's foes. The selections below indicate something of the range of the ways that knowledge could serve humanists either as a powerful tool or as a formidable weapon.

Plate 8 Perugino, *Christ Handing the Keys to St. Peter* (1481–2), Sistine Chapel, Vatican City. *Source*: Art Resource/Scala.

This painting by Pietro Perugino (ca. 1450–1523) is one of a series of wall-frescoes produced under Perugino's direction for the papal chapel consecrated by Sixtus IV (r. 1471–84). In the foreground is portrayed the founding moment of the papacy, when Jesus said to Simon Peter in the presence of the other disciples, "you are Peter, and on this rock I will build my church, and the gates of Hades will not prevail against it. I will give you the keys of the kingdom of heaven, and whatever you bind on earth will be bound in heaven, and whatever you loose on earth will be loosed in heaven" (Matthew 16:18–19, NRSV). Following Christ's death and resurrection, Peter became the leader of the Roman Church, and the popes are the direct heirs of his authority as Christ's vicar on earth. In the spacious geometric grid of the piazza in the middle ground of the painting are two scenes: on the left, Christ using a coin with the emperor's head stamped on it to pay the emperor's tax (Matthew 22:15–22); and on the right, the stoning of Christ in the temple complex of Jerusalem upon His having asserted that He is God (John 8:59 and 10:31). In both scenes, those surrounding Christ are portrayed in modern dress. The triumphal arches in the background, on either side of the temple, invoke the arch of Constantine, the first Roman emperor to convert to Christianity.

The painting takes on added meaning when viewed in context of the fresco program of the chapel. On one side wall are scenes from the life of Christ, while on the other are scenes from the life of Moses. Perugino's *Christ Handing the Keys to St. Peter* is situated directly opposite Sandro Botticelli's fresco of the *Punishment of Korah*, in which Moses chastises the sons of Aaron who have presumed to usurp priestly authority. On the arch of Constantine in the background of Botticelli's painting is inscribed in Latin, "Let no one arrogate to himself the honor [of the high priesthood], unless he has been called by God, just as Aaron was" (see Hebrews 5:4). This defense of priestly authority is echoed in the inscription on the triumphal arches in Perugino's fresco of the transfer of the keys, which reads: "You, Sixtus IV, unequal to Solomon in wealth [but] superior [to him] in religion, have consecrated this immense temple." Thus Sixtus's authority as the vicar of Christ – an authority prefigured jointly by that of Moses (as lawgiver) and that of Aaron (as chief priest) – both fulfills and transcends their examples, just as the New Testament both fulfills and transcends the Old.

Perugino's painting of *Christ Handing the Keys to St. Peter* came to be attributed a further significance in papal conclaves, which were held in the Sistine Chapel starting in 1484. At least by 1503, many believed (or at least hoped) that being stationed under certain frescoes could be auspicious for that cardinal's candidacy. In the event, in the conclave following the death of Alexander VI, Francesco Piccolomini of Siena, who had drawn the position under Perugino's fresco of the transfer of the keys, was elected Pope Pius III. When his death a few weeks later necessitated another conclave, the spot beneath that same fresco befell Cardinal Giuliano della Rovere (or, at least, so it was later claimed), who went on to be elected Pope Julius II. Belief in the power of this fresco seemed to receive further vindication in 1523, when Giulio de' Medici, positioned under it, was elected pope (Clement VII, r. 1523–34), and according to a later sixteenth-century source, Alessandro Farnese filled that spot in 1534, when he was chosen to succeed Clement (he became Paul III, r. 1534–49). The attribution of prophetic significance to Perugino's fresco is but one instance of the belief (normative in the Renaissance) in the transformative power of images.

11

Lorenzo Valla (1407–1457)

A talented theoretician of humanism and a fierce controversialist, Lorenzo Valla was born in Rome, where his father, a jurist, worked for the papacy. After teaching rhetoric in northern Italy, in 1435 he became attached to Alfonso of Aragon, king of Naples and Sicily. Finally, in 1448 he returned permanently to Rome, where he taught at the University and enjoyed the favor of Pope Nicholas V (r. 1447–55), himself a humanist. Valla's writings ranged widely, including a philological work, *On the Elegances of the Latin Language*; *The Reconstruction of Philosophy and Dialectic*, which attacked the use of Aristotle's categories and metaphysics by Scholastic theologians; and a new edition in Greek of the New Testament, based extensively upon Valla's own collation of Greek manuscripts.

Today Lorenzo Valla is best known as author of *On the Falsely Believed and Fictitious Donation of Constantine*, which appeared in 1440. The Donation, now universally agreed to be an eighth-century forgery, purported to be an account written by the Emperor Constantine (r. 306–37). It asserts that, out of gratitude for being cured of leprosy, Constantine willed temporal control over the western half of his empire to Pope Sylvester. Others before Valla had expressed doubts about the authenticity of the Donation, but his systematic attack upon it, using the tools of humanist textual criticism, was unprecedented. A highly effective polemic, Valla's tract on the Donation was by no means a disinterested work of scholarship: at precisely the time that he wrote it, his employer, Alfonso of Aragon, was waging war on Pope Eugenius IV over territories to which both laid claim. Nonetheless, Valla's tract stands as a model of the use of philology – not just as a tool for unlocking the meanings of texts, but as a powerful weapon for discrediting one's political rivals.

Questions

1   What is it about the language of the document that Valla finds objectionable?
2   How does the assessment of Constantine's character play into the argument?
3   In what ways might Valla's methods and assumptions have had wider repercussions? In other words, if textual-critical methods can determine which texts are authentic and how they should be read, what implications does that fact have for theology and for church traditions?
4   Eight years after writing this, Valla returned to favor with the papacy. But in 1520, shortly before he was excommunicated, Martin Luther read with enthusiasm an edition of Valla's tract on the Donation. What aspects of its argument and conclusions might Luther have found particularly congenial?

On the Donation of Constantine

I know that for a long time now men's ears are waiting to hear the offense with which I charge the Roman pontiffs. It is, indeed, an enormous one, due either to supine ignorance, or to gross avarice which is the slave of idols, or to pride of empire of which cruelty is ever the companion. For during some centuries now, either they have not known that the Donation of Constantine is spurious and forged, or else they themselves forged it, and their successors walking in the same way of deceit as their elders have defended as true what they knew to be false, dishonoring the majesty of the pontificate, dishonoring the memory of ancient pontiffs, dishonoring the Christian religion, confounding everything with murders, disasters and crimes. They say the city of Rome is theirs, theirs the kingdom of Sicily and of Naples,[1] the whole of Italy, the Gauls, the Spains, the Germans, the Britons, indeed the whole West; for all these are contained in the instrument of the Donation itself.[2] So all these are

---

1   Valla was in the service of the king of Sicily and of Naples when he wrote this.
2   The phrase "Italy and the western provinces," in the Donation of Constantine, meant to the writer of that document the Italian peninsula, including Lombardy, Venetia, Istria, and adjacent islands. Other countries probably did not occur to him as part of the Roman Empire. Valla, however, followed the current interpretation.

yours, supreme pontiff? And it is your purpose to recover them all? To despoil all kings and princes of the West of their cities or compel them to pay you a yearly tribute, is that your plan?

I, on the contrary, think it fairer to let the princes despoil you of all the empire you hold. For, as I shall show, that Donation whence the supreme pontiffs will have their right derived was unknown equally to Sylvester and to Constantine.

But before I come to the refutation of the instrument of the Donation, which is their one defense, not only false but even stupid, the right order demands that I go further back. And first, I shall show that Constantine and Sylvester were not such men that the former would choose to give, would have the legal right to give, or would have it in his power to give those lands to another, or that the latter would be willing to accept them or could legally have done so. In the second place, if this were not so, though it is absolutely true and obvious, [I shall show that in fact] the latter did not receive nor the former give, possession of what is said to have been granted, but that it always remained under the sway and empire of the Caesars. In the third place, [I shall show that] nothing was given to Sylvester by Constantine, but to an earlier Pope (and Constantine had received baptism even before that pontificate), and that the grants were inconsiderable, for the mere subsistence of the Pope. Fourth, that it is not true either that a copy of the Donation is found in the Decretum [of Gratian], or that it was taken from the History of Sylvester; for it is not found in it or in any history, and it is comprised of contradictions, impossibilities, stupidities, barbarisms and absurdities. Further, I shall speak of the pretended or mock donation of certain other Caesars. Then by way of redundance I shall add that even had Sylvester taken possession, nevertheless, he or some other pontiff having been dispossessed, possession could not be resumed after such a long interval under either divine or human law. Last [I shall show] that the possessions which are now held by the supreme pontiff could not, in any length of time, be validated by prescription.[...]

[*Here Valla quotes directly from the Donation:*]

"To the blessed Sylvester, his [Peter's] vicar, we by this present do give our imperial Lateran palace, then the diadem, that is, the crown of our head, and at the same time the tiara and also the shoulder-band, – that is, the strap that usually surrounds our imperial neck; and also the purple mantle and scarlet tunic, and all the imperial raiment; and the same rank as those presiding over the imperial cavalry; conferring also on him the imperial scepters, and at the same time all the standards and banners and the different imperial ornaments, and all the pomp of our imperial eminence, and the glory of our power.

"And we decree also, as to these men of different rank, the most reverend clergy who serve the holy Roman church, that they have that same eminence of distinguished power and excellence, by the glory of which it seems proper for our most illustrious Senate to be adorned; that is, that they be made patricians, consuls, – and also we have proclaimed that they be decorated with the other imperial dignities. And even as the imperial militia stands decorated, so we have decreed that the clergy of the holy Roman church be adorned. And even as the imperial power is ordered with different offices, of chamberlains, indeed, and door-keepers and all the bed-watchers, so we wish the holy Roman church also to be decorated. And, in order that the pontifical glory may shine forth most fully, we decree also that the holy clergy of this same holy Roman church may mount mounts adorned with saddle-cloths and linens, that is, of the whitest color; and even as our Senate uses shoes with felt socks, that is, they [the clergy] may be distinguished by white linen, and that the celestial [orders] may be adorned to the glory of God, just as the terrestrial are adorned."

O holy Jesus! This fellow, tumbling phrases about in his ignorant talk, – will you not answer him from a whirlwind? Will you not send the thunder? Will you not hurl avenging lightnings at such great blasphemy? Will you endure such wickedness in your household? Can you hear this, see this, let it go on so long and overlook it? But you are long-suffering and full of compassion. Yet I fear lest this your long-suffering may rather be wrath and condemnation, such as it was against those of whom you said, "So I gave them up unto their own hearts' lust: and they walked in their own counsels,"[3] and elsewhere, "Even as they did not like to retain me in their knowledge, I gave them over to a reprobate mind, to do those things which are not convenient."[4] Command me, I beseech thee, O Lord, that I may cry out against them, and perchance they may be converted.

O Roman pontiffs, the model of all crimes for other pontiffs! O wickedest of scribes and Pharisees, who sit in Moses' seat and do the deeds of Dathan and Abiram! Will the raiment, the habiliments, the pomp, the cavalry, indeed the whole manner of life of a Caesar thus befit the vicar of Christ? What fellowship has the priest with the Caesar? Did Sylvester put on this raiment; did he parade in this splendor; did he live and reign with such a throng of servants in his house? Depraved wretches! They did not know that Sylvester ought to have assumed the vestments of Aaron, who was the high priest of God, rather than those of a heathen ruler.

But this must be more strongly pressed elsewhere. For the present, however, let us talk to this sycophant about barbarisms of speech; for by the stupidity of his language his monstrous impudence is made clear, and his lie.

"We give," he says, "our imperial Lateran palace": as though it was awkward to place the gift of the palace here among the ornaments, he

3 Psalms 81:12.
4 Romans 1:28, with the person of the verb changed.

repeated it later where gifts are treated. "Then the diadem"; and as though those present would not know, he interprets, "that is, the crown." He did not, indeed, here add "of gold," but later, emphasizing the same statements, he says, "of purest gold and precious gems." The ignorant fellow did not know that a diadem was made of coarse cloth or perhaps of silk; whence that wise and oft-repeated remark of the king, who, they say, before he put upon his head the diadem given him, held it and considered it long and exclaimed, "O cloth more renowned than happy! If any one knew you through and through, with how many anxieties and dangers and miseries you are fraught, he would not care to pick you up; no, not even if you were lying on the ground!" This fellow does not imagine but that it is of gold, with a gold band and gems such as kings now usually add. But Constantine was not a king, nor would he have dared to call himself king, nor to adorn himself with royal ceremony. He was Emperor of the Romans, not king. Where there is a king, there is no republic. But in the republic there were many, even at the same time, who were "imperatores" [generals]; for Cicero frequently writes thus, "Marcus Cicero, imperator, to some other imperator, greeting": though, later on, the Roman ruler, as the highest of all, is called by way of distinctive title the Emperor.

"And at the same time the tiara and also the shoulder-band, – that is the strap that usually surrounds our imperial neck." Who ever heard "tiara" [phrygium] used in Latin? You talk like a barbarian and want it to seem to me to be a speech of Constantine's or of Lactantius'. Plautus, in the Menaechmi, applied "phrygionem" to a designer of garments; Pliny calls clothes embroidered with a needle "phrygiones" because the Phrygians invented them; but what does "phrygium" mean? You do not explain this, which is obscure; you explain what is quite clear. You say the "shoulder-band" is a "strap," and you do not perceive what the strap is, for you do not visualize a leather band, which we call a strap, encircling the Caesar's neck as an ornament. [It is of leather], hence we call harness and whips "straps": but if ever gold straps are mentioned, it can only be understood as applying to gilt harness such as is put around the neck of a horse or of some other animal. But this has escaped your notice, I think. So when you wish to put a strap around the Caesar's neck, or Sylvester's, you change a man, an Emperor, a supreme pontiff, into a horse or an ass.

"And also the purple mantle and scarlet tunic." Because Matthew says "a scarlet robe," and John "a purple robe,"[5] this fellow tries to join them together in the same passage. But if they are the same color, as the Evangelists imply, why are you not content, as they were, to name either one alone; unless, like ignorant folk today, you use "purple" for silk goods of a whitish color? The "purple" [purpura], however, is a fish in whose blood wool is

5   Matthew 27:28; John 19:2.

dyed, and so from the dye the name has been given to the cloth, whose color can be called red, though it may rather be blackish and very nearly the color of clotted blood, a sort of violet. Hence by Homer and Virgil blood is called purple, as is porphyry, the color of which is similar to amethyst; for the Greeks call purple "porphyra." You know perhaps that scarlet is used for red; but I would swear that you do not know at all why he makes it "coccineum" when we say "coccum," or what sort of a garment a "mantle" [chlamys] is.

But that he might not betray himself as a liar by continuing longer on the separate garments, he embraced them all together in a single word, saying, "all the imperial raiment." What! even that which he is accustomed to wear in war, in the chase, at banquets, in games? What could be more stupid than to say that all the raiment of the Caesar befits a pontiff!

But how gracefully he adds, "and the same rank as those presiding over the imperial cavalry." He says "seu" ["or" for "and"].[6] He wishes to distinguish between these two in turn, as if they were very like each other, and slips along from the imperial raiment to the equestrian rank, saying – I know not what! He wants to say something wonderful, but fears to be caught lying, and so with puffed cheeks and swollen throat, he gives forth sound without sense.

"Conferring also on him the imperial scepters." What a turn of speech! What splendor! What harmony! What are these imperial scepters? There is one scepter, not several; if indeed the Emperor carried a scepter at all. Will now the pontiff carry a scepter in his hand? Why not give him a sword also, and helmet and javelin?

"And at the same time all the standards and banners." What do you understand by "standards" [signa]? "Signa" are either statues (hence frequently we read "signa et tabulas" for pieces of sculpture and paintings; – for the ancients did not paint on walls, but on tablets) or military standards (hence that phrase "Standards, matched eagles"[7]). In the former sense small statues and sculptures are called "sigilla." Now then, did Constantine give Sylvester his statues or his eagles? What could be more absurd? But what "banners" [banna[8]] may signify, I do not discover. May God destroy you, most depraved of mortals who attribute barbarous language to a cultured age!

"And different imperial ornaments." When he said "banners," he thought he had been explicit long enough, and therefore he lumped the rest under a general term. And how frequently he drives home the word "imperial," as

---

6   Here, as was common in medieval Latin, "seu" is the equivalent of "et," and means "and." Valla's criticism is correct, but might go further in fixing the time of the forgery.

7   Lucan, *Pharsalia* i, 7.

8   In our best texts of the Donation this word is "banda," used in the eighth century for "colors" or "flags."

though there were certain ornaments peculiar to the Emperor over against the consul, the dictator, the Caesar!

"And all the pomp of our imperial eminence, and the glory of our power." "He discards bombast and cubit-long words,"[9] "This king of kings, Darius, the kinsman of the gods,"[10] never speaking save in the plural! What is this imperial "pomp"; that of the cucumber twisted in the grass, and growing at the belly? Do you think the Caesar celebrated a triumph whenever he left his house, as the Pope now does, preceded by white horses which servants lead saddled and adorned? To pass over other follies, nothing is emptier, more unbecoming a Roman pontiff than this. And what is this "glory"? Would a Latin have called pomp and paraphernalia "glory," as is customary in the Hebrew language? And instead of "soldiers" [milites] you say soldiery [militia[11]] which we have borrowed from the Hebrews, whose books neither Constantine nor his secretaries had ever laid eyes on!

But how great is your munificence, O Emperor, who deem it not sufficient to have adorned the pontiff, unless you adorn all the clergy also! As an "eminence of distinguished power and excellence," you say, they are "made patricians and consuls." Who has ever heard of senators or other men being made patricians? Consuls are "made," but not patricians. The senators, the conscript fathers, are from patrician (also called senatorial), equestrian, or plebeian families as the case may be. It is greater, also, to be a senator than to be a patrician; for a senator is one of the chosen counsellors of the Republic, while a patrician is merely one who derives his origin from a senatorial family. So one who is a senator, or of the conscript fathers, is not necessarily forthwith also a patrician. So my friends the Romans are now making themselves ridiculous when they call their praetor "senator," since a senate cannot consist of one man and a senator must have colleagues, and he who is now called "senator" performs the function of praetor. But, you say, the title of patrician is found in many books.[12] Yes; but in those which speak of times later than Constantine; therefore the "privilege" was executed after Constantine.

But how can the clergy become consuls?[13] The Latin clergy have denied themselves matrimony; and will they become consuls, make a levy of troops, and betake themselves to the provinces allotted them with legions and

9   Horace, *Ars Poetica* l. 97.
10   Julius Valerius, *Res Gestae Alexandri* i, 37.
11   At Rome in the eighth century, the time of the forgery, "militia" indicated a civil rank, rather than soldiers.
12   The allusion is to the title of Patrician given to Pepin and to his sons as defenders of the Roman See.
13   The office of consul as it existed in the Republic and the Empire disappeared in the time of the German invasions. The word was later applied quite differently, to a group, practically a social class, at Rome.

auxiliaries? Are servants and slaves made consuls? And are there to be not two, as was customary; but the hundreds and thousands of attendants who serve the Roman church, are they to be honored with the rank of general? And I was stupid enough to wonder at what was said about the Pope's transformation! The attendants will be generals; but the clergy soldiers. Will the clergy become soldiers or wear military insignia, unless you share the imperial insignia with all the clergy? [I may well ask,] for I do not know what you are saying. And who does not see that this fabulous tale was concocted by those who wished to have every possible license in the attire they were to wear? If there are games of any kind played among the demons which inhabit the air I should think that they would consist in copying the apparel, the pride and the luxury of the clergy, and that the demons would be delighted most by this kind of masquerading.

Which shall I censure the more, the stupidity of the ideas, or of the words? You have heard about the ideas; here are illustrations of his words. He says, "It seems proper for our Senate to be adorned" (as though it were not assuredly adorned), and to be adorned forsooth with "glory." And what is being done he wishes understood as already done; as, "we have proclaimed" for "we proclaim": for the speech sounds better that way. And he puts the same act in the present and in the past tense; as, "we decree," and "we have decreed." And everything is stuffed with these words, "we decree," "we decorate," "imperial," "imperial rank," "power," "glory." He uses "extat" for "est," though "extare" means to stand out or to be above; and "nempe" for "scilicet" [that is, "indeed" for "to wit"]; and "concubitores" [translated above, bed-watchers] for "contubernales" [companions or attendants]. "Concubitores" are literally those who sleep together and have intercourse; they must certainly be understood to be harlots. He adds those with whom he may sleep, I suppose, that he may not fear nocturnal phantoms.[14] He adds "chamberlains"; he adds "door-keepers."

It is not an idle question to ask why he mentions these details. He is setting up, not an old man, but a ward or a young son, and like a doting father, himself arranges for him everything of which his tender age has need, as David did for Solomon! And that the story may be filled in in every respect, horses are given the clergy, – lest they sit on asses' colts in that asinine way of Christ's! And they are given horses, not covered nor saddled with coverings of white, but decorated with white color. And what coverings! Not horse-cloths, either Babylonian or any other kind, but "mappulae" [translated above, saddle-cloths] and "linteamina" [linen cloths or sheets, translated above, linen]. "Mappae" [serviettes] go with the table, "linteamina" with the couch. And as though there were doubt as to their color, he

14 Where Valla's text of the Donation reads "concubitorum," another reads "excubiorum" [guards].

explains, "that is to say, of the whitest color." Talk worthy of Constantine; fluency worthy of Lactantius; not only in the other phrases, but also in that one, "may mount mounts"!

And when he had said nothing about the garb of senators, the broad stripe, the purple, and the rest, he thought he had to talk about their shoes; nor does he specify the crescents [which were on their shoes], but "socks," or rather he says "with felt socks," and then as usual he explains, "that is, with white linen," as though socks were of linen! I cannot at the moment think where I have found the word "udones" [socks], except in Valerius Martial, whose distich inscribed "Cilician Socks" runs:

> "Wool did not produce these, but the beard of an ill-smelling goat.
> Would that the sole in the gulf of the Cinyps might lie."[15]

So the "socks" are not linen, nor white, with which this two-legged ass says, not that the feet of senators are clad, but that senators are distinguished.

And in the phrase "that the terrestrial orders may be adorned to the glory of God, just as the celestial," what do you call celestial, what terrestrial? How are the celestial orders adorned?[16] You may have seen what glory to God this is. But I, if I believe anything, deem nothing more hateful to God and to the rest of humanity than such presumption of clergy in the secular sphere. But why do I attack individual items? Time would fail me if I should try, I do not say to dwell upon, but to touch upon them all. [...] But why need I say more in this case, absolutely self-evident as it is? I contend that not only did Constantine not grant such great possessions, not only could the Roman pontiff not hold them by prescription, but that even if either were a fact, nevertheless either right would have been extinguished by the crimes of the possessors, for we know that the slaughter and devastation of all Italy and of many of the provinces has flowed from this single source. If the source is bitter, so is the stream; if the root is unclean, so are the branches; if the first fruit is unholy, so is the lump.[17] And *vice versa*, if the stream is bitter, the source must be stopped up; if the branches are unclean, the fault comes from the root; if the lump is unholy, the first fruit must also be accursed. Can we justify the principle of papal power when we perceive it to be the cause of such great crimes and of such great and varied evils?

Wherefore I declare, and cry aloud, nor, trusting God, will I fear men, that in my time no one in the supreme pontificate has been either a faithful or a prudent steward, but they have gone so far from giving food to the household

15   Martial, XIV, 141 (140).
16   Valla for this part of his criticism uses the rather unintelligible order of words found in most texts of the Donation, instead of the more intelligible order which he used in his earlier quotations.
17   A reminiscence of Romans 11:16.

of God that they have devoured it as food and a mere morsel of bread! And the Pope himself makes war on peaceable people, and sows discord among states and princes. The Pope both thirsts for the goods of others and drinks up his own: he is what Achilles calls Agamemnon, Δημοβόρος βασιλεύς, "a people-devouring king." The Pope not only enriches himself at the expense of the republic, as neither Verres nor Catiline nor any other embezzler dared to do, but he enriches himself at the expense of even the church and the Holy Spirit as old Simon Magus himself would abhor doing. And when he is reminded of this and is reproved by good people occasionally, he does not deny it, but openly admits it, and boasts that he is free to wrest from its occupants by any means whatever the patrimony given the church by Constantine; as though when it was recovered Christianity would be in an ideal state, – and not rather the more oppressed by all kinds of crimes, extravagances and lusts; if indeed it can be oppressed more, and if there is any crime yet uncommitted!

And so, that he may recover the other parts of the Donation, money wickedly stolen from good people he spends more wickedly, and he supports armed forces, mounted and foot, with which all places are plagued, while Christ is dying of hunger and nakedness in so many thousands of paupers. Nor does he know, the unworthy reprobate, that while he works to deprive secular powers of what belongs to them, they in turn are either led by his bad example, or driven by necessity (granting that it may not be a real necessity) to make off with what belongs to the officers of the church. And so there is no religion anywhere, no sanctity, no fear of God; and, what I shudder to mention, impious men pretend to find in the Pope an excuse for all their crimes. For he and his followers furnish an example of every kind of crime, and with Isaiah and Paul, we can say against the Pope and those about him: "The name of God is blasphemed among the Gentiles through you, you who teach others, but do not teach yourselves; who preach against stealing and yourselves are robbers; who abhor idols, and commit sacrilege; who make your boast of the law and the pontificate, and through breaking the law dishonor God, the true pontiff."[18]

But if the Roman people through excess of wealth lost the well-known quality of true Romans; if Solomon likewise fell into idolatry through the love of women; should we not recognize that the same thing happens in the case of a supreme pontiff and the other clergy? And should we then think that God would have permitted Sylvester to accept an occasion of sin? I will not suffer this injustice to be done that most holy man, I will not allow this affront to be offered that most excellent pontiff, that he should be said to have accepted empires, kingdoms, provinces, things which those who wish to enter the clergy are wont, indeed, to renounce. Little did Sylvester possess, little also

18   Free quotations from Romans 2:21–4.

the other holy pontiffs, those men whose presence was inviolable even among enemies, as Leo's presence overawed and broke down the wild soul of the barbarian king, which the strength of Rome had not availed to break down nor overawe.[19] But recent supreme pontiffs, that is, those having riches and pleasures in abundance, seem to work hard to make themselves just as impious and foolish as those early pontiffs were wise and holy, and to extinguish the lofty praises of those men by every possible infamy. Who that calls himself a Christian can calmly bear this?

However, in this my first discourse I do not wish to urge princes and peoples to restrain the Pope in his unbridled course as he roams about, and compel him to stay within bounds, but only to warn him, and perhaps he has already learned the truth, to betake himself from others' houses to his own, and to put to port before the raging billows and savage tempests. But if he refuses, then I will have recourse to another discourse far bolder than this.[20] If only I may sometime see, and indeed I can scarcely wait to see it, especially if it is brought about by my counsel, if only I may see the time when the Pope is the vicar of Christ alone and not of Caesar also! If only there would no longer be heard the fearful cry, "Partisans for the Church," "Partisans against the Church," "The Church against the Perugians," "against the Bolognese"! It is not the church, but the Pope, that fights against Christians; the church fights against "spiritual wickedness in high places."[21] Then the Pope will be the Holy Father in fact as well as in name, Father of all, Father of the church; nor will he stir up wars among Christians, but those stirred up by others he, through his apostolic judgment and papal prerogative, will stop.[22]

19 A reference to the well-known interview in which Leo I persuaded Attila to desist from his invasion of Italy.
20 This other discourse did not appear.
21 Ephesians 6:12.
22 The manuscript on which this translation is based was finished December 7, 1451.

12

Marsilio Ficino (1433–1499)

Marsilio Ficino, whose father was Cosimo de' Medici's doctor, went on to become a critically important advocate of Platonic philosophy, which he initially encountered in Latin writings from ancient Rome and the Middle Ages. By the 1460s, following intensive study of Greek, he began translating Platonic writings into Latin, which made them accessible to the learned throughout Europe. In addition, he gained the patronage of Cosimo "The Elder" de' Medici (d. 1464), who asked him to translate Plato's works from a newly discovered manuscript, and in part to make the task easier, Cosimo provided him with a house in Florence, a villa in nearby Careggi, and a steady income.

Beyond his translations of Plato and his study of Neoplatonic writers (notably the third-century AD philosopher Plotinus), Ficino also gave public lectures and, in his own compositions, sought to integrate Platonic philosophy with Christian theology. A devout believer, he rendered pagan wisdom "safe" for fifteenth-century Europeans by treating Plato as a divinely inspired poet-theologian. Where Plato's words seemed to contradict Christian thought, Ficino read allegorically and found deeper meanings beneath the surface of the text. Making frequent use of medical metaphors, he presented Plato as a curer of souls.

The selection below is drawn from Ficino's *Three Books on Life* (1489). A bestseller that appeared in close to 30 editions over the following century and a half, this treatise deals specifically with how an intellectual can cultivate good health. Having himself suffered from what in our own time might be diagnosed as severe depression, Ficino had a personal stake in the efficacy of the cures he recommends. Although much of what he counsels may at first seem bizarre, it has its own internal logic in the context of medical astrology, a respected field of inquiry in the Renaissance. Through these remedies, Ficino seeks to restore balance and harmony within the human body, as well as between the individual human being and the order of the universe.

Questions

1 What do the five "special enemies of scholars" have in common? Why does each pose a threat?
2 Why is it that gold should be thought to revitalize old men? What do you make of the recommendation to consume gold along with golden wine and a fresh egg yolk?
3 Ficino writes of the need to preserve the "tree of the body" by keeping its roots moist. What is the point of the metaphor, and what ramifications might it have for his approach to medicine?
4 Consider Ficino's advice that the elderly consume human milk and blood. What assumptions underlie this advice? How might it make sense for a devoutly Christian Renaissance thinker to make such recommendations?
5 The elderly are enjoined to get some sun in the winter, and in the summer to spend time around bees. Why? Also, consider the foods that he recommends. What do they have in common, and why might these foods in particular help rejuvenate old people? What, more generally, is the place of harmony in Ficino's recommendations?
6 Like Valla, Ficino also sees knowledge as a source of power, but the two diverge both in the kind of power they seek and in the means they propose for obtaining it. Of what significance are the differences?

Three Books on Life

Book I

7

The Special Enemies of Scholars are Five: Phlegm, Black Bile, Sexual Intercourse, Gluttony, and Sleeping in the Morning

But to return from where we have been digressing now for quite a while, the road is very long which leads to truth and wisdom, full of heavy labors on land and sea. Hence people who undertake this journey are often at danger, as some poet might say, on land and sea. For if they sail on the sea, they are constantly tossed among the waves, that is, the two humors, namely phlegm and that noxious form of melancholy, as if between Scylla and Charybdis. Or if they journey on land, so to speak, three monsters immediately oppose them. The first monster is nourished by the earthly Venus and Priapus; the second, by Bacchus and Ceres; and the third, nocturnal Hecate often positions against us. Therefore Apollo must often be summoned from the heavens, Neptune from the sea, and Hercules from the land in order that Apollo may pierce such monsters, enemies of Pallas, with his shafts, Neptune may subdue them with his trident, and Hercules may crush and mangle them with his club.

The first monster is sexual intercourse, especially if it proceeds even a little beyond one's strength; for indeed it suddenly drains the spirits, especially the more subtle ones, it weakens the brain, and it ruins the stomach and the heart – no evil can be worse for one's intelligence. For why did Hippocrates judge sexual intercourse to be like epilepsy, if not because it strikes the mind, which is sacred;[1] and it is so harmful that Avicenna has said in his book *De animalibus*: "If any sperm should flow away through intercourse beyond that which nature tolerates, it is more harmful than if forty times as much blood should pour forth."[2] So it was with good reason that the ancients held the Muses and Minerva to be virgins. That Platonic saying has relevance here: When Venus threatened the Muses that, unless they celebrated the rites of love, she would send her son armed against them, "the Muses answered, 'O Venus, threaten Mars with such things, your Cupid does not fly among us.' "[3] Finally, nature has placed no sense farther from intelligence than touch.

The second monster is satiety in wine and food. For if wine is excessive or too hot and strong, it will fill the head with humors and very bad fumes. I pass over the fact that drunkenness makes men insane. And excessive food recalls all the power of nature first of all to the stomach to digest it. This renders nature unable to exert itself at the same time in the head and for reflection. In the next place, food badly digested dulls the sharpness of the mind with many dense vapors and with humors. But even if the food is sufficiently digested, nevertheless, as Galen says, "the mind that is choked up with fat and blood cannot perceive anything heavenly."[4]

---

1   Ficino errs in ascribing this judgment to Hippocrates. According to Galen, *Commentary* 1.4, it was Democritus who judged sexual intercourse to be like epilepsy. Concerning Ficino's remarks in the above passage, modern scholars have written: "It is remarkable that with regard to 'Venerei coitus' the Platonist Ficino departs from the views of the clinicians – to which, in this respect, even Hildegard of Bingen subscribed – and associates himself with the ascetic advice given by authors of a monastic and theological tendency" (R. Klibansky, E. Panofsky, and F. Saxl, *Saturn and Melancholy* [London, 1964], p. 267, n. 81).

2   Avicenna, *De animalibus* 3.3.

3   Diogenes Laertius, 3.33.

4   Ficino probably draws this quotation from Galen from its appearance in St. Jerome, *Contra Jovinianum* 2.11.

Finally, the third monster is to stay awake too often for much of the night, especially after dinner, with the result that you are forced to sleep even after sunrise. Since many scholars err in this and are deceived, therefore I will explain further how much it hurts the intelligence and I will give seven main reasons. The first reason is drawn from the heavens themselves, the second from the elements, the third from the humors, the fourth from the order of things, the fifth from the nature of the stomach, the sixth from the spirits, and the seventh from the phantasy.

First of all, three planets, as we said above, especially favor reflection and eloquence: the Sun, Venus, and Mercury. Since they run almost in step together, at the approach of night these planets flee from us, but with day approaching or now rising they arise again and revisit us. But after sunrise, they are immediately thrust into the twelfth house of heaven, which is assigned by astronomers to prison and darkness. Therefore it is not people who rise either at night, when they flee from us, or during the day after sunrise, when they enter the house of prison and darkness, who explore things most acutely and write and compose their findings most eloquently, but those people alone who, when they are either about to rise or now rising, themselves rise up with them to reflect and write.

The second reason, which is from the elements, is this: at sunrise the air is stirred, rarefied, and clear; but just the opposite happens at sunset. The blood and the spirits are compelled by necessity to imitate the motion and quality of the air because it surrounds them and is similar in nature.

The third reason, which is drawn from the humors, is this: at dawn the blood moves and rules; it is rarefied by motion and grows warm and clear; and the spirits characteristically imitate and follow the blood. But at the approach of night, that more dense and cold type of melancholy dominates, and phlegm, both of which without doubt render the spirits totally unfit for reflection.

The fourth reason, which is drawn from the order of things, will be this: day is assigned to wakefulness, night to sleep, since, when the sun either approaches our hemisphere or advances over it, it opens with its rays the passages of the body and spreads the humors and spirits from the center to the circumference, a thing which excites and leads to wakefulness and actions. But on the contrary, when the sun sets, all things are contracted, which by a certain natural order of things induces sleep, especially after the third or fourth part of the night. Therefore he who sleeps in the morning, when the sun and the world get up, and who is awake much of the night, when nature now commands us to sleep and to rest from labors – this man without doubt fights both with the order of the universe and especially with himself, while he is disturbed and distracted by contrary motions at the same time. Indeed, while there is movement on the part of the universe to the outer limits, he moves himself to the innermost. And, on the contrary, while there is attraction on the part of the universe to the most inward parts, he, meanwhile, draws himself back to externals. Such perverse order and contrary motions make both the entire body and the spirits and intelligence very unsteady.

In the fifth place, we argue from the nature of the stomach in this way: the stomach by the long action of daily air is quite dilated through open pores; when the spirits fly forth, it becomes at last exceedingly weak. Therefore, at the approach of night, it demands a new supply of spirits to sustain itself. This is why a person who begins long and difficult reflections at this time, has to strain to draw those spirits back to the head. When so divided, however, these spirits are not sufficient for either the stomach or the head. Indeed it is especially harmful, if, working at night after dinner, we concentrate too attentively for a long time on studies of this sort. For then the stomach needs many spirits for digesting food, as well as much heat. But these two by such work and study are diverted to the head; it happens as a result that they are sufficient for neither the brain nor the stomach. Add the fact that because of motion of this sort the head is filled with too-dense vapors coming from food; and food in the stomach without heat and spirit accumulates undigested and grows rotten, which again blocks up and injures the head. Finally, in the morning hours you must rise in order that each of your bodily parts may be purged of all the excrement retained during sleep. Then, worst of all, the person who had utterly interrupted his digestion by studying at night and likewise by sleeping in the morning is compelled to hinder the expulsion of excrement for a longer time – which, indeed, all physicians think is most harmful for the intelligence as well as the body. Rightly, therefore, those who against nature use night as day and, conversely again, day as night, like owls – these people also unwillingly imitate owls in this: that, just as the eyes of the owls grow weak under the light of the sun, so too the mental sharpness of these people grows weak beneath the splendor of truth.

In the sixth place, the same thing is proved from the spirits as follows: the spirits, especially all the most subtle ones, are eventually dispersed by daily fatigue. At night, therefore, few spirits are left, and they are dense and most unsuitable for literary studies, so that the intelligence, relying on these crippled wings, can fly only as do bats and owls. But, on the contrary, in the morning after sleep, with the spirits refreshed and with the bodily parts thus strengthened, so that they need the least help from the spirits, many subtle spirits are present; they serve the brain, and they are able to comply with it, since they are very little occupied with fostering and ruling the bodily parts.

Finally, the seventh reason is drawn from the nature of the phantasy as follows: Phantasy or imagination or apprehension ("cogitatio") or whatever other name it seems it ought to be called, is distracted and upset by many long and contrary imaginations, cogitations, and cares while it is awake. This distraction and confusion are too contrary to someone pursuing contemplation and requiring a completely tranquil and serene mind. Only during the quiet of night is that agitation finally calmed and put to rest. Therefore, at the approach of night we study with the mind always disturbed, but when night withdraws for the most part we give ourselves to study with a tranquil mind. A person who tries to judge truth with the mind too upset, is just like those people who suffer from dizziness and think everything is turning, as Plato said, when they themselves are turning.[5] This is why Aristotle in his *Economics* sensibly commands us to rise before dawn and asserts that it is most useful both for the health of the body and for the study of philosophy.[6] But this precept must be taken in such a way that we carefully avoid early morning indigestion by taking a quick and moderate dinner. Finally, that holy prophet David, the trumpet of the almighty God, never says that he rises to sing to his God with lyre and psalms in the evening, but always in the morning and at dawn.[7] Indeed we certainly ought to arise at that hour with our mind, and soon after also with our body, provided it can conveniently be done.

Book II

10
On Gold, Foods Made of Gold, and the Revitalization of Old Men

All writers place gold before everything else, as the most suitably mixed of all things and the most safe from decay – consecrated to the Sun because of its splendor and to Jupiter because of its temperedness; it can therefore marvelously temper the natural heat with moisture, save the humors from corruption, and bring a Solar and a Jovial power to the spirits and the bodily parts.[8] But nevertheless, they want to make the very hard substance of gold more fine and most quick to penetrate. For they know that cordials then especially refresh the hidden power of the heart, when nature incurs least work in attracting them. But in order that nature be fatigued as little as possible, they want the gold to be already in the finest form or to be used with the finest things. They think it would be best if the gold be made potable without mixing it with anything foreign; but if this cannot be done, they want it taken ground and reduced to leaves.

Here is how you will have the gold almost potable, I would say. Gather the flowers of borage, bugloss, and the melissa which we call "citraria," and

---

5 Plato, *Cratylus* 411b.
6 Aristotle, *Oeconomica* 1.6.5.
7 See Psalms 30:5 and 57:8.
8 In the Middle Ages, gold was seen to have an important role in the prolonging of life.

when the Moon enters Leo, Aries or Sagittarius and aspects the Sun or Jupiter, cook it with the whitest sugar dissolved in rose-water and carefully add three gold leaves per ounce. Take it on an empty stomach with a golden wine. Likewise take the moisture dripping from a capon which you have set over a fire or from which you have extracted it in some other way, together with a rose julep into which you have previously beaten some gold leaves. In addition, extinguish red-hot gold in very clear spring-water and beat some gold leaves into this water. Temper golden wine with it, and with a drink of this sort eat a fresh egg yolk.

You will easily maintain the moisture in the entire tree of the body if you preserve it in the roots. Therefore take the heart, the liver, the stomach, the testicles, and the brain of hens, chickens, and capons; cook them with a little water and a pinch of salt. When cooked, grind them out of all their flesh, and with all the broth, and sugar, add a fresh egg yolk; make a cake seasoned with a little cinnamon and saffron, and coated with gold. Eat this, when hungry, at least once every four days and by itself. though with a clear wine added for a drink.

11
On the Use of Human Milk and Blood for the Life of Old People

Immediately after the age of seventy and sometimes after sixty-three, since the moisture has gradually dried up, the tree of the human body often decays. Then for the first time this human tree must be moistened by a human, youthful liquid in order that it may revive. Therefore choose a young girl who is healthy, beautiful, cheerful, and temperate, and when you are hungry and the Moon is waxing, suck her milk; immediately eat a little powder of sweet fennel properly mixed with sugar. The sugar will prevent the milk from curdling and putrefying in the stomach; and the fennel, since it is fine and a friend of the milk, will spread the milk to the bodily parts.

Careful physicians strive to cure those whom a long bout of hectic fever has consumed, with the liquid of human blood which has distilled at the fire in the practice of sublimation. What then prevents us from sometimes also refreshing by this drink those who have already been in a way consumed by old age? There is a common and ancient opinion that certain prophetic old women who are popularly called "screech-owls" suck the blood of infants as a means, insofar as they can, of growing young again.[9] Why shouldn't our old people, namely those who have no [other] recourse, likewise suck the blood of a youth? – a youth, I say, who is willing, healthy, happy, and temperate, whose blood is of the best but perhaps too abundant. They will

9   See Ovid, *Fasti* 6:131–43.

suck, therefore, like leeches, an ounce or two from a scarcely-opened vein of the left arm; they will immediately take an equal amount of sugar and wine; they will do this when hungry and thirsty and when the Moon is waxing. If they have difficulty digesting raw blood, let it first be cooked together with sugar; or let it be mixed with sugar and moderately distilled over hot water and then drunk. At that time, the blood of a pig is also an effective aid in warming the stomach. A sponge soaked with hot wine should absorb this blood flowing from the pig's vein and, while hot, should immediately be applied to the stomach.

   Galen and Serapion say the bite of a mad dog is cured by drinking dog's blood, but it did not please them to assign a reason.[10] I, therefore, after investigating this for two days, am finally of the opinion that the poisonous saliva of a mad dog, pressed into the bite on a person's foot, climbs little by little through the veins to the heart like poison unless something draws it away in the meantime. If, therefore, that person has drunk the blood of another dog in the meantime, that undigested blood swims for many hours in the stomach, which finally drives it out through the bowels as something foreign. Meanwhile, that dog's blood diverts to the stomach the saliva which is taking hold of the upper bodily parts before it reaches the heart; for there is a power in canine blood to attract canine saliva and in saliva, in turn, to follow blood of a similar nature. Therefore the poison, put aside from the heart and absorbed by the blood swimming in the bowels, is drawn out together with the blood through the lower bodily parts and thus leaves the person safe. Why have I gone into all this? First of all, in order that I might reveal, within the material I have to discuss, the underlying cause for such an obscure fact; second, to point out that it is possible and indeed beneficial to drink blood, and that there is a power in human blood both to attract and, in turn, to follow human blood; and to reassure you that the blood of a youth drunk by an old person can be drawn to the veins and the bodily parts and can do a lot of good there.

12
The Diet, Dwelling, and Customs of Old People

If the patients are decrepit, they should remember that a weak nature ought not to be wearied with the weight of nourishment and distracted by too great diversity of foods; for by this bad habit even youth quickly turns into old age. Let them therefore split up their meals; let them refresh nature by food not so much abundant as frequent – provided, however, they afford an interval

10   This citation is not from Galen but from Dioscorides, *Liber virtutum simplicium medicinarum*, chap. 595. The Serapion is Serapion the Younger, an Arab physician of the twelfth century.

between for digestion; for often, even after the stomach itself has digested, unless the liver too has almost digested, it distracts and wearies nature to consume the nourishment; and when Old Age has been visited too often by occasion of this fatigue, he flies up prematurely. In winter, let old people like sheep seek places exposed to the sun; in summer, let them like birds revisit the pleasant places and rivers. Let them dwell continually among green and sweet-smelling plants; for these living and breathing things conspire [pun] to augment the human spirit. Let them habitually withdraw to places frequented by bees; in winter let them taste honey; for honey is a food especially friendly to old people, except when we are afraid of kindling choler. Also friendly are the following: the freshest cheese, dates, figs, raisins, capers, sweet pomegranates, jujubes, hyssop, scabious, betony; more friendly are pistachio-nuts. But best of all, as we have said, are pine nuts, from which they will get the most good if before they eat them they keep them twelve hours in tepid water, for this way they will not harm the stomach, and if besides, while they use them, they will also dwell among the pine-groves, olive-groves, and vines, or at least inhale the vapor of the pines and the smell. Likewise let gum and the gum-drops of the pine, with oil or wine, often besmear their bodies; for it is probable that trees endowed by nature with long life, especially if they stay green even in winter, will help you live long by their shade, their vapor, their fruit when new, their wood, and any timely use. Of long-lived animals, we have spoken above. But now it will perhaps lead you to the same end if you dwell chiefly with people who are healthy, whose nature is similar to yours when you are healthy, and who are your friends; and perhaps it is preferable if they are a little younger. But as to whether and how the frequent companionship of youths avails for a while to hold back old age, consult the chaste Socrates.[11]

13
What Means of Fomenting All the Parts of the Body the Elderly May Receive from the Planets

But rather [than Socrates], you old people who care about these things, consult Apollo, who judged Socrates to be the wisest of the Greeks.[12] Consult Jupiter besides, and Venus. Phoebus himself, the discoverer of the art of medicine, will give you the nutmeg for a fomentation to your stomach; Jupiter with Apollo, the mastic and the mint; and Venus, coral. Again, for

11 Socrates lived to an advanced age and maintained close friendships with youths such as Alcibiades. Ficino saw such friendships as models for his own friendship with Giovanni Cavalcanti. He says they kept Socrates young. He prefixes the epithet "chaste" as assurance to the reader that they remained, as it were, "Platonic."
12 Plato, *Apology* 21a.

fomenting your head, Phoebus will give you peony, frankincense, marjoram, and, in cooperation with Saturn, myrrh; Jupiter will give spikenard and mace; then Venus, sweet fennel and myrtle. For fomenting the heart, you receive from Phoebus citraria, saffron, aloe-wood, frankincense, amber, musk, doronicum, a little clove, citron-peel, and cinnamon. From Jupiter, the lily, bugloss, basil, mint, and roots of ben, both white and red. From Venus alone you receive myrtle, sandal, and the rose; and from Venus along with Saturn, coriander. Grind these up carefully. What pertains to the stomach, prepare it with oil of quince in the form of a wax-salve. But what pertains to the head, moisten it with oil of spikenard and besmear the back of the neck, the temples, and the forehead. Then what pertains to the heart, sprinkle it with golden wine and rose-water and apply it externally to the region of the heart. But we have somehow forgotten the liver, the prime necessity for the creation of the blood. To it, Phoebus will always administer agrimony and balm [opobalsamum]; Jupiter, pistachio-nuts and raisins; Venus, hepatica, endive, slag, and chicory. Finally, for fomenting the spleen, Saturn, your own planet, along with Jupiter, gives capers, scolopendrium, and tamarisk. Just so, Jupiter along with Venus cures the urinary bladder by pine, licorice, starch, cucumber seeds, mallows, wild mallows, manna, and cassia.

But you old people, do not flee so far from Saturn, though he is to be feared by the multitude. For to the same degree that he is foreign to young people, so he will be right at home with you. Therefore, that he too may enliven all your body as much as possible and make it strong, receive sometimes from him while he is reigning, and likewise from Phoebus at the same time, mummy[13] and the flesh of a roast goose. Soften these things with a little of the goose-fat, pound them carefully, cook them with honey of both chebule and Indic myrobalan; season them with amber, musk, and saffron. But above all, trust that these things are going to help you, believing that faith is the life of medicines that conduce to life. Hope thou in this, and that God is going to favor you when you supplicate him, and that the things created by him, especially the celestial things, have without a doubt a marvelous power to lengthen or preserve life.

13   Not comprised of mummified corpses, but of the pitchy substance by which mummies were preserved.

13

Laura Cereta (1469–1499)

The daughter of a lawyer and magistrate in Brescia in northern Italy, Laura Cereta received a humanist education both at home and at a nearby convent. Married at age 15 to a Venetian merchant, she was widowed only a year and a half later, and thereafter she devoted her life to learning. A formidable scholar, Cereta cultivated literary friendships both with men and with women. She appears to have taken part in informal gatherings of scholars in Brescia and elsewhere, but as a woman she could not pursue the kind of public career that lay open to male humanists such as Bruni or Valla. When she died at age 30, she left behind a volume including over 80 Latin letters, which would not be published until 1640.

The two letters below, written in the literary tradition that Petrarch had established, provide an opportunity for airing her concerns about how learned women are ill-treated both by men and by some women. While she has made up the names of the addressees – "Bibolo" suggests a man who drinks too much, and "Vernacula" a woman who knows only Italian – whether they are entirely fictional or based upon specific people remains an open question. These letters are impressive, polished compositions that demonstrate a mastery both of humanist Latin style and of the appropriation of historical examples to make points of contemporary relevance.

Questions

1 What is the tone of the first letter? Of what does Cereta accuse her male critic? How does her attitude toward him change toward the end of the letter?

2   In the letter to Bibolo Semproni, Cereta supports her argument with
    numerous examples. From what time periods and cultures does she
    draw them? (One of her immediate sources is Boccaccio's *Concerning
    Famous Women* [1361], which used many of the same examples, but
    with less of a polemical edge.) As she describes them, how do the
    deeds of great women compare with those of famous men?

3   How does the second letter, to Lucilia Vernacula, compare in tone to
    the first? What are her criticisms of other women? What do you
    imagine Cereta and Alessandra Strozzi might have thought of each
    other? How do they differ in the way they present themselves in
    writing, and why?

4   A leading expert has characterized Cereta as a "Renaissance feminist."
    Based upon your reading of these letters, to what extent do you view
    that characterization as accurate?

Two "familiar" letters

To Bibolo Semproni[1]

Your complaints are hurting my ears, for you say publicly and quite openly
that you are not only surprised but pained that I am said to show this
extraordinary intellect of the sort one would have thought nature would
give to the most learned of men – as if you had reached the conclusion, on
the facts of the case, that a similar girl had seldom been seen among the
peoples of the world. You are wrong on both counts, Semproni, and now that
you've abandoned the truth, you are going to spread information abroad that
is clearly false.

I think you should be deeply pained – no, you should actually be blushing
– you who are no longer now a man full of animus but instead a stone
animated by the scorn you have for the studies that make us wise, while you
grow weak with the sickness of debilitating leisure. And thus in your case, it is
not nature that goes astray but the mind, for which the path from the
appearance of virtue to villainy is a fairly easy one. In this manner, you

---

1   Cereta's correspondent might be either a real acquaintance whom she is addressing with a
comical nickname – Bibolo might be translated "tippler" – or a fictional creation and vehicle for
her polemic.

appear to be flattering a susceptible young girl because of the glory that has accrued to her – my – name. But the snare of flattery is seductive, for you who have always set traps for the sex that has been revered all throughout history have been ensnared yourself. And duped by your own madness, you are trying, by running back and forth, to trample me underfoot and smash me to the ground with your fists. Sly mockery is concealed here, and it is typical of the lowborn, plebeian mind to think that one can blind Medusa with a few drops of olive oil.[2] You would have done better to have crept up on a mole than a wolf, since the former, being shrouded in darkness, would see nothing clearly, while the latter's eyes radiate light in the dark.

In case you don't know, the philosopher sees with her mind; she furnishes paths with a window of reason through which she can ascend to a state of awareness. For Providence, the knower of the future, conquers marauding evil, trampling it with feet that have eyes. I would remain silent, believe me, if you, with your long-standing hostile and envious attitude towards me, had learned to attack me alone; after all, a ray of Phoebus' can't be shamed by being surrounded by mud. But I am angry and my disgust overflows. Why should the condition of our sex be shamed by your little attacks? Because of this, a mind thirsting for revenge is set afire; because of this, a sleeping pen is wakened for insomniac writing. Because of this, red-hot anger lays bare a heart and mind long muzzled by silence.

My cause itself is worthy: I am impelled to show what great glory that noble lineage which I carry in my own breast has won for virtue and literature – a lineage that knowledge, the bearer of honors, has exalted in every age.[3] For the possession of this lineage is legitimate and sure, and it has come all the way down to me from the perpetual continuance of a more enduring race.[4]

We have read that the breast of Ethiopian Sabba, imbued with divinity, solved the prophetic riddles of the Egyptian king Solomon.[5] The first writers believed that Amalthea, a woman erudite in the knowledge of the future,

2 See Boccaccio, *Concerning Famous Women* (hereafter *CFW*), chap. 20; Boccaccio's version of the Perseus–Medusa myth involves the hero's seduction of Queen Medusa, Boccaccio downplays as a mere fiction of the poets the queen's famous ability to turn men into stone.

3 *Generositas* (noble lineage, lineage, birth, nobility of stock) is the key image in Cereta's letter; the term suggests the notion of a noble race of learned women from which she, Laura, is descended. Note the prominence of the image of the female breast in Cereta; here her lineage itself is safeguarded "nostro pectore."

4 Here Cereta expresses the notion of women as a collectivity, as a race, breed, or generation "more enduring" than that of males. Note also her use of terms common in property and inheritance law: *legitima, hereditatis, possessio*, here applied to the intellectual and cultural legacy of generations of learned women.

5 See Boccaccio, *CFW*, chap. 41, on Saba, Sabba, or Nicaula, queen of Ethiopia; in Boccaccio, however, it is Queen Saba who comes to Solomon to consult his wisdom and not the other way around. In *CFW* Saba has a royal lineage and great wealth but she is not a seer.

sang responses near the banks that surround the Avernus, not far from Baiae. She, who as a Sybil was worthy of the gods of this lineage, sold books full of oracles to Priscus Tarquinius.[6] Thus the Babylonian prophetess Eriphila, looking into the future with her divine mind far removed, described the fall and the ashes of Troy, the fortunes of the Roman empire, and the mysteries of Christ, who would later be born.[7] Nicostrata, too, the mother of Evander and very learned in prophecy as well as literature, attained such genius that she was the first to show the alphabet to the first Latins in sixteen figures.[8] The enduring fame of Inachan Isis will flourish, for she alone of the Argive goddesses revealed to the Egyptians her own alphabet for reading.[9] But Zenobia, an Egyptian woman of noble erudition, became so learned not only in Egyptian but also in Latin and Greek literature that she wrote the histories of barbarian and foreign peoples.[10]

Shall we attribute illiteracy to Theban Manto, the prophesying daughter of Tiresias, and to Pyromantia, too, who was full of those Chaldaean arts when she spoke with the shades of the dead and foretold events in the future through the movements of flames, the flight of birds, and livers and entrails of animals?[11] Where did all the great wisdom of Tritonian Pallas come from, which enabled her to educate so many Athenians in the arts, if it was not that she succeeded in unraveling the mysteries of the scriptures of Apollo, the physician, to the delight of everyone?[12] Those little Greek women Phyliasia and Lasthenia were wonderful sources of light in the world of letters and they filled me with new life because they ridiculed the students of Plato, who frequently tied themselves in knots over the snare-filled sophistries of their arguments.[13]

Lesbian Sappho serenaded the stony heart of her lover with tearful poems, sounds I might have thought came from Orpheus' lyre or the plectrum of

6   See Boccaccio, CFW, chap. 24, on the Sibyl Amalthea, who lived at Cumae near Naples and the Avernus. According to legend, the Sibyl sold King Tarquinius of Rome three books of prophecies, having originally offered him six others which he refused.

7   See Boccaccio, CFW, chap. 19, on Eriphila or Herophile, the Sibyl. Cereta is faithful to Boccaccio.

8   See Boccaccio, CFW, chap. 25: Cereta's description agrees with Boccaccio's: Nicostrata's literary training and her intellectual acumen is connected in Boccaccio to her prophesying ability.

9   See Boccaccio, CFW, chap. 8, on Isis. Cereta's story of Isis's gift of "her own alphabet" (sua elementa) to the Egyptians agrees with Boccaccio.

10   See Boccaccio, CFW, chap. 98, on Zenobia. Boccaccio says Zenobia was believed to have written summaries of certain ancient histories, Cereta carries Boccaccio a step further by asserting that Zenobia was so erudite that she herself wrote histories.

11   See Boccaccio, CFW, chap. 28, on Manto. Cereta's remarks on the seer come straight out of CFW.

12   See Boccaccio, CFW, chap. 6, on the goddess Athene. Boccaccio credits the goddess with having invented or practiced every art and craft except divination. Cereta calls Apollo "physici" (doctor, physician).

13   Students of Plato. See Diogenes Laertius, Lives of the Philosophers.

Phoebus.[14] Soon the Greek tongue of Leontium, full of the Muses, emerged, and she, who had made herself agreeable with the liveliness of her writing, dared to make a bitter attack on the divine words of Theophrastus.[15] Nor would I omit here Proba, noted both for her exceptional tongue and her knowledge; for she wove together and composed histories of the Old Testament with fragments from Homer and Virgil.[16]

The majesty of the Roman state deemed worthy a little Greek woman, Semiramis, for she spoke her mind about the laws in a court of law and about kings in the senate.[17] Pregnant with virtue, Rome bore Sempronia, who, forceful in her eloquent poetry, spoke in public assemblies and filled the minds of her audiences with persuasive orations.[18] Hortensia, the daughter of Hortensius, and also an orator, was celebrated at a public meeting with equal elegance. Her grace of speech was so great that she persuaded the triumvirs, albeit with the tears of a loyal mother, to absolve the women of Rome from having to pay the debt levied against them.[19] Add also Cornificia, the sister of the poet Cornificius, whose devotion to literature bore such fruit that she was said to have been nurtured on the milk of the Castalian Muses and who wrote epigrams in which every phrase was graced with Heliconian flowers.[20] I will not mention here Cicero's daughter Tulliola or Terentia or Cornelia, Roman women who reached the pinnacle of fame for their learning; and accompanying them in the shimmering light

14 See Boccaccio, *CFW*, chap. 45, on Sappho. Cereta follows Boccaccio and makes her unresponsive lover an anonymous male.

15 See Boccaccio, *CFW*, chap. 58, on Leontium, Cereta is faithful to Boccaccio's text.

16 See Boccaccio, *CFW*, chap. 95, on Proba, about whom Cereta is fairly faithful to Boccaccio's portrait. Cereta makes her a speaker as well as a writer, but in Boccaccio there is no mention of Proba's oratory, and his emphasis is on Proba's exceptionality in comparison to most other women, whom he dismisses as idle and pleasure-seeking.

17 See Boccaccio, *CFW*, chap. 2, on Semiramis (Semiamira in Cereta). Cereta differs: Boccaccio says nothing about a connection between Rome and Semiramis, a queen who led her nation as its king and chief military leader, according to Boccaccio. Her sexual relationships and her incest with her son with which she is associated in most accounts of her life are suppressed in Cereta.

18 See Boccaccio, *CFW*, chap. 77, on the "Roman Sempronia." Cereta's Sempronia resembles Boccaccio's in her eloquence, classical training, and poetic skill but the sexual side of Sempronia's life – the dissolute Sempronia of Sallust's *Bellum Catilinae* – is suppressed.

19 See Boccaccio, *CFW*, chap. 82, on Hortensia. Cereta here follows Boccaccio but adds a detail of her own not in B.: namely, that she persuaded the triumvirs with her oratory and her "motherly tears." Again for Boccaccio the emphasis is on how exceptional Hortensia is for her sex: she seems, he remarks, to "be a man."

20 See Boccaccio, *CFW*, chap. 84, on Cornificia; Cereta's imagery and even diction come from Boccaccio. But as usual Boccaccio differs from Cereta by adding a passage at the end of his chapter on Cornificia in which he stresses the point that "most women" are really only good for sex and childbearing.

of silence will be Nicolosa of Bologna, Isotta of Verona, and Cassandra of Venice.[21]

All history is full of such examples. My point is that your mouth has grown foul because you keep it sealed so that no arguments can come out of it that might enable you to admit that nature imparts one freedom to all human beings equally – to learn.[22] But the question of my exceptionality remains. And here choice alone, since it is the arbiter of character, is the distinguishing factor. For some women worry about the styling of their hair, the elegance of their clothes, and the pearls and other jewelry they wear on their fingers. Others love to say cute little things, to hide their feelings behind a mask of tranquility, to indulge in dancing, and lead pet dogs around on a leash. For all I care, other women can long for parties with carefully appointed tables, for the peace of mind of sleep, or they can yearn to deface with paint the pretty face they see reflected in their mirrors. But those women for whom the quest for the good represents a higher value restrain their young spirits and ponder better plans. They harden their bodies with sobriety and toil, they control their tongues, they carefully monitor what they hear, they ready their minds for all-night vigils, and they rouse their minds for the contemplation of probity in the case of harmful literature. For knowledge is not given as a gift but by study. For a mind free, keen, and unyielding in the face of hard work always rises to the good, and the desire for learning grows in depth and breadth.

So be it therefore. May we women, then, not be endowed by God the grantor with any giftedness or rare talent through any sanctity of our own. Nature has granted to all enough of her bounty; she opens to all the gates of choice, and through these gates, reason sends legates to the will, for it is through reason that these legates can transmit their desires. I shall make a bold summary of the matter. Yours is the authority, ours is the inborn ability.[23] But instead of manly strength, we women are naturally endowed with cunning; instead of a sense of security, we are suspicious. Down deep we women are content with

21   Cicero's daughter Tullia (Tulliola), Cicero's wife Terentia (later the wife of Sallust), and Cornelia (the mother of Tiberius and Gaius Gracchi) are all Roman women who were legendary in the ancient world for their learning. Isotta Nogarola of Verona (b. 1418) and Cassandra Fedele of Venice (b. 1465) became legendary for their erudition during their own lifetimes. But what of the phrase "in the shimmering light of silence"? Cereta apparently didn't think modern Italian women scholars like Nogarola and Fedele got the press they deserved.

22   "Naturam discendi aeque omnibus unam impartiri licentiam": the idea that both women and men were born with the right to an education was a radical statement for any fifteenth-century thinker. On the controversy over women's intelligence and the exceptional-woman theory from Boccaccio, see Margaret King, *Women of the Renaissance* (Chicago, 1991), with further bibliography.

23   "Vestra est auctoritas, nostrum ingenium." One of Cereta's key feminist aphorisms, it suggests that the greatest source of tension between the sexes lies in an unjustifiable power differential: though men are born with the power to rule, women have superior intellectual gifts.

our lot. But you, enraged and maddened by the anger of the dog from whom you flee, are like someone who has been frightened by the attack of a pack of wolves. The victor does not look for the fugitive; nor does she who desires a cease-fire with the enemy conceal herself. Nor does she set up camp with courage and arms when the conditions are hopeless. Nor does it give the strong any pleasure to pursue one who is already fleeing.

Look, do you tremble from fear alone of my name? I am savage neither in mind nor hand. What is it you fear? You run away and hide in vain, for the traps that await you around every corner have been more cunningly set. Is it thus that you, a deserter, leave this city and our sight? Is it thus that, regretful of what you have done, you rely on flight as the first road to safety for yourself? May your shame then stay with you. My goodness towards men isn't always rewarded, and you may imagine in your disdain for women that I alone marvel at the felicitousness of having talent – I, who in the light of the well-deserved fame of other women, am indeed only the smallest little mouse. Therefore when you hide your envy under a bogus example, you clothe yourself with defensive words in vain.

For truth which is dear to God always emerges when falsehoods are overthrown. That road is twisted where you walk under the black gaze of an envious mind – far from human beings, from duties, and from God. Who will be surprised, do you think, Bibolo, if the lacerated and wounded heart of a girl who is filled with indignation bitterly rears itself up against your sarcasm and satire from this day on, now that your trifling arrogance has wounded her with bitter injuries? Do not think, most despicable of men, that I might believe I have fallen out of favor with Jove. I am a scholar and a pupil who has been lulled to sleep by the meager fire of a mind too humble. I have been too much burned, and my injured mind has accumulated too much passion; for tormenting itself with the defending of our sex, my mind sighs, conscious of its obligation. For all things – those deeply rooted inside us as well as those outside us – are being laid at the door of our sex.

In addition, I, who have always held virtue in high esteem and considered private things as secondary in importance, shall wear down and exhaust my pen writing against those men who are garrulous and puffed up with false pride. I shall not fail to obstruct tenaciously their treacherous snares. And I shall strive in a war of vengeance against the notorious abuse of those who fill everything with noise, since armed with such abuse, certain insane and infamous men bark and bare their teeth in vicious wrath at the republic of women,[24] so worthy of veneration. January 13, 1488.

24 "*Muliebris respublica* (womanly republic, republic of women) is an expression I have not seen elsewhere. While mine isn't a word for word translation, I did try to capture in English Cereta's prose rhythms, bombastic diction, and overstatement, and also the characterization of her opponents as viciously growling dogs ready to bite (*infestius mordaciusque delatrant*), which is so typical of the genre of invective." [Translator's note]

To Lucilia Vernacula

I should think that the tongues should be cut to pieces and the hearts brutally lacerated of people whose minds are so wicked and whose envious rage is so incredible that they deny in their ignorant rantings the possibility that any woman might master the most elegant elements of Roman oratory. I would pardon the morally hopeless and even people destined for a life of crime, whom wagging tongues are accustomed to castigate with obvious fury. But I cannot tolerate the gabbing and babbling women who, burning with wine and drunkenness, harm with their petulant talk not only their sex but themselves. These mindless women – these female counselors who emerge victorious from the cookshop jar after a prodigious vote among their neighbors – hunt down with their bilious poison those women who rise to greater distinction than they. The bold and undisguised passion these women have for destruction and disgrace, this hunger of theirs for calamity, which strives to smear even those who are completely above reproach, deserves to bring a worse disgrace on itself. For the man who does not take care to have himself absolved of wrongdoing wants his own moral lapses to be excused.

Besides, these women, being idle with time on their hands[1] and no interests of their own, occupy themselves with keeping watch over other people's business, and, like scarecrows hung up in the garden to get rid of sparrows, they shoot poison from the bows of their tongues[2] at those who cross their paths. What after all is the purpose of honor if I were to believe that the barking roars of these sharp-tongued women were worth tolerating, when decent and cultivated women always extol me with honorable words? I am not a woman who wants the shameful deeds of insolent people to slip through under the pardon of silence, either so that in the end I'll be said to approve of what I'm silent about or so that the very women who lead their lives with shame will continue to entice a great many people into their licentiousness as accomplices. Nor would I want, because of my speaking out, someone to criticize me for intolerance; even dogs are allowed to protect themselves from more aggressive fleas by crushing them with their nails. An infected sheep must always be isolated from the healthy flock. For the greatest number are often harmed by the least. Who would believe that disease in trees is caused by ants?

1   Cereta's indictment of the women gossips as lazy about their leisure time (*otio desides*) is interesting: they neglect that which is all-important to her: *otium*, the time when a woman is free from housework to study, write, and think.
2   Literally the "bow of their tongue" (*arcu linguae*), a strange metaphor, undoubtedly original with Cereta.

Those insolent women are therefore silent about every law of honor who, burning with the fires of hatred, would silently gnaw away at themselves, if they didn't feast in their slanderous talk on others. Mildew of the mind afflicts certain demented mothers, who being veritable Megaeras can't stand to hear even the epithet "learned women."[3] Their faces are spongy-looking, and in the vehemence of their speech they sometimes produce the words of a very large louse from their wrinkled cheeks, and sometimes in the presence of onlookers whose eyes grow round with horror at their thundering idiocies. Human error causes us to be ashamed and disgusted that those women who are themselves caught in a tangle of doubt have given up hope of attaining knowledge of the humane arts, when they could easily acquire such knowledge with skill and virtue. For an education is neither bequeathed to us as a legacy, nor does some fate or other give it to us as a gift. Virtue is something that we ourselves acquire; nor can those women who become dull-witted through laziness and the sludge of low pleasures ascend to the understanding of difficult things. But for those women who believe that study, hard work, and vigilance will bring them sure praise, the road to attaining knowledge is broad. Vale. November 1, 1487.

3   Megaera: the name of one of the Furies in Greek mythology.

14

Pietro Alcionio (ca. 1490–1528)

Pietro Alcionio first comes to notice as part of the humanist circle of the publisher Aldo Manuzio in Venice. In the early 1520s he published some translations of Aristotle from Greek into Latin, as well as a Latin dialogue on the topic of exile, with Medici family members figuring prominently among its interlocutors. Upon the election of his foremost patron, Giulio de' Medici, as Pope Clement VII (1523–34), Alcionio went to Rome where, by early 1527, he was lecturing at the University on the Greek orator Demosthenes.

That May, when Rome was sacked, Alcionio fled into the papal fortress, the Castel Sant' Angelo, where he wrote the following oration. Addressed to Pope Clement, who also was a refugee in the fortress, the oration exhorts the pontiff to follow a specific course of action: Clement, he says, should deny a petition by two chaplains, requesting that the corpse of the imperial commander Bourbon – who had died in the first assault from a gunshot that Benvenuto Cellini later claimed to have fired (see chapter 16 below) – be transported to Milan and buried in a place of honor.

Questions

1 Of what crimes is Bourbon accused, and how does Alcionio suggest that they should be punished? How compelling do you find his arguments?
2 What is the current situation in Rome? What future does Alcionio foresee for the city?

> 3 Like Cereta and Machiavelli, Alcionio supports his case with numerous examples from the classical past (although he also includes several late medieval figures). Whose behavior is Clement supposed to emulate, and why? On what bases is his authority said to depend?
> 4 "Deliberative" orations like this one were intended to persuade the listener to follow a particular course of action – in this case, to deny the petition for reburying Bourbon's corpse in a place of honor in Milan. Yet this oration also itemizes some serious criticisms of the very person that Alcionio seeks to persuade. What are those criticisms, and how do you suppose they might have been taken by Pope Clement?

An Oration Concerning the Sack of Rome

Among the greatest anguishes that I suffer in the destruction of this city and in your deplorable lot, o Clement, this one is not insignificant: that I see several out of the enemy army of Caesar's men[1] who are of such remarkable rashness and impudence that they dare daily to come into your presence, at that moment succeeding in getting favors and expecting remuneration from you – a thing that either allies are accustomed to expect from allies, or soldiers from their commander – even though they especially are the ones who, ordained in sacred orders, have overthrown the dignity of religion and, having taken up arms, invaded the city in order to subdue you, the head of our religion. And out of the number of those men, two such barbarians whom you see are present – domestic chaplains of Barbon,[2] the leader of Caesar's brigands – are requesting from you that with your complete favor they may dig up Barbon's body, which has been placed in the church of San Giacomo, and transport it to Milan.

Indeed, they have not appeared to understand how great a crime they committed at the outset, when they attended to him after he had been struck

Written in late May or early June, 1527, translated from a Latin manuscript in the Vatican Library, BAV Vat. Lat. 3436, fols. 35r–40r. The translation seeks to maintain insofar as possible the elegant Ciceronian sentence constructions of the original, which, however, is an unfinished rough draft.

1 "Caesar's men" refers here to the troops of the Emperor Charles V.
2 Alcionio frequently misspells *Borbonius*, the Latinized form of Bourbon (i.e., Charles, Constable of Bourbon), so as to make a pun on *Barbarus* ("Barbarian").

Plate 9   Sebastiano del Piombo (ca. 1485–1547), *Portrait of Clement VII* (ca. 1526), Museo Nazionale di Capodimonte, Naples. *Source*: Alinari/Art Resource, NY.

with a ball exploded out of a bronze firearm. Not long afterwards, they carried him, dead, into the chapel of your official home,[3] and then buried him at the church of San Giacomo, even though the impious and criminal

3   The Sistine Chapel in the Vatican Palace, where Bourbon's corpse was initially laid in state on the high altar, before being taken to the Spanish church of St. James (Santiago, or in Italian, San Giacomo).

leader was undeserving of all civilized obsequy. And certainly it seemed that there, exactly where he had fallen, he should have been left behind, so that he might be plucked to pieces by birds and nocturnal dogs; and that part of the ground which had caught him as he was falling should have been fenced in, like a desecrated neighborhood or field – clearly the sort of place that could not be restored to its former nature even by means of perpetual atonement. But since that man's great authority was in the hands of brigands like himself, seeing that while living he was obtaining easily those things which he desired with rash audacity, it is fitting that no one marvel if he felt that all those observances which were due to the pious and best men were owed also to him, as he was dying and then dead. Added onto this was the cruel insolence of the soldiers, who had given zealous assistance to him in the war. For these men, still armed, and high-spirited with both plunder and victory, were striking so much terror into many people of our order that these dared either to do or to say nothing the least bit openly. I myself would have done just that,[4] too, had I not decided at long last, provoked by the very arrogant demands of those priests, to disregard every risk to life so that I might defend the authority of our order, the reverence for sacred things, the honor of religion, and the divine majesty of God Himself.

Therefore, o Clement, I advise first that you should maintain to the end your jurisdiction, and likewise ours: that is to say, that you respond in no fashion to the wish of those priestlings; and that instead, as soon as possible, you should order a dash made to that place where Barbon's carcass has been set down, that it may indeed be dug up – not so that it may be transported to Milan (which is what those men want), but instead, after being dragged through the city with a hook imbedded in it, it should be flung into the Tiber. For that river is more suitable for receiving a man contaminated with such great crimes since, although it has been tainted so greatly with human bloodshed, nonetheless, because it flows with perennial movement, it can cast away such a great foulness; but the earth of Milan, if it is holy, will be rendered profane once the enemy of all sacred things has been taken in; if, however, the place is already profane earth, neither shall it be considered a part of the world, nor shall [it] be called any longer by the name of the element.[5]

To be sure, it is clear that laws have been established by the holy popes for the welfare of citizens, the safety of cities, and the happy and peaceful life of the people. But they have considered no law to be more apt for this very thing than that which inspires fear of having been denied burial and the due ceremonies of the funeral procession. For since the human alone of all animals joins the perception of present circumstances with foresight and

4 i.e., Alcionio, too, would have remained silent.
5 In classical thought, earth is one of the four elements from which all things below the moon are formed (the other three are water, air, and fire).

with the hope of future things, he cannot help but be greatly anxious concerning that matter which can bear witness to a life lived properly or disgracefully.

Now, the whole force of this matter is contained in the honor or disgrace of burial. Indeed, so great is the inviolability of every tomb that it makes sacred even the very place in which it is enclosed, nor can it be moved or taken away by any force; and even as other things are destroyed, so tombs are made more sacred with age. Therefore, those very judicious Caesars, from whom there still survive many things both properly thought out and wisely said concerning the well-being of humans, decreed that it is lawful for a corpse to be transported to another [place] on the authority of the ruler of the province, if the force of a river should uncover the remains, or if there should be another just and necessary motive. They therefore wanted the authority of transporting a corpse to be in the hands of the ruler, because if the corpse had been treated with burial, whether in the ignorance of the ruler or with his favor, once he had changed his mind, there still lay within the same man's power the right of exhuming it, and of stripping it of the covering of the earth, as though of a mother, by which it was being enveloped. What [does all this matter]? [It matters] in this way, Clement: that not only with you not knowing, but also against your will, the body of that brigand was brought onto your property. But it is clear by surer and also more just reason that such a body must be exhumed, since that place has not been consecrated, for it is of such a type that it can be put under a bond by religion only in accordance with the owner's wish.

Now, they admittedly will say what I heard [them] say on another occasion: namely, that Bourbon never strove or took pains that such great destruction of the city would follow, nor that priests would be afflicted so terribly and you yourself, Clement, be oppressed so impiously and wretchedly – and that for this reason, he proposed conditions of peace. A fine defense of the villainy of Bourbon! It is neither right nor lawful to believe, o Clement, that this enemy of sacred things and plunderer of all religions, who had passed over the Appenines with so large a multitude of brigands, sought anything other than that which happened, that is to say, the final death of the republic, and also that you, along with all possessions, might serve as spoils of war for the most-cruel enemy. Indeed, what conditions of peace were offered can be seen to have been offered with the intent that, once a delay had been imposed in taking consultation, you might look less to the interests of your affairs; then also, so that after some semblance of mildness would first have been sought, nothing would be so terrible and cruel that he would not undertake it for our destruction; not so that the welfare of the city might remain intact or so that your dignity might remain inviolate. And indeed [he sought terms of peace] all the more so because already he was feeling that your army was picking at the tail end of his own army, and so would be present not long after that. Is it not true therefore that he was all the more wanting you to give up lasting peace in the hope of a present peace? Is it not true that, under the pretext of concord, he was striving to sow the seeds of everlasting discord? Why, if he was desiring peace when he was on the far side of the Appenines, did he so defiantly repudiate your ambassadors of peace? Why did he belittle the money offered as wages not for your soldiers, but (a thing which hardly seems worthy of belief) for his own? Why did he, barbaric and arrogant with regard to your authority and will, also show himself deaf to the entreaties of Lannoy?[6]

Undoubtedly that leader always sought after this thing: that just as he himself was without a fatherland, and had oppressed France with a pro-longed attack of military force, so too you, o Clement, might be without a fatherland, liberty, and even life; then, too, that he might capture the city, plunder the captured, destroy the plundered, and ruin all Italy with a most destructive and grievous war. In fact, the consciousness of these crimes would have discouraged the mind of anyone except Barbon, who had become so thick-skinned with the practice of brigandry that he was accustomed to bring to bear equal audacity and stubbornness for contriving every abominable, heinous deed. O detestable priests, does such a man seem to you as needing to be treated with the honor of burial in any temple in Italy? This man who, once he had formed an army of sorts out of every variety of barbarians, has violated with sacrileges the temples of Italy and even of this most sacred city, has defiled them with slaughter, and has deformed them with the greatest destructions?

And what is more, we read that it was decreed in the assembly at Varese that people who either divert or intercept pious payments intended for shrines are to be thrown out of the sanctuaries. All the learned think that this decree must be understood with regard to living men performing that type of crime, in whom of course breath is still alive, and in whom there can be the will to purge the soul and to do penance. But when he was living, Bourbon was not only the instigator that payments of such a kind might not be made, he also plundered those payments that had been made and, dying, he did not give any indication of a troubled mind concerning that matter. And will you, o Clement, allow to be received, dead, into any temple him who with such cursing savageness wrenched loose all the honor of sacred things, and cast down from its station even most-holy religion itself? But what is the reason why our ancestors decreed what needed to be done by them with such great harshness and strictness against those who would appropriate pious and holy payments? Obviously, because it was supposed they were being condemned as murderers of paupers and of people of the lower ranks. For he

---

6   Charles de Lannoy, the viceroy of Naples on behalf of Charles V, had sought unsuccessfully to secure Bourbon's compliance with the truce that Lannoy had just made with Pope Clement.

who despises paupers and miserable ones, if he is a Christian, is regarded as both to be despised and to be reckoned as good for nothing. Now, if he is the murderer and assassin of those men, one should call in an executioner for the living man to avenge the crime; but against the one having been struck down and put to death by the executioner, by all means the dogs need to be brought in, who should mangle the body, pull to pieces the entrails, and most cruelly dismember all the parts.

Therefore, o Clement, make use of the favor of the immortal gods who, even if you are a captive and a person of shattered fortune, all things having been ruined, nonetheless wish unimpaired power to have been left to you of passing judgment concerning sacred matters, and that thing by the authority of the priesthood, with which you are recognized as endowed. Make use also of the laws which earlier popes proposed and, once the laws had been confirmed in public assemblies of Christians, the popes ordained as entirely to be observed. By these, certainly, it is decreed that no man, even one having died piously, is to be buried within the temple, but either in the atrium, or in the portico, or in the hall. Moreover, in the highest part of the temple near the greatest altar, certainly no place is to be left which may stand open for burying, lest that august honor of the divine sacrifice which is accustomed to be performed there should be defiled, and lest the holy place of worship should be polluted.

O audacity which must not be endured! O singular rashness! You vile priestlings, you have laid Bourbon in state at that main altar of San Giacomo, which he wanted in every way overturned, near the container where is preserved that consecrated wafer in which Christ is present, which we have seen more than once thrown down onto the earth and trampled in the sight of the saints, whose ceremonies, sacred rites, and religion he violated with such turpitude. Nearby, you set up his helmet, breastplate, and greaves, so that the overbearingness of that most filthy monster should be more evident and more attested, relying upon which he had struck at a friendly pope and, so impiously armed, had come for the purpose of stabbing prelates and priests of every rank, and for despoiling and demolishing the holiest temples of the city.

But in fact, among previous popes there were not missing those whose remarkable piety and exceptional wisdom both are honored, who approved the practice of burying bodies in temples, because they were hoping that those who from the people of our kind would have been buried there would be more pleasing to God, since especially they were hoping that with the intercession of the holy martyrs, who were lying nearby, there was nothing belonging to their own salvation which they could not easily obtain from God. But who now will be the holy martyrs who may commend to God the remains of that impious and destructive pest? Surely not those whose bones and bodily remains he destroyed in the plundering of temples? Surely not the priests and other very holy men whom he harassed, beat, killed, and tore to pieces, not so that they might discard the vessel of Christ and the steadfast defense of that religion (that thing which the ancient Caesars in Rome used to do), but so that he might carry away the holy vestments, chalices, incense boxes, and other implements necessary for performing the divine sacrifice that had been brought out from the chapels, and that he might wrench out whatever of gold and silver had been preserved for many years?

"Barbon," they say, "was from the foremost nobility of France; he can also adduce in his family distinguished examples of ancestors, the honor of glorious deeds, and the splendor of kings. Therefore, greater consideration must be had of that man, and it appears that an action must not be taken against him with the same kind of severity with which it is taken against private citizens." Surely no one denies that the man's ancestors were so illustrious and distinguished by the greatness of their house that they alone could uphold the dignity of the Gallic nobility. But is it not true that he has beclouded the household glory of such great honors and the celebrity of his lineage, first by devising a plot to kill Francis the king of France, and then by undertaking the plan to oppress the pope? On account of the former matter, he was proclaimed an enemy and proscribed as one. He was branded throughout all France with the name of a traitor, and his estate was confiscated, and his goods were exposed for sale by the voice of an auctioneer.[7]

By us, however, nothing else has been decreed against him except what is usual to be decreed against those who have spoken and done all things by which both the true religion has been polluted, and the authority of the popes can be adjudged as betrayed; and if these more recent decrees, by which citizens have been brought to ruin, may not appear enough to someone to render [Bourbon] odious to all posterity in times to come, this man should think over with himself in his heart the fatal predations of [Bourbon] in Cisalpine Gaul, Aemilia, and Etruria. Why, at last, should I bring up for reconsideration this devastation of Rome, these slaughterings, these conflagrations, these plunderings, these failures to punish crimes, [or] the flights, agitations, and bereavements of citizens, which flowed from that source? Will not these things always be adjudged sufficiently deserving that the name of that man be obscured by the death of people [now living], and utterly extinguished by the forgetfulness of posterity?

In the past, those who on their own behalf had done a deed less deserving of punishment were kept at a distance from temples; but those, too, who had defended, or cared for with a sense of loyalty, or given shelter to a person thinking wrongly about religion, used to be driven not only out of temples, but also out of the society of Christians. Still, our ancestors wished a place left

---

7   This refers to Bourbon's disgrace in France, which led to his entering the service of the Emperor Charles V. Pending success in the Italian campaign, Bourbon was promised Milan as his reward.

for pardon and clemency even in such great harshness of laws, for they thus assessed the man having the wrong idea as needing to be reminded of piety once and again; but if he had not obeyed the one kindly warning him, he would pay the penalty with public burning for his defiance and for a mind obstinate in upholding an erroneous interpretation of religion. Those who were ripping apart the truth of religion even made use of books, commentaries, and debates to weaken our position. O Clement, what do you adjudge as having been decreed concerning those who, as barbarians, also begirt with the weapons of barbarians, have now even attacked us, brought hostile action, squandered away the possessions of priests, demanded blood, and dashed down, crushed, and almost destroyed even the pope himself? You should know, I say, that nothing else has been decreed except that which needs to be decreed against Saracens, against Carthaginians, against Moors, and against Turks and other peoples threatening to Christians: certainly we are accustomed to curse the name of these people, avoid their company, censure them while living, and either set out the half-dead ones to be torn to pieces by dogs, or burn them in the streets, or fling them into the sea. Moreover, a sure and precise law of religion, the long existence of precedents, the authority of sacred literature, and the uninterrupted glory of the historical record assure the credibility of this matter.

But indeed, the divine wisdom of our ancestors is manifest not only in this thing, but also in decreeing that, if by chance a false interpreter of religion had been buried by a friend ignorant of the matter, that man would not be able to obtain pardon unless he would have dug up the dead body, even with his own hands, and had left it exhumed as a thing detestable and needing to be cursed. They add also that the place in which that man had first been buried would be forever unconsecrated, and could not by any reckoning be made sanctified. And unquestionably, prudently and rightly they deemed that this crime must be punished so very relentlessly, lest any impurity of corrupt people should, on account of their condition, displace from its position the dignity of our order and the outstanding honor of religion. But if those most steadfast and by far most innocent of all ancient men had felt that they were unequal to uphold the authority of such great matters, then mindful of that freedom which ought to be characteristic of priests, they brought to an end that very authority by an honorable death, rather than by disreputable and most foul servitude.

Neither, however, will this deed be unusual, o Clement, if you will have ordered that the enemy, Bourbon, must be honored with no kind of burial. I will not pursue here the stories about Polynices whom, by order of Creon, all people were required to leave unburied as an enemy of the king. However, his sister Antigone, by no means fearing the command, buried him; on that account, she was laid to rest under the earth as a living woman. Is it not true that the victorious Sulla commanded that the remains of Marius, which had been laid down near the Anio River, be scattered? "You must not deal with us," they say, "according to the examples of those who were devoid of the Christian religion, for we are disposed by its authority and injunction toward total forbearance, toward complete meekness of spirit, and toward granting all indulgence with affability and with readiness, and the harshness of popes ought not to extend beyond death." O Clement, an immense number of examples are read, having been consigned to the public records of popes, which pertain very much to refuting the wish of those awful men. However, satisfied with a few examples, I will show that they are ignorant of the true course of that glory, in undertaking which, the Christian priest can admirably be placed in the right light.

The German Emperor Frederick II, a small cushion having been stuffed into his mouth by his son Manfred, and having been killed by the same illegitimate one, was left unburied or, what some write, was buried with too little religious ceremony, and that on the authority of Pope Innocent IV, because of the fact that he had harassed all the popes of his time with undutiful warfare; and once those had been scorned, he even had chosen for priestly ministries those whom it was not behooving to be chosen, and he consecrated with pontifical ceremony the chosen ones; then, also, he presented them with those insignia which were seen to be fitting for entering the priesthood. Why should I bother to mention Ezzelino the transpadine tyrant, who in military service had learned that training of the same Frederick, so that he was the continual enemy of priests, the plunderer of sanctuaries, the mocker of the pope's majesty, the disturber of the common peace, the executioner of the city-states of Italy, and the despiser of religion and of God? But after he had seen that some among his men were being butchered, others being slit, others being massacred, and the half-dead and those lying on the ground were often being stabbed, the wound being repeated, then the man himself, his left leg pierced by a dart, and he having been thrown prostrate, the weapon of Soncino dashed against his head, lacked burial, as a person cursed with everlasting punishments, having been both assailed by Alexander IV with dreadful curses and vexed with every kind of execration. Not dissimilar, also, was the harshness of Clement IV toward Conradin, by whose despotism, which was not only cruel and overbearing but also disgraceful and shameful, Apulia, Samnium, and Campania were being crushed down. For Charles, the king of Naples, struck down with an axe this man conquered in battle; then, obedient to the authority of that very Clement, he exposed him as food for wild animals. So, also, Martin V at first did not wish that Braccio, having been conquered in the battle of Amiternum, and killed, and brought into the territory of the Romans, later be buried. Lest he appear imbued with just as much cruelty as the villainy of Braccio was requiring, he permitted him to be buried in land at the first milestone from the city, which was neither fettered nor bound by any religious scruple.

See, o Clement, how great is the dignity of your priesthood, how great is the power of the pontifical role which you uphold, and how indisputably great is the Divine Will, so that you may keep firm hold of those things. Back then, no man dared to contrive anything which might appear possibly to have been done against the will of those popes, and justified revenge seemed to have been undertaken against those who had stirred up long and destructive wars in Italy, and who had exercised savage cruelty with an intolerable kind of frenzy: for they had driven out of the cities some old distinguished families, and had destroyed others; they had tortured with sleeplessness and starvation some infants who had been snatched away from the bosom of mothers, and even had torn out their eyes in the sight of the parents; and others, they had killed. They had dragged out noble matrons and chaste virgins to that point to which unbridled lust and a singular matchless desire of defiling all things had driven them on. They had burned up the most venerable churches, and stolen gold, silver, gems, crafted vessels, and every furnishing with which, in the observances of sacred rituals and on feast days, the altars of the saints were accustomed to be splendidly adorned. They had contaminated altars with the blood of priests, and had broken to pieces what had been contaminated.

But indeed, why should we be amazed if the Roman pontiffs, who are called "maximi" for this reason, because it is accepted that they hold the supreme power, have shown themselves so very invincible, steadfast, severe, and strict against their enemies, who had been both subverting established opinion about religion and polluting the true worship of the gods? After all, priests beyond the seas and private citizens acted likewise to the Byzantine Emperor Michael who, however, had followed our religion with magnificent and pious observance. They had prohibited a monument to be set up in a holy place, because at the Council at Lyons he had followed the authority of the Latins in the interpretation of religion. Nor did any kinsman among the right-thinking satraps of the deceased emperor or any friend of those paltry Greeks dare to obstruct in any way that decree of perverse and impious religion, sacred rites, and holy things; and certainly the patronage of divine things among transmarine provincials was a thing of distinguished authority and grace.[8]

It remains, o Clement, that I should warn you that on no account ought you to judge that I have been enraged to such a degree against the cause of Bourbon on account of the personal injuries that I have received; because I have judged that the fortunes which the foreign enemies plundered, the household belongings they snatched away, and so many (that which those priestlings say) serious, almost fatal, wounds which they inflicted when I was

---

8   Here, the manuscript was repeatedly revised and evidently left unfinished, and its meaning is ambiguous.

defending you and your official residence – these things are able to shake me in no way, ever, as often as I turn my attention (that which I always do) to the universal and wretched disasters of the citizens, and to the most burdensome and sorrow-causing destruction of the entire city, toward which we have looked out from this fortress with infinite tears. Therefore, the public matter at hand inflames my hatred against you. The blood of so many priests, poured out so impiously, renders me stern, implacable, and rigorous toward you. The honor, also, of the violated divine will of God arouses in me this steadfastness. Finally, those bones and buried remains of the holy martyrs, which Bourbon dug up and scattered, bring it about that I am an adviser to the pope himself, that retaliation in kind must also be rendered to Bourbon: namely, that he must be exhumed, torn to pieces, and, in accordance with the custom of the ancient Romans, thrown into the Tiber.

But if, Clement, you decide that I must not be listened to, at least you should look upon the authority of those popes whom I have mentioned; for, relying on their authority (and thus on yours), you will not henceforth be able to forgo your right; indeed, you should confirm the power of the Roman pontificate both by this very thing and by other most beautiful examples of justice, dignity, greatness of soul, and constancy. For thus you will put to the test those things which have been spread around about your pontificate by the conversations of very judicious people: that up to this time it has been disastrous for the liberty of Italy, fatal to the health of the city, sorrowful for the dignity of religion, and offensive and pestiferous to the universal church of God; and that fortune bears out their claim (indeed, the fortune which embraced you as a private citizen is not the same as that which has embraced you as a prince).

All good men, furthermore, will judge that you are undeserving that the voices of distressed citizens should burst out anymore against your name – for if it is fitting that, following the custom of the ancient popes, you now listen to unbiased voices and, indeed, those of your intimates; if you will have repudiated bad counselors, by whose insane judgment and perverse advice you have run your pontificate; if you have not been at the same time both the author and overturner of your laws; if you will have administered the grain supply in such a way that neither you nor your own people are discerned to reduce it to profit and booty – then, you will have claimed back the languishing and nearly dead memory of famous and learned men from silence and from the most adverse thing created of fate. If you will have decreed rewards for the vigilances and the efforts of those who, as virtue guides, are striving to become free; if you both approve men in the priestly estate and will have read about those to whom all eternity is clearly indebted, having proposed that they be not only followed, but also equalled by you (for although they originated as private citizens of their fatherland, nonetheless they were living in such a way that they were being surpassed neither by kings with regard to magnificence, justice, and splendor of lofty mind, nor even by the popes themselves with regard to purity, modesty, and commendation of religion) – then, this your pitiable lot will have God as an avenger and certainly a zealous deliverer Who, as I incline to believe, wanted you to be vexed with imprisonment, with the loss of most-valued possessions and with such great evils, in order that you might know that liberality and innocence, not arms, would have been a most faithful protection for you. For by the protection of those virtues, you would have had at least no barbarians as enemies (let me be silent about the others), and if ever you had, you would have been in the end the object of their reverence. But by your reliance upon arms, you provoked the most monstrous barbarians, for whom you were, in the end, the object of plunder and of ridicule.

For this reason we hope, o Clement, that your prudence, made miserable by terrible dangers and a life full of tribulation, will finally become good judgment that is glorious for you and salutary for the human race. On that account, once all your plans have been brought back to this high degree of goodness or of beneficence, you will relieve our miseries, and at the same time, with the manifest gratitude of all, you will auspiciously take charge of those things which pertain both to restoring the city, which had been abandoned to fires and greater catastrophes without laws, without law-courts, without justice, and without good faith; and to protecting the authority of your priesthood. I have had my say.

Part VI
Patronage, Art, and Culture

Introduction to Part VI

In the Italian Renaissance, the production of artworks often took place in social contexts that belie the nineteenth-century myth of the artist as an isolated genius expressing ideas that well up from within the individual. Major commissions, from Giotto's wall-frescoes in the Arena Chapel in Padua to Michelangelo's Sistine Chapel ceiling, did not spring forth fully formed, like Athena from the head of Zeus. Instead, they required a workshop in which the production of art was a shared enterprise that involved discrete stages as well as extensive delegation of responsibilities.[1] In addition, in small commissions as well as large ones, patrons – the individuals or institutions who hired an artist for a particular project – could play a significant role not only in the choice of subject of an artwork, but also in the style of its execution. In the two selections below, consider the ways that patrons and artists interacted in the creative process.

1   Thus the distinguished historian of art William E. Wallace, in an op-ed piece in the *New York Times* in the 1990s, likened Michelangelo's role to that of the CEO of a corporation today.

Plate 10 Cellini, *Perseus with the Head of Medusa* (1545–53), Loggia dei Lanzi, Florence. *Source*: Scala/Art Resource, NY.

Benvenuto Cellini (1500–71) received the commission for this bronze statue from Cosimo I de' Medici (1519–74), who in 1537 had succeeded Alessandro de' Medici as duke of Florence. An administrator highly effective at consolidating power in his own hands, Cosimo I set about expanding and strengthening the Florentine territorial state, while at the same time seeking through patronage to demonstrate that Florentine culture was as vibrant as ever. Cellini played a part in that demonstration, as did his friend Benedetto Varchi, who advised him on the project. Varchi, a humanist historian and philogist who had favored the expulsion of the Medici from Florence in 1527, had been brought back to the city by Cosimo I in 1543 to adorn the ducal court. Cellini's own lofty aspiration for the commission was that the sculpture should rival or even surpass Donatello's *Judith and Holofernes* and Michelangelo's *David*, each of which was displayed nearby: the *David* in front of the Palazzo della Signoria, and the *Judith and Holofernes*, which was then in another arch of the Loggia dei Lanzi, directly opposite from where the *Perseus* was to stand. In addition, Cellini sought to put to shame the marble *Hercules and Cacus* (1534), by his archenemy Baccio Bandinelli, which was also close by.

When the *Perseus* was unveiled in April 1554, it became a triumph not only for the vainglorious Cellini (on whose career, see the introduction to chapter 16 below) but also for Duke Cosimo. Indeed, while the bronze statue was recognized as an outstanding work of art (thereby bringing honor to both artist and patron), it also was less vulnerable to anti-Medicean political readings than had been the proximate works by Donatello, Michelangelo, and Bandinelli. When defeated on occasion by a resurgent republic, the Medici rulers of Florence had been compared variously to the slain tyrants Goliath and Holofernes. When ensconced as rulers in the mid-1530s, by contrast, the Medici lords of Florence were likened to Bandinelli's *Hercules*, lording it over the defeated. But now, as art historian John Shearman has demonstrated, Cellini's *Perseus* played a role in Cosimo I de' Medici's strategy "to neutralize the encoded political message of existing images by making them more emphatically works of art in an open-air gallery."[1] Thus the symbolic center of Florence came to have fewer republican associations, as a Medicean "prince" strove to make his own small part of the world "safe" for autocracy.

1 John Shearman, *Only Connect: Art and the Spectator in the Italian Renaissance* (Princeton, 1992), p. 52. The summary above is based substantially upon Shearman's exposition in ibid., pp. 44–58.

15

Isabella d'Este (1474–1539)

Isabella d'Este was one of the outstanding Renaissance patrons of art and literature. The daughter of Duke Ercole I of Ferrara and Eleonora of Aragon, she received a humanist education and was exposed early on to the elevated culture of the Ferrarese court. In 1490 she married Francesco Gonzaga II, the marquis of Mantua (1466–1519), with whom she had six children. During Francesco's absences for military and political missions, she governed effectively in his stead, and she also played an active role in promoting the careers of her children.

While she herself enjoyed courtly diversions including dancing and playing music, she also read widely and developed a keen appreciation for art. She is most famous as a collector of both art and antiquities, which she sought out energetically, at times commissioning new paintings to add to her collections. In the letters below, we can glimpse Isabella's efforts (often successful, but not always so) to obtain works by some of the most famous artists of her day.

Questions

1 How does the tone differ from one letter to another? To what extent does the status of the recipient matter to Isabella? What are the roles of intermediaries in the process?
2 What image of Isabella emerges from the letters? What do you imagine it would be like to work for her?
3 Based on these letters, to what extent do you think that Isabella played a role in shaping the final artistic product? In other words, did artist and

patron collaborate in designing the project, or did the artist make the rules? Or, did that differ from case to case?

4   Consider the epistolary genre. Like the letters of Alessandra Strozzi and Laura Cereta, those of Isabella d'Este prod the reader to think or act in certain ways. How do their strategies of persuasion differ? Compare and contrast their approaches to exercising power in spheres traditionally dominated by men.

Selected letters on collecting art

64[1]

Letter of Michele Vianello to Isabella d'Este, 5 March 1501

My most illustrious and excellent respected Lady

On my arrival here I saw Giovanni Bellini about the commission Your Ladyship gave me at my departure. After telling him of the requirement and desire of Your illustrious Ladyship and the story in the manner you wished, the said Giovanni Bellini replied that he was under an obligation to the illustrious government [of Venice] to continue the work he had begun in the palace; that he could never leave it from early morning until after dinner. However, he would make or steal time during the day to do this work for Your Excellency in order to serve you and for the sake of the love I bear him. I still warn you that the said Giovanni Bellini has a great deal of work on his hands, so that it will not be possible for you to have it as soon as you wanted. I am asking whether he will be able to get it done within a year and a half, and it will depend on how much he can do. As to the price, he asked me for 150 ducats, but he will reduce it to 100 ducats, and this is all that can be done; so Your illustrious Ladyship knows what has been attempted in the matter. I await a reply from Your illustrious Ladyship, to whom I offer and recommend myself for ever. Please recommend me to the illustrious lordship of my Lord your husband.

> Your most illustrious and excellent Ladyship's servant
> Michele Vianello

1   The letter numbering is drawn from D. S. Chambers, ed., *Patrons and Artists in the Italian Renaissance* (London, 1971).

65
Letter of Michele Vianello to Isabella d'Este, 25 June 1501

My most illustrious Lady

Today I have received your letter from Ziprian, Your Excellency's courier, and from the same I received 25 ducats to give Giovanni Bellini, who is at his villa. He will be back at his house here, they tell me, within five days. I will be with him immediately, and that Your Excellency may know that I have your service in mind, I have spoken to him several times about this picture. He told me that he was very anxious to serve Your Ladyship, but about the story Your Ladyship gave him, words cannot express how badly he has taken it, because he knows Your Ladyship will judge it in comparison with the work of Master Andrea [Mantegna], and for this reason he wants to do his best. He said that in the story he cannot devise anything good out of the subject at all, and he takes it as badly as one can say, so that I doubt whether he will serve Your Excellency as you wish. So if it should seem better to you to allow him to do what he likes, I am most certain that Your Ladyship will be very much better served. Therefore I beg Your Ladyship will be pleased to give me your views, because he will not do anything until I hear from you.

From Your Ladyship's servant
Michele Vianello

66
Letter of Isabella d'Este to Michele Vianello, 28 June 1501

Messer Michele

If Giovanni Bellini is so unwilling to do this story as you write, we are content to leave the subject to his judgment, so long as he paints some ancient story or fable with a beautiful meaning. We should be very glad if you would urge him to make a start on this work, so that we have it within the time he has estimated, and sooner if possible. The size of the picture has not been altered since you were here and saw the place where it was to go in the studio. Nevertheless, to be on the safe side I am sending you the measurements again, and Gian Cristoforo our sculptor will write to you about this.

Mantua, 28 June 1501

67
Letter of Isabella d'Este to Michele Vianello, 15 September 1502

Messer Michele

You may remember that many months ago we gave Giovanni Bellini a commission to paint a picture for the decoration of our studio, and when it ought to have been finished we found it was not yet begun. Since it seemed clear that we should never obtain what we desired, we told him to abandon the work, and give you back the 25 ducats which we had sent him before, but now he begs us to leave him the work and promises to finish it soon. As till now he has given us nothing but words, we beg that you will tell him in our name that we no longer care to have the picture, but that if instead he would paint a Nativity, we should be well content, as long as he does not keep us waiting any longer, and will count the 25 ducats which he has already received as half payment. This, it appears to us, is really more than he deserves, but we are content to leave this to your judgment. We want this Nativity to contain the Madonna and Our Lord God and St. Joseph, together with a St. John and Baptist and the [usual] animals. If he refuses to agree to this, you will ask him to return the 25 ducats, and if he will not give back the money you will take proceedings.

68
Letter of Michele Vianello to Isabella d'Este, 3 November 1502

Most illustrious and excellent Lady

I have just received a letter from Your Ladyship in which you tell me about the picture by Giovanni Bellini. I have had the measurements of the picture from Messer Battista Scola and I at once went to find him and tell him Your Ladyship's wish about the Nativity scene, and that Your Ladyship wished a St. John the Baptist to appear in the scene. He replied that he was happy to serve Your Excellency, but that the said saint seemed out of place in this Nativity, and that if it pleases Your illustrious Ladyship he will do a work with the infant Christ and St. John the Baptist and something in the background with other fantasies which would be much better. So we left it at that: if this pleases Your Ladyship please let me know. because I will do whatever Your Ladyship commands. As to the price, he agreed to take 50 ducats, and anything more which may seem fair to Your Excellency. So I ordered the canvas to be primed and he promised to begin very soon.

69
Letter of Isabella d'Este to Michele Vianello, 12 November 1502

Messer Michele

As Bellini is resolved on doing a picture of the Madonna and Child and St. John the Baptist in place of the Nativity scene, I should be glad if he would also include a St. Jerome with the other subjects which occur to him; and about the price of 50 ducats we are content, but above all urge him to serve us quickly and well.

70
Letter of Isabella d'Este to Giovanni Bellini, 9 July 1504

Master Giovanni Bellini

If the picture which you have done for us corresponds to your fame, as we hope, we shall be satisfied and will forgive you the wrong which we reckon you have done us by your slowness. But hand it over to Lorenzo da Pavia, who will pay you the 25 ducats owing on completion of the work, and we beg you to pack it in such a way that it can be carried here easily and without risk of damage. If we can oblige you in anything we will willingly do so when we have seen that you have served us well.

Farewell
Mantua, 9 July 1504

71
Letter of Isabella d'Este to Giovanni Bellini, 19 October 1505

Master Giovanni

You will remember very well how great our desire was for a picture of some story painted by your hand, to put in our studio near those of your brother-in-law Mantegna; we appealed to you for this in the past, but you could not do it on account of your many other commitments. Instead of the story which first you had promised to do, we resigned ourselves to taking a Nativity scene instead, which we like very much and are as fond of as any picture we possess. But the Magnificent Pietro Bembo was here a few months ago, and hearing of the great desire which we cherish continually, encouraged us to hope it might yet be gratified. He thought that some of the works which have been keeping you busy had now been delivered, and knowing your sweet nature in obliging everyone, especially those in high places, he was able to promise us satisfaction. Since the time of this conversation we have been ill with fever and unable to attend to such things, but now we are better it has occurred to us to write begging you to consent to painting a picture, and we will leave the poetic invention for you to make up if you do not want us to give it to you. As well as the proper and honorable payment, we shall be under an eternal obligation to you. When we hear of your agreement, we will send you the measurements of the canvas and an initial payment.

Mantua, 19 October 1505

72
Letter of Pietro Bembo to Isabella d'Este, 1 January 1506

I have been with Bellini recently and he is very well disposed to serve Your Excellency, as soon as the measurements of the canvas are sent to him. But the invention, which you tell me I am to find for his drawing, must be adapted to the fantasy of the painter. He does not like to be given many written details which cramp his style; his way of working, as he says, is always to wander at will in his pictures, so that they can give satisfaction to himself as well as to the beholder. Nevertheless he will achieve both ends by hard work. In addition to this, spurred by my great devotion and service to Your Excellency, I beg your good offices about a matter which I have much at heart, with as great a hope of being heard as the desire I always have to do you service. With Messer Francesco Cornelio,[2] brother of the most reverend Cardinal, I observe a close kinship and a most dear and familiar friendship, no less than if he were my brother. He has in addition many very singular qualities, so that I hold him infinitely high in honor, and desire to please him. Since he is, like all lofty and gentle souls, passionately fond of rare things, he arranged some time ago with Messer Andrea Mantegna to have several canvases painted for him at the price of 150 ducats. He gave him an advance of 25 ducats, having first sent him the measurements, and the work was welcomed by Messer Andrea, so that he went ahead. Now he tells me that Messer Andrea refuses to go on with it for that price, and asks a much larger sum, which seems to Messer

2   Francesco Cornaro affected the name Cornelius to imply descent from the Roman family of that name. One of the paintings under discussion is presumably *The Triumph of Scipio* in the National Gallery, London.

Francesco the greatest novelty in the world, as it appears to everyone he tells about it. This is especially so because he possesses letters of Messer Andrea in which he particularly confirmed the said agreement they made together. Messer Andrea alleges that the work turns out to be bigger than he had estimated, so he wants more payment. I therefore beg and implore Your Ladyship to persuade Messer Andrea to keep faith with Messer Francesco and make a start on the pictures he has undertaken for him; above all he should be reminded that he who is called the *Mantegna* of the world ought above all men to keep (*mantenere*) his promises, so that there should not be the like discord when he does otherwise, being and not being Mantegna at the same time. M. Francesco does not take issue about one hundred or two hundred florins for something which merits so little gold (thank God he has abundant means for a man of his rank), but takes issue against being made a fool of and derided. Should your Excellency think that the work, once delivered, deserves a much higher reward, he will act in such a way that Messer Andrea will not be able to call him boorish, and he wants to stand by Your Ladyship's judgment, and that she should commit him to whatever seems right and pleasing to her. But that he should now say – the bargain having been arranged long ago and the advance payment accepted – "I no longer want it thus, but like this; do not imagine that the work is going ahead" – Messer Andrea should for God's sake see that these matters are no more burdensome to him than damaging to Messer Francesco, who would not want his pictures except that it is a very important issue for him. Messer Francesco is in no doubt of obtaining this favor from you by my intercession, reckoning that I can do much more with you and that Messer Andrea should and can deny you nothing. It will be most highly appreciated by me if Your Ladyship deigns to act in such a way that Messer Francesco is confirmed in the estimated price; it will show that I am not excluded from the grace of Your most illustrious Ladyship, which [token] I will certainly receive in place of a very great benefice. I hope also that Messer Andrea's courtesy and good nature (*gentilezza*), from which two virtues he never strays far, will mean that your Ladyship has little trouble in this task. Nevertheless I promise you that all the help Your Ladyship gives in resolving the matter of Messer Francesco's pictures with Messer Andrea, Messer Francesco will gratefully repay by helping on your business with Giovanni Bellini, with whom he is usually able to do a great deal. In the meantime he and I remain obliged to Your most illustrious Ladyship, to whose grace we both kiss our hands.

In Venice, 1 January 1506
Your most illustrious Ladyship's servant
Pietro Bembo

73
Letter of Isabella d'Este to Francesco Malatesta, 15 September 1502

Francesco

Since we desire to have in our *camerino* pictures with a story by the excellent painters now in Italy, among whom Perugino is famous, we want you to approach him, or use a friend of his if it seems better, and see if he is willing to undertake a picture according to the story or invention we will give him. The figures will be as small as you know the others are in the said *camerino*. And if he accepts the offer to serve us, find out what he wants as payment; and if he will apply himself to work soon, we will then send him the measurements of the picture with our fantasy. Please reply with diligence.

Mantua, 15 September 1502

74
Letter of Francesco Malatesta to Isabella d'Este, 23 September 1502

My most illustrious Lady

I see Your Ladyship writes to me that I must look for Perugino, the famous painter, and wishes for a picture by his hand. I find that he is at present working in Siena, and is not coming here for eight or ten days. When he returns, I will talk to him and I will use all the diligence I know to make him willing to serve Your Ladyship. It is true that I have heard he is a slow man; I might put it this way, he hardly ever finishes a work he has once begun, so long does he take.

I have heard of another famous painter, who is also much praised, called Filippo di Fra Filippino and I wanted to talk to him. He told me that he could not begin such a work for the next six months, being busy on other works and that perhaps having finished these he could serve Your Ladyship.

Another, Alessandro Botticelli, has been much praised to me as a very good painter and a man who serves willingly and is not so encumbered as the former. I have spoken to him and he says that he will take on the commission at once and serve Your Ladyship gladly.

It has occurred to me to send this news to your Ladyship so that you can choose whichever pleases you the most. I continually recommend myself.

Your servant,
Francesco de' Malatesta

75
Letter of Francesco Malatesta to Isabella d'Este, 24 October 1502

My most illustrious Lady

I have just been with the painter Perugino, about whom Your Ladyship wrote to me some days ago concerning your wish to have a picture by his hand for your *camerino*. The said Perugino says that he will accept the job of doing it, and will compel himself to serve Your Ladyship well. And he asks for you to send the measurements of the picture and similarly the figures to go on it, and to write out the story or subject of the painting as you want it to be. He will then send a reply about the price and the time that it will take him to do it. He says he will use the utmost diligence to serve Your Ladyship both for his own honor and your entire satisfaction.

> And, most illustrious Lady, I remain your servant,
> Francesco Malatesta

76
Instructions of Isabella d'Este to Perugino, 19 January 1503

Drawn up at Florence in the parish of Santa Maria in Campo in the below-mentioned house, in the presence of Bernardo Antonio di Castiglione, Florentine citizen, and Fra Ambrogio, Prior of the Order of Jesuati, near Florence, witnesses.

Lord Francesco de' Malatesta of Mantua, procurator of the Marchioness of Mantua, in the best manner he was able, commissioned from Master Perugino, painter, there present, the undertaking on his own behalf and that of his heirs to make a painting on canvas, 2 1/2 *braccia* high and 3 *braccia* wide, and the said Pietro, the contractor, is obliged to paint on it a certain work of Lasciviousness and Modesty (in conflict) with these and many other embellishments, transmitted in this instruction to the said Pietro by the said Marchioness of Mantua, the copy of which is as follows:

Our poetic invention, which we greatly want to see painted by you, is a battle of Chastity against Lasciviousness, that is to say, Pallas and Diana fighting vigorously against Venus and Cupid. And Pallas should seem almost to have vanquished Cupid, having broken his golden arrow and cast his silver bow underfoot; with one hand she is holding him by the bandage which the blind boy has before his eyes, and with the other she is lifting her lance and about to kill him. By comparison Diana must seem to be having a closer fight with Venus for victory. Venus has been struck by Diana's arrow only on the surface of the body, on her crown and garland, or on a veil she may have around her; and part of Diana's raiment will have been singed by the torch of Venus, but nowhere else will either of them have been wounded. Beyond these four deities, the most chaste nymphs in the trains of Pallas and Diana, in whatever attitudes and ways you please, have to fight fiercely with a lascivious crowd of fauns, satyrs and several thousand cupids; and these cupids must be much smaller than the first [the god Cupid], and not bearing gold bows and silver arrows, but bows and arrows of some baser material such as wood or iron or what you please. And to give more expression and decoration to the picture, beside Pallas I want to have the olive tree sacred to her, with a shield leaning against it bearing the head of Medusa, and with the owl, the bird peculiar to Pallas, perched among the branches. And beside Venus I want her favorite tree, the myrtle, to be placed. But to enhance the beauty a fount of water must be included, such as a river or the sea, where fauns, satyrs and more cupids will be seen, hastening to the help of Cupid, some swimming through the river, some flying, and some riding upon white swans, coming to join such an amorous battle. On the bank of the said river or sea stands Jupiter with other gods, as the enemy of Chastity, changed into the bull which carried off the fair Europa; and Mercury as an eagle circling above its prey, flies around one of Pallas' nymphs, called Glaucera, who carries a casket engraved with the sacred emblems of the goddess. Polyphemus, the one-eyed Cyclops, chases Galatea, and Phoebus chases Daphne, who has already turned into a laurel tree; Pluto, having seized Proserpina, is bearing her off to his kingdom of darkness, and Neptune has seized a nymph who has been turned almost entirely into a raven.

I am sending you all these details in a small drawing, so that with both the written description and the drawing you will be able to consider my wishes in this matter. But if you think that perhaps there are too many figures in this for one picture, it is left to you to reduce them as you please,[3] provided that you do not remove the principal basis, which consists of the four figures of Pallas, Diana, Venus and Cupid. If no inconvenience occurs I shall consider myself well satisfied; you are free to reduce them, but not to add anything else. Please be content with this arrangement.

And to this manner and form the parties are referred.

Master Pietro promised Lord Francesco to devote himself with his skill to achieving the said picture over a period from now until the end of next June, without any exception of law or deed; Lord Francesco promised, in the said names, to pay for the making of the said work a hundred gold florins, in large gold florins, to the said Lord [sic] Pietro, with the agreement that of the said sum twenty gold florins, in large gold florins, should be given at present to the said Lord Pietro, painter; which the said Lord Pietro in the presence of me,

---

3   He did. Polyphemus and Pluto, for instance, seem to be missing from the painting.

the notary, and of the witnesses written above, acknowledged he had received of the said Lord Francesco, and the remainder the said Lord Francesco promised to pay to the said Lord Pietro when the said Lord Pietro completes the said work to perfection and shall give it to Lord Francesco Malatesta of Mantua. And the said Lord Pietro is obliged to complete the said work himself, bearing all the expenses for the same; with an agreement that in the event of the death of the said Master Pietro, should it happen that the said work is not completed, the heirs of the said Master Pietro shall be obliged to restore the said sum of 20 large gold florins to the said Lord Francesco Malatesta, or however much more he has had; or else, in the event of the said work not being completed on account of the death of the said Lord Pietro, that the said Lord Francesco shall be obliged to receive the said work in the form and style so far devised for it, and the said work must be valued by two experienced painters and he must take it for the price they estimate.

77
Letter of Perugino to Isabella d'Este, 10 December 1503

Most Excellent Madam

Having learnt the story which Your Ladyship commissioned from me a short while ago, it seems to me that the drawing sent to me does not correspond very well with the size of the figures, which seem to me to be very small and the height of the picture seems too great in proportion to them. I want to know what is the size of the figures in the other stories which are to go beside it, because if the whole scheme is to turn out well all the measurements must agree, or there must be very little difference. Therefore please arrange for me to be sent this information, so that I can give satisfaction to Your Excellency as is my desire. Nothing else; I recommend myself humbly, praying God keeps you well.

Florence, 10 December 1503
Your Excellency's faithful servant, Pietro Perugino

78
Letter of Isabella d'Este to Perugino, 12 January 1504

Excellent friend

The enclosed paper, and the thread wound round it together give the length of the largest figure on Master Andrea Mantegna's picture, beside which yours will hang. The other figures smaller than this can be as you please. You know how to arrange it. We beg you above all to hasten with the work; the sooner we have it, the more we shall be pleased.

79
Letter of Perugino to Isabella d'Este, 24 January 1504

My most illustrious Lady, Marchioness of Mantua, greeting and infinite recommendations

I sent a letter to you a month and a half ago and I have never had a reply to the said letter. I will repeat what it is about in this: I have drawn some of your figures, which come out very small; I would like Your Ladyship to send me the size of the other stories which are to accompany my story, so that they should conform; and so that the principal figures are all of one size, otherwise they will contradict each other a great deal, one being big and another small. So send me the measurements of the other figures in the other stories that you have had done, and I will at once show my diligence. Nothing further; I recommend myself to Your Ladyship.

24 January 1504
Your Pietro Perugino, painter in Florence

80
Letter of Isabella d'Este to Paride Ceresara,[4] 10 November 1504

Lord Paride Ceresara

Messer Paride – we do not know who finds the slowness of these painters more wearisome, we who fail to have our *camerino* finished, or you who have to devise new schemes every day, which then, because of the bizarre ways of these painters, are neither done as soon nor drawn in entirety as we would have wished; and for this reason we have decided to try our new painters in order to finish it in our lifetime.

---

4 Paride (Paris) Ceresara, of a Mantuan family, was a fairly well-known poet of the court circle.

81
Letter of Isabella d'Este to Agostino Strozzi,[5] Abbot of Fiesole, 19 February 1505

Your Reverence

Domenico Strozzi has informed me that Perugino is not following the scheme for our picture laid down in the drawing. He is doing a certain nude Venus and she was meant to be clothed and doing something different. And this is just to show off the excellence of his art. We have not, however, understood Domenico's description very well, nor do we remember exactly what the drawing was like; so we beg you to examine it well together with Perugino, and likewise the instructions that we sent him in writing. And do your utmost to prevent him departing from it, because by altering one figure he will pervert the whole sentiment of the fable. The instruction was sent as information of what he had to do, so that he could better understand the significance of the fable and not stray from it. We know that Your Reverence will understand it clearly and will know how to correct him if any trouble prevails; but should you be in any doubt you could write to me so that we can clarify it with Messer Paride [Ceresara], who was the author.

82
Letter of Agostino Strozzi to Isabella d'Este, 22 February 1505

My most illustrious and excellent Lady

If Your Excellency's expectation and the hope I have raised in my letters to have your picture by Perugino next Easter should not be fulfilled, you will understand that my utmost solicitude and diligence have not been lacking. But the behavior of this man, unknown to me formerly, I fear will make me seem a liar to Your illustrious Ladyship. It is already about a fortnight since he left Florence, and I cannot discover where he has gone nor when he is going to return. His wife and household either do not know where he is or are unwilling to tell me. I think myself that he has gone to do some work outside Florence and that when it is about Easter he will return. And he intends to finish the work hastily and spoil it, which will cause me unbeliev-

---

5   Apparently a descendant of the branch of the Strozzi family who had fled to Mantua in 1382. Agostino Strozzi, formerly a canon of San Bartolomeo, Mantua, had been well known as a preacher with literary interests before becoming Abbot at Fiesole.

able annoyance and displeasure, because he wanted Your Excellency to be well served, as he was certain he was able and had intended to show, meaning to apply himself with the requisite diligence and to spend the time reasonably needed on it. I do not know what more to say or promise to Your Ladyship: not a day passes without my sending one of us to find out about him, and while he was working on the picture not a week passed without my going to see him at least once. As soon as he returns, should God so please that he does return, I shall be on to him, and I will not fail you in all the diligence of which I am capable so that Your illustrious Ladyship may be well served. I should have thought it might have been a good idea to send him some money to fire his zeal into finishing the work soon and making a good job of it, had he gone on with it. Now I do not know what to say of this man, who does not seem to have the wit to make any distinction between one person and another. I shall be very astonished if art can accomplish in him what nature has been incapable of showing.

I shall not fail with all my strength to labor that you shall be well served.

From our abbey of Fiesole, 22 February 1505
Your illustrious Ladyship's most dedicated
Agostino Strozzi

83
Letter of Perugino to Isabella d'Este, 14 June 1505

Most Illustrious and Exalted Lady, Most Worshipful Lady

I have received the 80 ducats promised me as the price of the picture from the bearer Zorzo, sent by Your Ladyship, and I have consigned the said picture to him; in this I hope I have used sufficient diligence to satisfy both Your exalted Ladyship and my honor, which I have always placed before profit. And I humbly beseech God to grant me the grace of having pleased Your Ladyship, because I have the greatest desire both to serve and please you in whatever I can; and thus I ever offer myself to Your exalted Ladyship as a good servant and friend. And I have done it in tempera because Andrea Mantegna did his that way, so I have been told. If I can do anything else for Your exalted Ladyship I am ready, and I humbly recommend myself to Your Ladyship. Christ keep you in happiness.

Written on 14 June 1505 by your most humble servant
Pietro Perugino, painter in Florence

84
Letter of Isabella d'Este to Perugino, 30 June 1505

The picture has reached me safely, and pleases me, as it is well drawn and colored; but if it had been more carefully finished, it would have been more to your honor and our satisfaction, since it is hung near those of Mantegna, which are painted with rare delicacy. I am sorry that the painter Lorenzo of Mantua advised you not to employ oils, for I should have preferred this method, as it is more effective. Nonetheless, I am, as I said before, well satisfied, and remain kindly disposed towards you.

85
Letter of Isabella d'Este to Fra Pietro da Novellara, 27 March 1501

Most Reverend Father

If Leonardo, the Florentine painter, is now in Florence, we beseech Your Reverence to find out what sort of life he is leading; whether (as we have been informed) he has begun some new work, and what sort of work this is. And if you think he will be staying there for some time, Your Reverence might then sound him as to whether he will take on a picture for our "studio." And if he is pleased to do this, we will leave both the subject and the time of doing it to him. But if you find him unwilling, you might at least induce him to do a little picture of the Madonna, holy and sweet as is his natural manner.

Please also beg him to send us another sketch of our portrait,[6] because our illustrious lord and husband has given away the one which he left us here. For all of this we shall be no less grateful to Your Reverence than to Leonardo. Offering etc.

Mantua, 27 March 1501

86
Letter of Fra Pietro da Novellara to Isabella d'Este, 3 April 1501

Most illustrious and excellent Lady

I have just received a letter from Your Excellency, and I will do as you write with the utmost speed and diligence. But from what I hear Leonardo's life is

6   During his short stay at Mantua in 1500 Leonardo had done a charcoal sketch of her: See Plate 11.

Plate 11   Leonardo da Vinci (1452–1519), *Study for a Portrait of Isabella d'Este*, The Louvre, Paris. *Source*: Réunion des Musées Nationaux/Art Resource, NY.

changeable and very erratic, so that he seems to live just from one day to the next. Since coming to Florence he has only done one sketch, a cartoon depicting the infant Christ about one year old, almost jumping out of his mother's arms to seize hold of a lamb, and he seems to be squeezing it. The mother, almost rising from the lap of St. Anne, is taking hold of the child to draw him away from the little lamb, a spotless creature signifying the Passion. It looks as though St. Anne, rising slightly from her seat, wants to restrain her daughter from parting the child and the little lamb; perhaps she symbolizes the Church, not wishing to prevent the Passion of Christ. And these figures are life-size, but they are on a small cartoon because all are either seated or bending over, one of them being slightly in front of the other on the left-hand side; and this sketch is not yet finished. He has done nothing else, except that his two apprentices are painting portraits and he sometimes adds a few touches. He is working hard at geometry and has absolutely no patience to spare for painting. I am only writing this so that Your Excellency may know that I have received your letter. I will perform the commission and send you the news very shortly; and I pray God to keep your Excellency in His Grace.

Florence, 3 April 1501
Fra Petrus Nuvolara, Vicar-General of the Carmelites

87
Letter of Fra Pietro da Novellara to Isabella d'Este, 14 April 1501

Most illustrious and excellent Lady

This Holy Week I have succeeded in learning the painter Leonardo's intentions by means of his pupil, Salai, and some of his other friends, who, to make him more known to me, took me to see him on Wednesday in Holy Week. In short, his mathematical experiments have so distracted him from painting that he cannot bear the sight of a paintbrush. Still, I endeavored as skillfully as I could to make him understand Your Excellency's point of view. Then, finding him well disposed to gratify you, I frankly told him everything, and we came to this conclusion: if he can, as he hopes, break off his engagement with the King of France without falling into disfavor, within a month at the longest, he would serve Your Excellency sooner than any other person in the world. But in any case, as soon as he has finished a certain little picture which he is painting for one Robertet, a favorite of the King of France, he will do your portrait immediately and send it to you. I left two good petitioners with him. The little picture which he is painting is a Madonna, seated as winding [thread on] spindles, and the Child, with his foot on the basket of spindles, has taken up the winder, and looks attentively at the four rays in the shape of a cross, as if wishing for the cross, and holds it tight, laughing and refusing to give it to his mother, who seems to be trying to take it from him. This is all I have been able to settle with him [Leonardo]. I preached my sermon yesterday; God grant it may bring forth much fruit in proportion to the copious numbers who heard it.

Fra Petrus de Novellara
Florence, 14 April 1501

88
Letter of Isabella d'Este to Leonardo da Vinci,[7] 14 May 1504

To Master Leonardo da Vinci, painter

Master Leonardo – Hearing that you are staying in Florence, we have conceived the hope that something we have long desired might come true: to have something by your hand. When you were here and drew our portrait in charcoal, you promised one day to do it in color. But because this would be almost impossible, since it would be inconvenient for you to move here, we beg you to keep your good faith with us by substituting for our portrait another figure even more acceptable to us: that is, to do a youthful Christ of about twelve years old, which would be the age he was when he disputed with the doctors in the Temple, and executed with that sweetness and soft ethereal charm which is the peculiar excellence of your art. If we are gratified by you in this strong desire of ours, you shall know that beyond the payment, which you yourself shall fix, we shall remain so obliged to you that we shall think of nothing else but to do you good service, and from this very moment we offer ourselves to act at your convenience and pleasure. Expecting a favorable reply, we offer ourselves to do all your pleasure.

Mantua, 14 May 1504

89
Letter of Isabella d'Este to Leonardo da Vinci, 31 October 1504

To Master Leonardo Vinci, painter

Master Leonardo: Some months ago we wrote to you that we wanted to have a young Christ, about twelve years old, by your hand; you have replied through Messer Angelo Tovaglia that you would do this gladly; but owing to the many commissioned works you have on your hands, we doubt whether you have remembered ours. Wherefore it has occurred to us to send you these few lines, begging you that when you are tired of the Florentine historical theme, you will turn to doing this little figure for us by way of recreation, which will be doing us a very gracious service and of benefit to yourself.

Farewell
Mantua, 31 October 1504

7   Enclosed in a letter to Angelo Tovaglia.

90

Letter of Alessandro Amadori, Canon of Fiesole and Uncle of Leonardo, to Isabella d'Este, 3 May 1506

My most illustrious and respected Lady

Since I came back to Florence I have been acting all the time as Your Ladyship's proctor with my nephew Leonardo da Vinci. I do not cease to urge him to make an effort to satisfy Your Ladyship's desire concerning the figure for which you asked him, and which he promised several months ago in his letter to me which I showed to Your Excellency. He has promised that he will begin the work shortly in order to satisfy Your Ladyship's desire; and commends himself very warmly to your graces. And if while I am in Florence you could signify whether you would prefer to have one figure rather than another I will take care that Leonardo satisfies your taste. Above all it is my desire to oblige you. I visited Madonna Argentina[8] this afternoon, and she was very glad to hear of Your Ladyship's safe arrival at Mantua. I added that Your Ladyship commended and offered yourself to her and she was much obliged, and it occurred to her to write the enclosed note to Your Ladyship. Nothing else occurs to me at present. May God prosper Your Excellency, to whom I humbly commend myself.

Florence, 3 May 1506

Your servant, Alessandro Amadori

91

Letter of Taddeo Albano to Isabella d'Este, 8 November 1510

Most illustrious and excellent and my most respected Lady

I understood that as Your Excellency wrote in your letter of the twenty-fifth of last month that you had heard that a picture of a very beautiful and singular night scene was to be found among the belongings and inheritance of a certain Giorgio of Castelfranco,[9] you wanted to see if you could have it. To which I reply to your Excellency that the said Giorgio died some days ago, of plague, and out of my wish to do you service, I have spoken to several of my friends who had very close dealings with him, who inform me that no such picture is among his inheritance. It is true that the said Giorgio did one for Messer Taddeo Contarini, which according to information I have had is not as perfect as you would wish. The said Giorgio did another night picture

8   Wife of Piero Soderini, Standardbearer of Justice or first magistrate of the republic from 1502 to 1512.
9   i.e., the painter Giorgione.

for a Vittorio Becharo, which I understand is better designed and finished than Contarini's. But this Becharo is not to be found here at present, and from what I have been told neither picture is for sale at any price; they had them painted for their own enjoyment. So I regret not being able to satisfy your Ladyship's desire etc.

At Venice, 8 November 1510
Your Servant, Taddeo Albano

92
Letter of Isabella d'Este to Matteo Ippoliti, 24 May 1512

Federico Gonzaga, Isabella d'Este's child, was kept in the papal court for several years as a hostage for his father's political loyalty. In this letter, his mother's expressed preference for Raphael to paint his portrait is hardly surprising: few artists could have been more congenial to her taste for "sweetness."

Because I had to give away the portrait of our son Federico which was done at Bologna, we want another one, especially since we hear he has grown even more handsome and more graceful. We want you to see whether the painter Raphael, son of Giovanni Santi of Urbino, is in Rome, and ask him whether he is willing to paint him in armor from the chest down. If Raphael is not to be found, seek the next best painter, because we do not want a second-rate man to do the portrait but a good master. We will treat him with honor and courtesy, as you know to be our custom, and warn him to do it life-size and as quickly as possible. You could do nothing to please me better.

24 May 1512

16

Benvenuto Cellini (1500–1571)

Cellini was famous in his own time as a goldsmith, medal-maker, and sculptor whose outstanding creations included a jeweled golden salt-cellar, portrait medals of Pope Clement VII, and a bronze statue of Perseus holding aloft the severed head of the Medusa (see plate 10). Today he is known most widely for his autobiography, begun in 1558, but not published until a century and a half later. From a family of craftsmen, Cellini trained in Florence to be a goldsmith, and in subsequent years he worked in a variety of cities, including Siena, Rome, Padua, Ferrara, and Paris. He numbered among his patrons some of the most powerful people in Europe, including King Francis I, Pope Clement VII, and Pope Paul III. Yet his personal flamboyance cost him the good will of many who had initially supported him, and he was frequently in trouble with the law. For example, in 1523 in Florence he was prosecuted for sodomy; in Rome over a decade later, he was charged with murdering another goldsmith; and in 1545 in Paris he was accused of embezzling some of the silver entrusted to him for making candle-sticks. In all three instances, he rapidly left town, only to find new patrons – and develop new enmities – elsewhere.

Cellini took to writing only after he had lost the favor of Cosimo I of Florence. Thus his patron's loss has become our gain, for his autobiography is one of the liveliest reads in Renaissance literature. The following passage centers on Cellini's activities during the sack and occupation of Rome in 1527.

Questions

1 What social position does Cellini see himself as occupying? Whom does he view as peers? Whom does he ridicule as beneath him?

2   Not shy about self-congratulation, Cellini makes many bold claims about his accomplishments, including an assertion that he fired the shot that killed Bourbon in the sack of Rome. How reliable do you think his account is of this and other achievements? How does he portray other people's perceptions of him?

3   Would a career like Cellini's have been possible a century earlier? If so, who resembles him? If not, what changed since the time of Cosimo "The Elder" de' Medici that facilitated the rise and professional survival of a figure like Cellini?

4   The genre of autobiography has at times been used for painful self-scrutiny, as for example in the early chapters of Augustine's *Confessions*. Clearly, however, agonizing introspection is not a mode that Cellini finds congenial. What do you think motivates him to write? Finally, is there anything distinctly "Renaissance" about his autobiography?

Autobiography I, 34–9

34

The whole world was now in warfare.[1] Pope Clement had sent to get some troops from Giovanni de' Medici, and when they came, they made such disturbances in Rome, that it was ill living in open shops.[2] On this account I retired to a good snug house behind the Banchi, where I worked for all the friends I had acquired. Since I produced few things of much importance at that period, I need not waste time in talking about them. I took much pleasure in music and amusements of the kind. On the death of Giovanni de' Medici in Lombardy, the Pope, at the advice of Messer Jacopo Salviati, dismissed the five bands he had engaged; and when the Constable of Bourbon knew there were no troops in Rome, he pushed his army with the utmost energy up to the city. The whole of Rome upon this flew to arms. I happened to be intimate with Alessandro, the son of Piero del Bene, who, at the time

1   As the chapter begins, the Imperial army commanded by Charles of Bourbon is advancing toward Rome, which they would conquer and sack on May 6, 1527.
2   These troops, called the black bands, had entered Rome in October 1526. They were disbanded in March 1527.

when the Colonnesi entered Rome, had requested me to guard his palace.[3] On this more serious occasion, therefore, he prayed me to enlist fifty comrades for the protection of the said house, appointing me their captain, as I had been when the Colonnesi came. So I collected fifty young men of the highest courage, and we took up our quarters in his palace, with good pay and excellent appointments.

Bourbon's army had now arrived before the walls of Rome, and Alessandro begged me to go with him to reconnoiter. So we went with one of the stoutest fellows in our company; and on the way a youth called Cecchino della Casa joined himself to us. On reaching the walls by the Campo Santo, we could see that famous army, which was making every effort to enter the town. Upon the ramparts where we took our station, several young men were lying killed by the besiegers; the battle raged there desperately, and there was the densest fog imaginable. I turned to Alessandro and said: "Let us go home as soon as we can, for there is nothing to be done here; you see the enemies are mounting, and our men are in flight." Alessandro, in a panic, cried: "Would God that we had never come here!" and turned in maddest haste to fly. I took him up somewhat sharply with these words: "Since you have brought me here, I must perform some action worthy of a man"; and directing my arquebus where I saw the thickest and most serried troop of fighting men, I aimed exactly at one whom I remarked to be higher than the rest: the fog prevented me from being certain whether he was on horseback or on foot. Then I turned to Alessandro and Cecchino, and bade them discharge their arquebuses, showing them how to avoid being hit by the besiegers. When we had fired two rounds apiece, I crept cautiously up to the wall, and observing among the enemy a most extraordinary confusion, I discovered afterwards that one of our shots had killed the Constable of Bourbon; and from what I subsequently learned, he was the man whom I had first noticed above the heads of the rest.[4]

Quitting our position on the ramparts, we crossed the Campo Santo, and entered the city of St. Peter's; then coming out exactly at the church of Santo Agnolo, we got with the greatest difficulty to the great gate of the castle; for the generals Renzo da Ceri and Orazio Baglioni were wounding and

3   Cellini here refers to the attack made upon Rome by the great Ghibelline house of Colonna, led by their chief captain, Pompeo, in September 1526. They took possession of the city and drove Clement into the Castel Sant' Angelo, where they forced him to agree to terms favoring the Imperial cause. It was customary for Roman gentlemen to hire armed men for the defense of their palaces when any extraordinary disturbance was expected, as, for example, following the death of a pope.

4   All historians of the sack of Rome agree in saying that Bourbon was shot dead while placing ladders against the outworks near the shop Cellini mentions. But the honor of firing the arquebus which brought him down cannot be assigned to any one in particular. Very different stories were current on the subject.

slaughtering everybody who abandoned the defense of the walls.[5] By the time we had reached the great gate, part of the foemen had already entered Rome, and we had them in our rear. The castellan had ordered the portcullis to be lowered, in order to do which they cleared a little space, and this enabled us four to get inside. On the instant that I entered, the captain Pallone de' Medici claimed me as being of the Papal household, and forced me to abandon Alessandro, which I had to do, much against my will. I ascended to the keep, and at the same instant Pope Clement came in through the corridors into the castle; he had refused to leave the palace of St. Peter earlier, being unable to believe that his enemies would effect their entrance into Rome.[6] Having got into the castle in this way, I attached myself to certain pieces of artillery, which were under the command of a bombardier called Giuliano Fiorentino. Leaning there against the battlements, the unhappy man could see his poor house being sacked, and his wife and children outraged; fearing to strike his own folk, he dared not discharge the cannon, and flinging the burning fuse upon the ground, he wept as though his heart would break, and tore his cheeks with both his hands.[7] Some of the other bombardiers were behaving in like manner; seeing which, I took one of the matches, and got the assistance of a few men who were not overcome by their emotions. I aimed some swivels and falconets at points where I saw it would be useful, and killed with them a good number of the enemy. Had it not been for this, the troops who poured into Rome that morning, and were marching straight upon the castle, might possibly have entered it with ease, because the artillery was doing them no damage. I went on firing under the eyes of several cardinals and lords, who kept blessing me and giving me the heartiest encouragement. In my enthusiasm I strove to achieve the impossible; let it suffice that it was I who saved the castle that morning, and brought the other bombardiers back to their duty.[8] I worked hard the

---

5   Renzo da Ceri (Renzo Orsini), a distinguished military commander, had been entrusted with Rome's defense, in which capacity he proved utterly ineffective. Orazio Baglioni, of the semi-princely Perugian family, was a distinguished Condottiere. He subsequently obtained the captaincy of the Bande Nere, and died fighting near Naples in 1528. Orazio murdered several of his cousins in order to acquire the lordship of Perugia. His brother Malatesta undertook to defend Florence in the siege of 1530, and sold the city by treason to Clement.

6   Paolo Giovio, a humanist and historian employed by the pope, relates how he accompanied Clement in his flight from the Vatican to the castle. While passing some open portions of the gallery, he threw his violet mantle and cap of a Monsignore over the white stole of the Pontiff, for fear he might be shot at by the soldiers in the streets below.

7   The short autobiography of Raffaello da Montelupo, a man in many respects resembling Cellini, confirms this part of our author's narrative. It is one of the most interesting pieces of evidence regarding what went on inside the castle during the sack of Rome. Montelupo was also a gunner, and commanded two pieces.

8   This is an instance of Cellini's exaggeration. He did more than yeoman's service, no doubt. But we cannot believe that, without him, the castle would have been taken.

whole of that day; and when the evening came, while the army was marching into Rome through the Trastevere, Pope Clement appointed a great
Roman nobleman named Antonio Santacroce to be captain of all the
gunners. The first thing this man did was to come to me, and having greeted
me with the utmost kindness, he stationed me with five fine pieces of artillery
on the highest point of the castle, to which the name of the Angel specially
belongs. This circular eminence goes round the castle, and surveys both Prati
and the town of Rome. The captain put under my orders enough men to help
in managing my guns, and having seen me paid in advance, he gave me
rations of bread and a little wine, and begged me to go forward as I had
begun. I was perhaps more inclined by nature to the profession of arms than
to the one I had adopted, and I took such pleasure in its duties that I
discharged them better than those of my own art. Night came, the enemy
had entered Rome, and we who were in the castle (especially myself, who
have always taken pleasure in extraordinary sights) stayed gazing on the
indescribable scene of tumult and conflagration in the streets below. People
who were anywhere else but where we were, could not have formed the least
imagination of what it was. I will not, however, set myself to describe that
tragedy, but will content myself with continuing the history of my own life
and the circumstances which properly belong to it.

35

During the course of my artillery practice, which I never intermitted through
the whole month passed by us beleaguered in the castle, I met with a great
many very striking accidents, all of them worthy to be related. But since I do
not care to be too prolix, or to exhibit myself outside the sphere of my
profession, I will omit the larger part of them, only touching upon those I
cannot well neglect, which shall be the fewest in number and the most
remarkable. The first which comes to hand is this: Messer Antonio Santacroce had made me come down from the Angel, in order to fire on some
houses in the neighborhood, where certain of our besiegers had been seen to
enter. While I was firing, a cannon shot reached me, which hit the angle of a
battlement, and carried off enough of it to be the cause why I sustained no
injury. The whole mass struck me in the chest and took my breath away. I lay
stretched upon the ground like a dead man, and could hear what the
bystanders were saying. Among them all, Messer Antonio Santacroce
lamented greatly, exclaiming: "Alas, alas! we have lost the best defender
that we had." Attracted by the uproar, one of my comrades ran up; he was
called Gianfrancesco, and was a bandsman, but was far more naturally given
to medicine than to music. On the spot he flew off, crying for a stoop of the
very best Greek wine. Then he made a tile red-hot, and cast upon it a good

handful of wormwood; after which he sprinkled the Greek wine; and when the wormwood was well soaked, he laid it on my breast, just where the bruise was visible to all. Such was the virtue of the wormwood that I immediately regained my scattered faculties. I wanted to begin to speak, but could not; for some stupid soldiers had filled my mouth with earth, imagining that by so doing they were giving me the sacrament; and indeed they were more like to have excommunicated me, since I could with difficulty come to myself again, the earth doing me more mischief than the blow. However, I escaped that danger, and returned to the rage and fury of the guns, pursuing my work there with all the ability and eagerness that I could summon.

Pope Clement, by this, had sent to demand assistance from the Duke of Urbino, who was with the troops of Venice; he commissioned the envoy to tell his Excellency that the Castle Sant' Angelo would send up every evening three beacons from its summit, accompanied by three discharges of the cannon thrice repeated, and that so long as this signal was continued, he might take for granted that the castle had not yielded. I was charged with lighting the beacons and firing the guns for this purpose; and all this while I pointed my artillery by day upon the places where mischief could be done. The Pope, in consequence, began to regard me with still greater favor, because he saw that I discharged my functions as intelligently as the task demanded. Aid from the Duke of Urbino never came; on which, as it is not my business, I will make no further comment.[9]

36

While I was at work upon that diabolical task of mine, there came from time to time to watch me some of the cardinals who were invested in the castle, and most frequently the Cardinal of Ravenna and the Cardinal de' Gaddi.[10] I often told them not to show themselves, since their nasty red caps gave a fair mark to our enemies. From neighboring buildings, such as the Torre de' Bini, we ran great peril when they were there; and at last I had them locked off, and gained thereby their deep ill-will. I frequently received visits also from

9   Francesco Maria Della Rovere, Duke of Urbino, commanded a considerable army as general of the Church, and was now acting for Venice. Why he effected no diversion while the Imperial troops were marching upon Rome, and why he delayed to relieve the city, was never properly explained. Folk attributed his impotent conduct partly to a natural sluggishness in warfare, and partly to his hatred for the house of Medici. Leo X had deprived him of his dukedom, and given it to a Medicean prince. It is to this that Cellini probably refers in the cautious phrase which ends the chapter.

10   Benedetto Accolti of Arezzo, Archbishop of Ravenna in 1524, obtained the hat in 1527, three days before the sack of Rome. He was a distinguished man of letters. Niccolò Gaddi was created Cardinal on the same day as Accolti.

the general, Orazio Baglioni, who was very well affected toward me. One day while he was talking with me, he noticed something going forward in a drinking-place outside the Porta di Castello, which bore the name of Baccanello. This tavern had for a sign a sun painted between two windows, of a bright red color. The windows being closed, Signor Orazio concluded that a band of soldiers were carousing at table just between them and behind the sun. So he said to me: "Benvenuto, if you think that you could hit that wall an ell's breadth from the sun with your demi-cannon here, I believe you would be doing a good stroke of business, for there is a great commotion there, and men of much importance must probably be inside the house." I answered that I felt quite capable of hitting the sun in its center, but that a barrel full of stones, which was standing close to the muzzle of the gun, might be knocked down by the shock of the discharge and the blast of the artillery. He rejoined: "Don't waste time, Benvenuto. In the first place, it is not possible, where it is standing, that the cannon's blast should bring it down; and even if it were to fall, and the Pope himself was underneath, the mischief would not be so great as you imagine. Fire, then, only fire!" Taking no more thought about it, I struck the sun in the center, exactly as I said I should. The cask was dislodged, as I predicted, and fell precisely between Cardinal Farnese[11] and Messer Jacopo Salviati. It might very well have dashed out the brains of both of them, except that just at that very moment Farnese was reproaching Salviati with having caused the sack of Rome, and while they stood apart from one another to exchange opprobrious remarks, my gabion fell without destroying them. When he heard the uproar in the court below, good Signor Orazio dashed off in a hurry; and I, thrusting my neck forward where the cask had fallen, heard some people saying: "It would not be a bad job to kill that gunner!" Upon this I turned two falconets toward the staircase, with mind resolved to let blaze on the first man who attempted to come up. The household of Cardinal Farnese must have received orders to go and do me some injury; accordingly I prepared to receive them, with a lighted match in hand. Recognizing some who were approaching, I called out: "You lazy lubbers, if you don't pack off from there, and if but a man's child among you dares to touch the staircase, I have got two cannon loaded, which will blow you into powder. Go and tell the Cardinal that I was acting at the order of superor officers, and that what we have done and are doing is in defense of them priests,[12] and not to hurt them." They made away; and then came Signor Orazio Baglioni, running. I bade him stand back, else I'd murder him; for I knew very well who he was. He drew back a little, not without a certain show of fear, and called out: "Benvenuto, I am your friend!" To this I answered: "Sir, come up, but come alone, and then come as you like." The

11   Cardinal Alessandro Farnese, who in 1534 became Pope Paul III.
12   "Loro preti." Perhaps their priests.

general, who was a man of mighty pride, stood still a moment, and then said angrily: "I have a good mind not to come up again, and to do quite the opposite of that which I intended toward you." I replied that just as I was put there to defend my neighbors, I was equally well able to defend myself too. He said that he was coming alone; and when he arrived at the top of the stairs, his features were more discomposed than I thought reasonable. So I kept my hand upon my sword, and stood eyeing him askance. Upon this he began to laugh, and the color coming back into his face, he said to me with the most pleasant manner: "Friend Benvenuto, I bear you as great love as I have it in my heart to give; and in God's good time I will render you proof of this. Would to God that you had killed those two rascals; for one of them, is the cause of all this trouble, and the day perchance will come when the other will be found the cause of something even worse." He then begged me, if I should be asked, not to say that he was with me when I fired the gun; and for the rest bade me be of good cheer. The commotion which the affair made was enormous, and lasted a long while. However, I will not enlarge upon it further, only adding that I was within an inch of revenging my father on Messer Jacopo Salviati, who had grievously injured him, according to my father's frequent complaints. As it was, unwittingly I gave the fellow a great fright. Of Farnese I shall say nothing here, because it will appear in its proper place how well it would have been if I had killed him.

37

I pursued my business of artilleryman, and every day performed some extraordinary feat, whereby the credit and the favor I acquired with the Pope was something indescribable. There never passed a day but what I killed one or another of our enemies in the besieging army. On one occasion the Pope was walking round the circular keep,[13] when he observed a Spanish Colonel in the Prati; he recognized the man by certain indications, seeing that this officer had formerly been in his service; and while he fixed his eyes on him, he kept talking about him. I, above by the Angel, knew nothing of all this, but spied a fellow down there, busying himself about the trenches with a javelin in his hand; he was dressed entirely in rose-color; and so, studying the worst that I could do against him, I selected a gerfalcon which I had at hand; it is a piece of ordnance larger and longer than a swivel, and about the size of a demi-culverin. This I emptied, and loaded it again with a good charge of fine powder mixed with the coarser sort; then I aimed it exactly at the man in red, elevating prodigiously, because a piece of that

13 The main body of the Castel Sant' Angelo, so called because of the statue of an angel at its top.

caliber could hardly be expected to carry true at such a distance. I fired, and hit my man exactly in the middle. He had trussed his sword in front,[14] for swagger, after a way those Spaniards have; and my ball, when it struck him, broke upon the blade, and one could see the fellow cut in two fair halves. The Pope, who was expecting nothing of this kind, derived great pleasure and amazement from the sight, both because it seemed to him impossible that one should aim and hit the mark at such a distance, and also because the man was cut in two, and he could not comprehend how this should happen. He sent for me, and asked about it. I explained all the devices I had used in firing; but told him that why the man was cut in halves, neither he nor I could know. Upon my bended knees I then besought him to give me the pardon of his blessing for that homicide; and for all the others I had committed in the castle in the service of the Church. Thereat the Pope, raising his hand, and making a large open sign of the cross upon my face, told me that he blessed me, and that he gave me pardon for all murders I had ever perpetrated, or should ever perpetrate, in the service of the Apostolic Church. When I left him, I went aloft, and never stayed from firing to the utmost of my power; and few were the shots of mine that missed their mark. My drawing, and my fine studies in my craft, and my charming art of music, all were swallowed up in the din of that artillery, and if I were to relate in detail all the splendid things I did in that infernal work of cruelty, I should make the world stand by and wonder. But, not to be too prolix, I will pass them over. Only I must tell a few of the most remarkable, which are, as it were, forced in upon me.

To begin then: pondering day and night what I could render for my own part in defense of Holy Church, and having noticed that the enemy changed guard and marched past through the great gate of Santo Spirito, which was within a reasonable range, I thereupon directed my attention to that spot; but, having to shoot sideways, I could not do the damage that I wished, although I killed a fair percentage every day. This induced our adversaries, when they saw their passage covered by my guns, to load the roof of a certain house one night with thirty gabions, which obstructed the view I formerly enjoyed. Taking better thought than I had done of the whole situation, I now turned all my five pieces of artillery directly on the gabions, and waited till the evening hour, when they changed guard. Our enemies, thinking they were safe, came on at greater ease and in a closer body than usual; where-upon I set fire to my blow-pipes.[15] Not merely did I dash to pieces the gabions which stood in my way; but, what was better, by that one blast I slaughtered more than thirty men. In consequence of this maneuver, which I repeated twice, the soldiers were thrown into such disorder, that being, moreover, encumbered with the spoils of that great sack, and some of them desirous of

14 "S'aveva messo la spada dinanzi." Perhaps was bearing his sword in front of him.
15 "Soffioni," the cannon being like tubes to blow a fire up.

enjoying the fruits of their labor, they oftentimes showed a mind to mutiny and take themselves away from Rome. However, after coming to terms with their valiant captain, Juan de Urbina,[16] they were ultimately compelled, at their excessive inconvenience, to take another road when they changed guard. It cost them three miles of march, whereas before they had but half a mile. Having achieved this feat, I was entreated with prodigious favors by all the men of quality who were invested in the castle. This incident was so important that I thought it well to relate it, before finishing the history of things outside my art, the which is the real object of my writing; forsooth, if I wanted to ornament my biography with such matters, I should have far too much to tell. There is only one more circumstance which, now that the occasion offers, I propose to record.

38

I shall skip over some intervening circumstances, and tell how Pope Clement, wishing to save the tiaras and the whole collection of the great jewels of the Apostolic Camera, had me called, and shut himself up together with me and the Cavalierino in a room alone. This Cavalierino had been a groom in the stable of Filippo Strozzi; he was French, and a person of the lowest birth; but being a most faithful servant, the Pope had made him very rich, and confided in him like himself. So the Pope, the Cavaliere, and I, being shut up together, they laid before me the tiaras and jewels of the regalia; and his Holiness ordered me to take all the gems out of their gold settings. This I accordingly did; afterwards I wrapt them separately up in bits of paper, and we sewed them into the linings of the Pope's and the Cavaliere's clothes. Then they gave me all the gold, which weighed about two hundred pounds, and bade me melt it down as secretly as I was able. I went up to the Angel, where I had my lodging, and could lock the door so as to be free from interruption. There I built a little draught-furnace of bricks, with a largish pot, shaped like an open dish, at the bottom of it; and throwing the gold upon the coals, it gradually sank through and dropped into the pan. While the furnace was working, I never left off watching how to annoy our enemies; and as their trenches were less than a stone's-throw right below us, I was able to inflict considerable damage on them with some useless missiles, of which there were several piles, forming the old munition of the castle. I chose a swivel and a falconet, which were both a little damaged in the muzzle, and filled them with the

16   This captain was a Spaniard, who played a very considerable figure in the war, distinguishing himself at the capture of Genoa and the battle of Lodi in 1522, and afterwards acting as Lieutenant-General to the Prince of Orange. He held Naples against Orazio Baglioni in 1528, and died before Spello in 1529.

projectiles I have mentioned. When I fired my guns, they hurtled down like mad, occasioning all sorts of unexpected mischief in the trenches. Accordingly I kept these pieces always going at the same time that the gold was being melted down; and a little before vespers I noticed some one coming along the margin of the trench on muleback. The mule was trotting very quickly, and the man was talking to the soldiers in the trenches. I took the precaution of discharging my artillery just before he came immediately opposite; and so, making a good calculation, I hit my mark. One of the fragments struck him in the face; the rest were scattered on the mule, which fell dead. A tremendous uproar rose up from the trench; I opened fire with my other piece, doing them great hurt. The man turned out to be the Prince of Orange, who was carried through the trenches to a certain tavern in the neighborhood, whither in a short while all the chief folk of the army came together.

When Pope Clement heard what I had done, he sent at once to call for me, and inquired into the circumstance. I related the whole, and added that the man must have been of the greatest consequence, because the inn to which they carried him had been immediately filled by all the chiefs of the army, so far at least as I could judge. The Pope, with a shrewd instinct, sent for Messer Antonio Santacroce, the nobleman who, as I have said, was chief and commander of the gunners. He bade him order all us bombardiers to point our pieces, which were very numerous, in one mass upon the house, and to discharge them all together upon the signal of an arquebus being fired. He judged that if we killed the generals, the army, which was already almost on the point of breaking up, would take to flight. God perhaps had heard the prayers they kept continually making, and meant to rid them in this manner of those impious scoundrels.

We put our cannon in order at the command of Santacroce, and waited for the signal. But when Cardinal Orsini[17] became aware of what was going forward, he began to expostulate with the Pope, protesting that the thing by no means ought to happen, seeing they were on the point of concluding an accommodation, and that if the generals were killed, the rabble of the troops without a leader would storm the castle and complete their utter ruin. Consequently they could by no means allow the Pope's plan to be carried out. The poor Pope, in despair, seeing himself assassinated both inside the castle and without, said that he left them to arrange it. On this, our orders were countermanded; but I, who chafed against the leash, when I knew that they were coming round to bid me stop from firing, let blaze one of my demicannons, and struck a pillar in the courtyard of the house, around which I

17　Franciotto Orsini was educated in the household of his kinsman Lorenzo de' Medici. He followed the profession of arms, and married; but after losing his wife took orders, and received the hat in 1517.

saw a crowd of people clustering. This shot did such damage to the enemy that it was like to have made them evacuate the house. Cardinal Orsini was absolutely for having me hanged or put to death; but the Pope took up my cause with spirit. The high words that passed between them, though I well know what they were, I will not here relate, because I make no profession of writing history. It is enough for me to occupy myself with my own affairs.

39

After I had melted down the gold, I took it to the Pope, who thanked me cordially for what I had done, and ordered the Cavalierino to give me twenty-five crowns, apologizing to me for his inability to give me more. A few days afterwards the articles of peace were signed. I went with three hundred comrades in the train of Signor Orazio Baglioni toward Perugia; and there he wished to make me captain of the company, but I was unwilling at the moment, saying that I wanted first to go and see my father, and to redeem the ban which was still in force against me at Florence. Signor Orazio told me that he had been appointed general of the Florentines; and Sir Pier Maria del Lotto, the envoy from Florence, was with him, to whom he specially recommended me as his man.[18]

In course of time I came to Florence in the company of several comrades. The plague was raging with indescribable fury. When I reached home, I found my good father, who thought either that I must have been killed in the sack of Rome, or else that I should come back to him a beggar. However, I entirely defeated both these expectations; for I was alive, with plenty of money, a fellow to wait on me, and a good horse. My joy on greeting the old man was so intense, that, while he embraced and kissed me, I thought that I must die upon the spot. After I had narrated all the devilries of that dreadful sack, and had given him a good quantity of crowns which I had gained by my soldiering, and when we had exchanged our tokens of affection, he went off to the Eight to redeem my ban. It so happened that one of those magistrates who sentenced me, was now again a member of the board. It was the very man who had so inconsiderately told my father he meant to march me out into the country with the lances. My father took this opportunity of addressing him with some meaning words, in order to mark his revenge, relying on the favor which Orazio Baglioni showed me.

Matters standing thus, I told my father how Signor Orazio had appointed me captain, and that I ought to begin to think of enlisting my company. At

18   Pier Maria di Lotto of S. Miniato was notary to the Florentine Signoria. He collected the remnants of the Bande Nere, and gave them over to Orazio Baglioni, who contrived to escape from S. Angelo in safety to Perugia.

these words the poor old man was greatly disturbed, and begged me for God's sake not to turn my thoughts to such an enterprise, although he knew I should be fit for this or yet a greater business, adding that his other son, my brother, was already a most valiant soldier, and that I ought to pursue the noble art in which I had labored so many years and with such diligence of study. Although I promised to obey him, he reflected, like a man of sense, that if Signor Orazio came to Florence, I could not withdraw myself from military service, partly because I had passed my word, as well as for other reasons. He therefore thought of a good expedient for sending me away, and spoke to me as follows: "Oh, my dear son, the plague in this town is raging with immitigable violence, and I am always fancying you will come home infected with it. I remember, when I was a young man, that I went to Mantua, where I was very kindly received, and stayed there several years. I pray and command you, for the love of me, to pack off and go thither; and I would have you do this today rather than tomorrow."

Part VII

The End of the Renaissance

Introduction to Part VII

It is difficult to determine the endpoint of a cultural movement, especially of one so widely diffused and influential as the Italian Renaissance. Often an important event, such as the excommunication of Luther in 1521, or the sack of Rome in 1527, has served as a convenient *terminus ad quem*. Underlying such choices has been a sense that in the sixteenth century, Italy was beginning a slow decline into irrelevance that would be reversed only in the *Risorgimento*. Recent scholarship, however, has demonstrated the continuing vitality of the Italian economy, a surprising degree of political autonomy (for example, in Cosimo I de' Medici's Tuscany) despite Habsburg overlordship, and a symbiosis between high culture and Catholic reform rather than a simple opposition of one to the other. Nor did cultural creativity, whether in art, music, or humanism, disappear so quickly as has often been assumed.

Surely one indicator of meaningful change can be found in the perceptions of those living at the time. Petrarch had believed that he lived at the beginning of a new age. Leonardo Bruni, who credited Petrarch with having "opened the way," saw himself as participating in the new age. At least by the 1520s, however, we encounter some nostalgic visions that suggest that the golden age of Italian Renaissance culture might already be a thing of the past. In the final selections below, consider how we ought to interpret this perception of loss. Do such writings signal the end of Renaissance culture, or are they a further articulation of that culture? Or, might they perhaps be both at once?

17

Baldassare Castiglione (1478–1529)

Baldassare Castiglione, who was born in the duchy of Mantua, received a classical education in Milan before pursuing a diplomatic career. Initially working for Francesco Gonzaga (Isabella d'Este's husband), he later spent a decade in the service of the duchy of Urbino, and his final appointment came from Pope Clement VII, whom he served from 1525 to 1529 as papal nuncio to the court of Charles V in Spain. His fame rests, however, on the *Book of the Courtier*, a dialogue in Italian set in the court of Urbino in 1506. Although he wrote the dialogue mostly in the following decade, he continued revising it until its publication in 1528. Immensely popular, the book was translated into several languages within the next half-century, and it inspired the composition of many other "courtesy" books.

In Castiglione's dialogue, a group of aristocrats are gathered for an evening of conversation. Although he has named the interlocutors for particular individuals who could all have been present at the time, he has taken liberties in how he represents them. The game they select for their diversion is to imagine in words the perfect Courtier. This ideal figure, they assert, should have a variety of skills, ranging from horsemanship and military prowess to being able to speak and write well. In all that he does, however, the Courtier must appear graceful and natural, avoiding any hint of affectation. Thus he is to "practice in all things a certain *sprezzatura* [nonchalance], so as to conceal all art and make whatever is done or said appear to be without effort and almost without any thought about it" (I, 27). The selection that follows, drawn from the last quarter of the dialogue, concerns the ways in which the ideal Courtier may act as adviser to his prince.

Plate 12 Raphael (1483–1520), *Portrait of Baldassare Castiglione*, The Louvre, Paris. *Source*: Réunion des Musées Nationaux/Art Resource, NY.

Renowned today above all for his narrative frescoes in the Vatican *stanze*, such as the *Disputà* and the *School of Athens*, Raphael also painted a number of portraits. These include some likenesses of famous patrons, such as Popes Julius II and Leo X; yet he also painted more intimate portraits of his friends, including a double portrait of Andrea Navagero and Agostino Beazzano, which by 1530 adorned the house in Padua of another mutual friend, Pietro Bembo. Here, the artist portrays Castiglione from a close perspective that fosters a sense of intimacy. The sitter's pose, with hands folded and head turned slightly to engage the viewer, imitates the *Mona Lisa*, which Leonardo da Vinci had brought with him to Rome in 1513. Some have claimed that the muted colors, as well as the sitter's understated and unassuming countenance, portray the author as the ideal figure that his *Book of the Courtier* describes. But the sitter's distinguished attire, which includes black velvet and beaver, displays wealth conspicuously, and the expressive facial features, including eyes fixed upon the

Questions

1   Is the dialogue nostalgic for the past, hopeful for the future, or possibly both at once? In what ways, if any, is Castiglione's own career as a diplomat and a leader of troops during the "crisis of Italy" relevant to the dialogue?

2   Rather than being a "yes-man" who endorses everything that his prince says, the ideal Courtier is supposed to "bring him to the path of virtue," enticing the prince to the good by using "salutary deception." To what extent does this advice resemble that of Machiavelli? In what ways does it differ? Would it be fair to characterize the cultivation of *sprezzatura* (nonchalance), too, as a kind of deception? Is the Courtier ultimately too concerned with keeping up appearances?

3   The speakers consider at length whether virtue can be learned, an issue debated among philosophers in the western tradition at least since Plato and Aristotle. What positions are put forth here, and with what resolution? What, for Castiglione, is the role of morality in effective governance? How might his contemporary, Machiavelli, have responded?

4   The Courtier's role as adviser to the prince looks to be quite a difficult one – more difficult, perhaps, than actually being the prince. Is this ideal attainable? Does it matter whether or not one can attain it, or is that beside the point?

5   From its outset, Renaissance humanism was concerned with the emulation of models, including not only literary and artistic models of style, but also models of human behavior. Through imitating examples of greatness, attractively presented, one could be inspired to become better. Is the ideal Courtier's grace and nonchalance primarily decorative? Or, might there be something rhetorically persuasive about it? And if so, whom might it have been intended to persuade?

spectator, do not appear to accord with the dialogue's emphases on indirection and concealment. In the Renaissance, while some portraits of political leaders served as political propaganda, the genre encompassed as well more intimate portraits like this one. When in 1516 Castiglione left Rome for Mantua, where he would be married later that year, he took with him the portrait by Raphael. Three years later, when Federico Gonzaga sent him back to Rome as an ambassador, Castiglione left the portrait with his wife in Mantua, where his virtual presence could remind her and the couple's infant son of their shared affection.[1]

1   This summary follows the interpretation of Shearman (1992), pp. 132–7 (see note to plate 10).

Book of the Courtier IV, 4–26

[Signor Ottaviano Fregoso is speaking:]

[4] "So, to continue the reasoning of these gentlemen. which I wholly approve and confirm, I say that, among the things which we call good, there are some which, simply and in themselves, are always good, such as temperance, fortitude, health, and all the virtues that bring tranquillity of mind; others, which are good in various respects and for the end to which they are directed, such as law, liberality, riches, and other like things. Therefore I think that the perfect Courtier, such as Count Ludovico and messer Federico have described him, may indeed be good and worthy of praise, not, however, simply and in himself, but in regard to the end to which he is directed. For indeed if by being of noble birth, graceful, charming, and expert in so many exercises, the Courtier were to bring forth no other fruit than to be what he is, I should not judge it right for a man to devote so much study and labor to acquiring this perfection of Courtiership as anyone must do who wishes to acquire it. Nay, I should say that many of those accomplishments that have been attributed to him (such as dancing, merry-making, singing, and playing) were frivolities and vanities and, in a man of any rank, deserving of blame rather than of praise; for these elegances of dress, devices, mottoes, and other such things as pertain to women and love (although many will think the contrary), often serve merely to make spirits effeminate, to corrupt youth, and to lead it to a dissolute life; whence it comes about that the Italian name is reduced to opprobrium, and there are but few who dare, I will not say to die, but even to risk any danger. And certainly there are countless other things, which, if effort and study were put into them, would prove much more useful, both in peace and in war, than this kind of Courtiership taken in and for itself. But if the activities of the Courtier are directed to the good end to which they ought to be directed, and which I have in mind, I feel certain that they are not only not harmful or vain, but most useful and deserving of infinite praise.

[5] "Therefore, I think that the aim of the perfect Courtier, which we have not spoken of up to now, is so to win for himself, by means of the accomplishments ascribed to him by these gentlemen, the favor and mind of the prince whom he serves that he may be able to tell him, and always will tell him, the truth about everything he needs to know, without fear or risk of displeasing him; and that when he sees the mind of his prince inclined to a wrong action, he may dare to oppose him and in a gentle manner avail himself of the favor acquired by his good accomplishments, so as to dissuade

him of every evil intent and bring him to the path of virtue. And thus, having in himself the goodness which these gentlemen attributed to him, together with readiness of wit, charm, prudence, knowledge of letters and of many other things – the Courtier will in every instance be able adroitly to show the prince how much honor and profit will come to him and to his from justice, liberality, magnanimity, gentleness, and the other virtues that befit a good prince; and, on the other hand, how much infamy and harm result from the vices opposed to these virtues. Hence, I think that even as music, festivals, games, and the other pleasant accomplishments are, as it were, the flower; so to bring or help one's prince toward what is right and to frighten him away from what is wrong are the true fruit of Courtiership. And because the real merit of good deeds consists chiefly in two things, one of which is to choose a truly good end to aim at, and the other is to know how to find means timely and fitting to attain that good end – it is certain that a man aims at the best end when he sees to it that his prince is deceived by no one, listens to no flatterers or slanderers or liars, and distinguishes good from evil, loving the one and hating the other.

[6] "I think too that the accomplishments attributed to the Courtier by these gentlemen may be a good means of attaining that end – and this because, among the many faults that we see in many of our princes nowadays, the greatest are ignorance and self-conceit. And the root of these two evils is none other than falsehood: which vice is deservedly odious to God and to men, and more harmful to princes than any other; because they have the greatest lack of what they would most need to have in abundance – I mean, someone to tell them the truth and make them mindful of what is right: because their enemies are not moved by love to perform these offices, but are well pleased to have them live wickedly and never correct themselves; and, on the other hand, their enemies do not dare to speak ill of them in public for fear of being punished. Then among their friends there are few who have free access to them, and those few are wary of reprehending them for their faults as freely as they would private persons, and, in order to win grace and favor, often think of nothing save how to suggest things that can delight and please their fancy, although these things be evil and dishonorable; thus, from friends these men become flatterers, and, to gain profit from their close association, always speak and act in order to please, and for the most part make their way by dint of lies that beget ignorance in the prince's mind, not only of outward things but of himself; and this may be said to be the greatest and most monstrous falsehood of all, for an ignorant mind deceives itself and inwardly lies to itself.

[7] "From this it results that, besides never hearing the truth about anything at all, princes are made drunk by the great license that rule gives; and by a

profusion of delights are submerged in pleasures, and deceive themselves so and have their minds so corrupted – seeing themselves always obeyed and almost adored with so much reverence and praise, without ever the least contradiction, let alone censure – that from this ignorance they pass to an extreme self-conceit, so that then they become intolerant of any advice or opinion from others. And since they think that to know how to rule is a very easy thing, and that to succeed therein they need no other art or discipline save sheer force, they give their mind and all their thoughts to maintaining the power they have, deeming true happiness to lie in being able to do what one wishes. Therefore some princes hate reason or justice, thinking it would be a kind of bridle and a way of reducing them to servitude, and of lessening the pleasure and satisfaction they have in ruling if they chose to follow it, and that their rule would be neither perfect nor complete if they were obliged to obey duty and honor, because they think that one who obeys is not a true ruler.

"Therefore, following these principles and allowing themselves to be trans-ported by self-conceit, they become arrogant, and with imperious counten-ance and stern manner, with pompous dress, gold, and gems, and by letting themselves be seen almost never in public, they think to gain authority among men and to be held almost as gods. And to my mind these princes are like the colossi that were made last year at Rome on the day of the festival in Piazza d'Agone,[1] which outwardly had the appearance of great men and horses in a triumph, and which within were full of tow and rags. But princes of this kind are much worse in that these colossi were held upright by their own great weight, whereas these princes, since they are ill-balanced within and are heedlessly placed on uneven bases, fall to their ruin by reason of their own weight, and pass from one error to a great many: for their ignorance, together with the false belief that they cannot make a mistake and that the power they have comes from their own wisdom, brings them to seize states boldly, by fair means or foul, whenever the possibility presents itself.

[8] "But if they would take it upon themselves to know and do what they ought, they would then strive not to rule as they now strive to rule, because they would see how monstrous and pernicious a thing it is when subjects, who have to be governed, are wiser than the princes who have to govern. Take note that ignorance of music, of dancing, of horsemanship, does no harm to anyone; nevertheless, one who is not a musician is ashamed and dares not sing in the presence of others, or dance if he does not know how, or ride if he does not sit his horse well. But from not knowing how to govern peoples there come so many woes, deaths, destructions, burnings, ruins, that it may be said to be the deadliest plague that exists on earth. And yet some

---

1 The modern Piazza Navona.

princes who are so very ignorant of government are not ashamed to attempt to govern, I will not say in the presence of four or six men, but before the whole world, for they hold such a high rank that all eyes gaze upon them and hence not only their great but their least defects are always seen. Thus, it is recorded that Cimon was blamed for loving wine, Scipio for loving sleep, Lucullus for loving feasts. But would to God that the princes of our day might accompany their sins with as many virtues as did those ancients; who, even though they erred in some things, yet did not flee from the promptings and teachings of anyone who seemed to them able to correct those errors; nay, they made every effort to order their lives on the model of excellent men: as Epaminondas on that of Lysias the Pythagorean, Agesilaus on that of Xenophon, Scipio on that of Panaetius, and countless others. But if some of our princes should happen upon a strict philosopher, or anyone at all who might try openly and artlessly to reveal to them the harsh face of true virtue, and teach them what good conduct is and what a good prince's life ought to be, I am certain they would abhor him as they would an asp, or indeed would deride him as a thing most vile.

[9] "I say, then, that, since the princes of today are so corrupted by evil customs and by ignorance and a false esteem of themselves, and since it is so difficult to show them the truth and lead them to virtue, and since men seek to gain their favor by means of lies and flatteries and such vicious ways – the Courtier, through those fair qualities that Count Ludovico and messer Federico have given him, can easily, and must, seek to gain the good will and captivate the mind of his prince that he may have free and sure access to speak to him of anything whatever without giving annoyance. And if he is such as he has been said to be, he will have little trouble in succeeding in this, and will thus be able always adroitly to tell him the truth about all things; and also, little by little, to inform his prince's mind with goodness, and teach him continence, fortitude, justice, and temperance, bringing him to taste how much sweetness lies hidden beneath the slight bitterness that is at first tasted by anyone who struggles against his vices; which are always noxious and offensive and attended by infamy and blame, just as the virtues are beneficial, smiling, and full of praise. And he will be able to incite his prince to these by the example of the famous captains and other excellent men to whom the ancients were wont to make statues of bronze, of marble, and sometimes of gold, and to erect these in public places, both to honor these men and to encourage others, so that through worthy emulation they may be led to strive to attain that glory too.

[10] "In this way the Courtier will be able to lead his prince by the austere path of virtue, adorning it with shady fronds and strewing it with pretty flowers to lessen the tedium of the toilsome journey for one whose strength is

slight; and now with music, now with arms and horses, now with verses, now with discourse of love, and with all those means whereof these gentlemen have spoken, to keep his mind continually occupied in worthy pleasures, yet always impressing upon him also some virtuous habit along with these enticements, as I have said, beguiling him with salutary deception; like shrewd doctors who often spread the edge of the cup with some sweet cordial when they wish to give a bitter-tasting medicine to sick and over-delicate children.

"Thus, by using the veil of pleasure to such an end, the Courtier will reach his aim in every time and place and activity, and for this will deserve much greater praise and reward than for any other good work that he could do in the world. For there is no good more universally beneficial than a good prince, nor any evil more universally pernicious than a bad prince: likewise, there is no punishment atrocious and cruel enough for those wicked courtiers who direct gentle and charming manners and good qualities of character to an evil end, namely to their own profit, and who thereby seek their prince's favor in order to corrupt him, turn him from the path of virtue, and bring him to vice; for such as these may be said to contaminate with a deadly poison, not a single cup from which one man alone must drink, but the public fountain that is used by all the people."

[11] Signor Ottaviano was silent, as if he did not wish to say more; but signor Gasparo said: "It does not seem to me, signor Ottaviano, that this goodness of mind and this continence and the other virtues which you would have our Courtier teach his prince can be learned; but I think that to those who have them they have been given by nature and by God. And that this is so, you will see that there is not a man in the world so wicked and evil by nature, nor so intemperate and unjust, as to confess himself to be such when he is asked; nay, everyone, no matter how wicked, is pleased to be thought just, continent, and good: which would not happen if these virtues could be learned; for it is no disgrace not to know what one has made no effort to know, but it seems blameworthy indeed not to have that with which we should be adorned by nature. Thus, everyone tries to hide his natural defects, both of mind and of body; which is seen in the blind, the crippled, and the twisted, and in others who are maimed or ugly; for, although these defects can be ascribed to nature, yet everyone is displeased at the thought that he has them, because it seems that nature herself bears witness to that imperfection, as if it were a seal and token of wickedness in him. This opinion of mine is also confirmed by the story that is told of Epimetheus, who knew so badly how to apportion the gifts of nature among men that he left them much more wanting in everything than all other creatures: wherefore Prometheus stole from Minerva and from Vulcan that artful knowledge whereby men gain their livelihood; but they did not yet know how to congregate in cities and

live by a moral law, for this knowledge was guarded in Jove's stronghold by most watchful warders who so frightened Prometheus that he dared not approach them; wherefore Jove took pity on the misery of men who were torn by wild beasts because, lacking civic virtues, they could not stand together; and sent Mercury to earth to bring them justice and shame, so that these two things might adorn their cities and unite the citizens. And he ordained that these should not be given to men like the other arts, in which one expert suffices for many who are ignorant (as in the case of medicine), but that they should be impressed upon every man; and he established a law that all who were without justice and shame should be exterminated and put to death as public menaces. So you see, signor Ottaviano, that these virtues are granted to men by God, and are not learned, but are natural."

[12] Then signor Ottaviano said, laughing: "Would you have it, then, signor Gasparo, that men are so unhappy and perverse in their judgments that they have by industry found an art whereby to tame the natures of wild beasts, bears, wolves, lions, and are thereby able to teach a pretty bird to fly wherever they wish and to return of its own will from the woods and from its natural freedom to cages and to captivity – and that by the same industry they cannot, or will not, devise arts to help themselves and to improve their minds by diligence and study? This, to my way of thinking, would be as if physicians were to put all their efforts into finding the method of healing sore nails and milk scab in children, and were to leave off treating fevers, pleurisy, and other grave maladies; and how out of all reason that would be, everyone may consider.

"Therefore I hold that the moral virtues are not in us entirely by nature, for nothing can ever become accustomed to that which is naturally contrary to it; as we see in a stone, which, even though it were thrown upward ten thousand times, would never become accustomed to move so by itself; and if the virtues were as natural to us as weight is to a stone, we should never become accustomed to vice. Nor, on the other hand, are the vices natural in this sense, else we should never be able to be virtuous; and it would be too wrong and foolish to punish men for those defects that proceed from nature without any fault on our part; and this error would be committed by the laws, which do not inflict punishment on evildoers on account of their past error (since what is done cannot be undone), but have regard to the future, to the end that he who has erred may err no more nor by his bad example be the cause of others erring. And thus the laws do assume that virtues can be learned, which is very true; for we are born capable of receiving them and of receiving the vices too, and hence through practice we acquire the habit of both, so that first we practice virtue or vice and then we are virtuous or vicious. The contrary is noted in things that are given us by nature, which we first have the power to practice and then do practice: as with the senses;

for first we are able to see, hear, and touch, then we do see, hear, and touch, although many of these activities are improved by discipline. Wherefore good masters teach children not only letters, but also good and seemly manners in eating, drinking, speaking, and walking, with appropriate gestures.

[13] "Therefore, as in the arts, so likewise in virtue it is necessary to have a master who, by his teaching and good reminders, shall stir and awaken in us those moral virtues of which we have the seed enclosed and planted in our souls; and, like a good husbandman, cultivate them and open the way for them by removing from about us the thorns and tares of our appetites which often so overshadow and choke our minds as not to let them flower or produce those fair fruits which alone we should desire to see born in the human heart.

"In this way, then, justice and shame, which you say Jove sent upon earth to all men, are natural in each one of us. But even as a body without eyes, however robust it may be, often goes astray in moving toward some object, so the root of these virtues which are potentially innate in our minds, often comes to nothing if it is not helped by cultivation. For if it is to pass to action and to a perfect operation, nature alone does not suffice, as has been said, but the practice of art and reason is required to purify and clear the soul by lifting from it the dark veil of ignorance, from which almost all the errors of men proceed – because if good and evil were well recognized and understood, no one would fail to prefer good and eschew evil. Hence, virtue can almost be called a kind of prudence and a knowledge of how to choose the good, and vice a kind of imprudence and ignorance that brings us to judge falsely; for men never choose evil, thinking it to be evil, but are deceived by a certain semblance of the good."

[14] Then signor Gasparo replied: "There are, however, many who know well that they are doing evil and yet do it; and this because they put the present pleasure which they feel before the punishment which they fear will befall them: like thieves, murderers, and other such men."

Signor Ottaviano said: "True pleasure is always good and true suffering always evil; therefore these men deceive themselves in taking false pleasure for true, and true suffering for false; wherefore through false pleasures they often incur true sufferings. Therefore the art that teaches how to distinguish the true from the false can indeed be learned; and the virtue by which we choose what is truly good and not what falsely appears so can be called true knowledge, more profitable to human life than any other, because it removes ignorance from which, as I have said, all evils spring."

[15] Then messer Pietro Bembo said: "I do not see why signor Gasparo should grant you, signor Ottaviano, that all evils are born of ignorance; and that there are not many who know well that they are sinning when

they sin, and do not at all deceive themselves regarding true pleasure or true suffering. For it is certain that men who are incontinent judge reasonably and rightly, and know that what they are brought to by their lusts in despite of duty is evil, and therefore resist and set reason against appetite, whence arises the struggle of pleasure and pain against the judgment. Finally reason gives up, overcome by too strong an appetite, like a ship that for a while resists the stormy seas but at last, beaten by the too furious violence of the winds, with anchor and rigging broken, lets herself be driven at Fortune's will, without helm or any guidance of compass to save her.

"Therefore the incontinent commit their errors with a certain ambiguous remorse and, as it were, in despite of themselves; which they would not do if they did not know that what they are doing is evil, but they would follow appetite lavishly without any struggle on the part of reason, and would then be not incontinent but intemperate, which is much worse: for incontinence is said to be a lesser vice because it has some part of reason in it; and likewise continence is said to be an imperfect virtue because it has a part of passion in it. Therefore in this I think we cannot say that the errors of the incontinent proceed from ignorance, or that they deceive themselves and do not sin, when they well know that they are sinning."

[16] Signor Ottaviano replied: "Truly, messer Pietro, your argument is fine; nonetheless, it strikes me as being specious rather than true. For even though the incontinent do sin in this ambiguous way, reason struggling with appetite in their minds, and, although what is evil seems evil to them, yet they do not have a perfect recognition of it nor do they know it as thoroughly as they would need to know it. Hence, they have a vague notion rather than any certain knowledge of it, and so allow their reason to be overcome by passion; but if they had true knowledge of it, it is certain that they would not err: since that by which appetite conquers reason is always ignorance, and true knowledge can never be overcome by passion (which pertains to the body and not to the soul); and passion becomes virtue if rightly ruled and governed by reason, otherwise it becomes vice. But reason has such power that it always brings the senses to obey it, and extends its rule by marvelous ways and means, provided ignorance does not seize upon what reason ought to possess. So that, although the spirits, nerves, and bones have no reason in them, yet when a movement of the mind begins in us, it is as if thought were spurring and shaking the bridle on our spirits, and all our members make ready: the feet to run, the hands to grasp or to do what the mind thinks. This, moreover, is plainly seen in many who sometimes, without knowing it, eat some loathsome and disgusting food, which seems most dainty to their taste, and then when they learn what thing it was not only suffer pain and distress of mind, but the body so follows the judgment of the mind that perforce they cannot help vomiting that food."

[17] Signor Ottaviano was proceeding with his discourse, but the Magnifico Giuliano interrupted him, saying: "If I have heard aright, signor Ottaviano, you said that continence is an imperfect virtue because it has a part of passion in it; and when there is a struggle in our minds between reason and appetite, I think that the virtue which fights and gives victory to reason ought to be esteemed more perfect than that which conquers when no lust or passion opposes it; for in the latter instance the mind seems not to abstain from evil out of virtue, but to refrain from doing evil because it has no wish to do the thing."

Then signor Ottaviano said: "Which captain would you judge to be of greater worth, the one who by fighting openly puts himself in danger and yet conquers the enemy, or the one who by his ability and knowledge deprives them of their strength, reducing them to such a point that they cannot fight, and conquering them so, without any battle or any danger whatsoever?"

"The one," said the Magnifico Giuliano, "who conquers more in safety is without doubt more to be praised, provided that this safe victory of his is not due to the cowardice of the enemy."

Signor Ottaviano replied: "You have judged well; and hence I say to you that continence may be compared to a captain who fights manfully, and, although the enemy is strong and powerful, still conquers them even though not without great difficulty and danger; but temperance, free of all perturbation, is like that captain who conquers and rules without opposition; and, having not only put down but quite extinguished the fire of lust in the mind wherein it abides, like a good prince in time of civil war, temperance destroys her seditious enemies within, and gives to reason the scepter and entire dominion.

"Thus, this virtue does no violence to the mind, but very gently infuses it with a vehement persuasion which inclines it to honorable things, renders it calm and full of repose, and in all things even and well tempered, and informed throughout by a certain harmony with itself that adorns it with a tranquillity so serene as never to be disturbed; and in all things becomes most obedient to reason and ready to direct its every movement accordingly, and to follow it wherever reason may wish to lead, without the least recalcitrance, like a tender lamb which always runs and stops and walks near its mother and moves only when she moves. This virtue, then, is very perfect, and is especially suited to princes because from it many other virtues spring."

[18] Then messer Cesare Gonzaga said: "I do not know what virtues befitting a prince can spring from this temperance, if temperance is what removes the passions from the mind, as you say. Perhaps this would be fitting in a monk or hermit; but I am not at all sure that it becomes a prince who is magnanimous, liberal, and valiant in arms, never to feel, regardless of what is done to

him, either wrath or hate or good will or scorn or lust or passion of any kind; or that without these he could have authority over citizens or soldiers."

Signor Ottaviano replied: "I did not say that temperance entirely removes and uproots the passions from the human mind. Nor would this be well, because even in the passions there are some good elements; but temperance brings under the sway of reason that which is perverse in our passions and which stands against what is right. Therefore it is not well to extirpate the passions altogether in order to get rid of disturbances; for this would be like issuing an edict that no one must drink wine, in order to suppress drunkenness, or like forbidding everyone to run because in running we sometimes fall. Note that those who tame horses do not prevent them from running and jumping, but have them do so at the right time and in obedience to the rider. Hence, the passions, when moderated by temperance, are an aid to virtue, just as wrath aids fortitude, and as hatred of evildoers aids justice, and likewise the other virtues too are aided by the passions; which if they were wholly taken away, would leave the reason weak and languid, so that it could effect little, like the master of a vessel abandoned by the winds and in a great calm.

"Therefore, do not marvel, messer Cesare, if I have said that many other virtues are born of temperance, for when a mind is attuned to this harmony, then through the reason it easily receives true fortitude, that makes it intrepid and safe from every danger, and almost puts it above human passions. And this is true no less of justice (pure virgin, friend of modesty and of the good, queen of all the other virtues), because she teaches us to do what we ought to do and to shun what we ought to shun; and therefore she is most perfect, because the other virtues perform their works through her, and because she is helpful to whomsoever possesses her, and to others as well as to himself: and, without her, as it is said, Jove himself could not rule his kingdom well. Magnanimity also follows upon these and makes them all greater; but it cannot stand by itself because whoever has no other virtue cannot be magnanimous. Then the guide of these virtues is prudence, which consists of a certain judgment in choosing well. And linked into this happy chain are also liberality, magnificence, desire for honor, gentleness, pleasantness, affability, and many other virtues that there is not time now to name. But if our Courtier will do what we have said, he will find them all in his prince's mind, and every day will see beautiful flowers and fruits put forth there, such as are not found in all the exquisite gardens of the world; and within him he will feel very great satisfaction, remembering that he gave his prince, not what fools give (which is gold or silver, vases, garments, and the like, whereof he who gives them is in great want of them and he who receives them has them in greatest abundance), but gave him that virtue which perhaps among all human things is the greatest and rarest, that is, the manner and method of right rule: which of itself alone would suffice to make men happy and to bring back once again to earth that Golden Age which is recorded to have existed once upon a time when Saturn ruled."

[19] When signor Ottaviano here made a slight pause as if to rest, signor Gasparo said: "Which do you think, signor Ottaviano, is the happier rule and the more capable of bringing back to earth that golden age you mention: the rule of so good a prince or the government of a good republic?"

Signor Ottaviano replied: "I should always prefer the rule of a good prince because such rule is more according to nature, and (if we may compare small things with things infinitely great) more like that of God who singly and alone governs the universe. But, apart from this, you see that in those things that are made by human skill, such as armies, great fleets, buildings, and the like, the whole is referred to one man who governs as he wishes. So too in our body, where all the members do their work and fulfill their functions at the command of the heart. In addition to this, moreover, it seems right that people should be ruled by a single prince, as is the case also with many animals, to whom nature teaches such obedience as a very salutary thing. Note that deer, cranes, and many other birds, when they migrate, always choose a leader whom they follow and obey; and bees, almost as if they had discourse of reason, obey their king with as much reverence as the most obedient people on earth; and hence all this is very certain proof that the rule of a prince is more in keeping with nature than that of republics."

[20] Then messer Pietro Bembo said: "To me it seems that since liberty has been given us by God as a supreme gift, it is not reasonable that it should be taken from us, or that one man should have a larger portion of it than another: which happens under the rule of princes, who for the most part hold their subjects in the closest bondage. But in well-ordered republics, this liberty is fully preserved: besides which, both in judging and in deliberating, one man's opinion happens more often to be wrong than the opinion of many men; because the disturbance that arises from anger or indignation or lust more easily enters the mind of one man than that of the many, who are like a great body of water, which is less subject to corruption than a small body. I will say too that the example of the animals does not seem appropriate to me; for deer, cranes, and other animals do not always choose to follow and obey the same one, but they change and vary, giving rule now to one, now to another, and come in this way to a kind of republic rather than to monarchy; and this can be called true and equal liberty, when those who sometimes command obey in their turn. Nor do I think that the example of the bees is pertinent, for their king is not of their own species; and therefore whoever wishes to give men a truly worthy lord would need to find one of another species and of a more excellent nature than the human, if men are to be bound in reason to obey him, like the herds which obey, not an animal of

their own kind, but a herdsman who is a man, and is of a higher species than theirs. For these reasons, signor Ottaviano, I hold that the rule of a republic is more desirable than that of a king."

[21] Then signor Ottaviano said: "Against your opinion, messer Pietro, I wish only to cite one argument; namely, that there are only three kinds of right rule: one is monarchy; another, the rule of the good, whom the ancients called optimates; the third, popular government. And the excess and opposing vice, so to speak, into which each of these kinds of rule falls when it comes to ruin and decay is when monarchy becomes tyranny; when the rule of the optimates changes into government by a few who are powerful and not good; and when popular government is seized by the rabble, which brings general confusion and surrenders the rule of the whole to the caprice of the multitude. Of these three kinds of bad government, it is certain that tyranny is the worst of all, as could be proved by many arguments: thus, it follows that monarchy is the best of the three kinds of good government, because it is the opposite of the worst; for, as you know, those things that result from opposite causes are themselves opposites.

"Now as to what you said about liberty, I answer that we ought not to say that true liberty is to live as we like, but to live according to good laws. Nor is obeying less natural or less useful or less necessary than commanding; and some things are born and devised and ordained by nature to command, as others are to obey. It is true that there are two modes of ruling: the one absolute and violent, like that of masters toward their slaves, and in this way the soul commands the body; and the other is more mild and gentle, like that of good princes over the citizens by means of laws, and in this way the reason commands the appetite: and both of these modes are useful, for the body is by nature made apt for obeying the soul, and likewise appetite for obeying the reason. There are many men, moreover, whose actions pertain only to the body; and such men differ as much from virtuous men as the soul differs from the body; and, even though they are rational creatures, they have only such share of reason as to be able to recognize this, but do not possess it or derive profit from it. These, therefore, are naturally slaves, and it is better and more useful for them to obey than to command."

[22] Then signor Gasparo said: "The discreet and virtuous, and those who are not by nature slaves, in what mode are they to be ruled?"

Signor Ottaviano replied: "By the gentle kind of rule, kingly and civic. And to such men it is well sometimes to give the charge of those offices for which they are suited, so that they too may be able to command and govern those who are less wise than themselves, yet in such a way that the chief rule shall depend entirely upon the supreme ruler. And since you said that it is an easier thing for the mind of a single man to be corrupted than that of many, I say that it is also easier to find one good and wise man than many. And we must think that a king of noble race will be good and wise, inclined to the virtues by his natural instinct and by the illustrious memory of his forebears, and practiced in good behavior; and even if he is not of another species higher than the human (as you have said of the king of bees), being aided by the teachings and the training and skill of so prudent and good a Courtier as these gentlemen have devised, he will be very just, continent, temperate, strong, and wise, full of liberality, magnificence, religion, and clemency. In fine, he will be most glorious and dear to men and to God, by Whose grace he will attain the heroic virtue that will bring him to surpass the limits of humanity and be called a demigod rather than a mortal man: for God delights in and protects, not those princes who try to imitate Him by a show of great power and by making themselves adored of men, but those who, besides the power they wield, strive to make themselves like Him in goodness and wisdom, by means of which they may wish and be able to do good and be His ministers, distributing for the welfare of mortals the benefits and gifts they receive from Him. Hence, just as in the heavens the sun and the moon and the other stars exhibit to the world, as in a mirror, a certain likeness of God, so on earth a much liker image of God is seen in those good princes who love and revere Him and show to the people the splendid light of His justice accompanied by a semblance of His divine reason and intellect; and with such as these God shares His righteousness, equity, justice, and goodness, and more happy blessings than I could name, that give to the world a much clearer proof of divinity than the sun's light or the continual turning of the heavens and the various courses of the stars.

[23] "Thus, men have been put by God under princes, who for this reason must take diligent care in order to render Him an account of them like good stewards to their lord, and love them and look upon every good and evil thing that happens to them as happening to themselves. and procure their happiness above every other thing. Therefore the prince must not only be good but also make others good, like the square used by architects, which not only is straight and true itself, but also makes straight and true all things to which it is applied. And it is a very great proof that the prince is good if his people are good, because the life of the prince is a norm and guide for the citizens, and all behavior must needs depend on his behavior; nor is it fitting for an ignorant man to teach, or for a disorderly man to give orders, or for one who falls to raise others up.

"Hence, if the prince is to perform these duties well, he must put every effort and care into acquiring knowledge; let him then erect within himself and in every regard follow steadfastly the law of reason (not one inscribed on paper or in metal, but graven upon his very mind) so that it will always be not only familiar to him but ingrained in him and that he will live with it as with a part of himself; so that day and night in every place and time, it may admonish him and speak to him within his heart, removing from him those turbulences that are felt by intemperate minds which – because they are oppressed on the one hand, as it were, by a very deep sleep of ignorance, and on the other, by the turmoil which they undergo from their perverse and blind desires – are shaken by a restless frenzy as a sleeper sometimes is by strange and horrible visions.

[24] "Moreover, when greater power is joined to an evil will, greater harm is also joined; and when the prince can do whatever he desires, then there is great danger that he may not desire what he ought. Hence, Bias well said that the office shows the man: for just as vases that are cracked cannot readily be detected so long as they are empty, yet if liquid be put into them, show at once just where the defect lies – in like manner corrupt and depraved minds rarely disclose their defects save when they are filled with authority; because they are then unable to bear the heavy weight of power, and so give way and pour out on every side greed, pride, wrath, insolence, and those tyrannical practices which they have within them. Thus, they recklessly persecute the good and the wise and exalt the wicked; and they allow no friendships in their cities nor unions nor understandings among the citizens, but encourage spies, informers, and murderers in order to make men afraid and cowardly, sowing discord to keep men disunited and weak. And from these ways come endless harm and ruin to the unhappy people; and often cruel death (or at least continual fear) comes to the tyrants themselves; because good princes do not fear for themselves but for those whom they rule, while tyrants fear those whom they rule; hence, the greater the number of people they rule and the more powerful they are, the more fear they feel and the more enemies they have. How fearful and of what an uneasy mind was Clearchus, tyrant of Pontus, whenever he went into the market place or theater, or to some banquet or other public place; who, as it is written, was wont to sleep shut up in a chest! Or that other tyrant, Aristodemus the Argive, who made his bed into a kind of prison: for in his palace he had a little room suspended in air, so high that it could only be reached by a ladder; and there he slept with his woman, whose mother would remove the ladder at night and replace it in the morning.[2]

"The life of the good prince must be an entirely different life from this, free and secure, and as dear to his citizens as their own life, and so ordered as to partake of both the active and the contemplative life, in the measure that is suited to the welfare of his people."

---

2   The examples here derive from Plutarch's *On the Ignorant Prince*.

[25] Then signor Gasparo said: "And which of these two ways of life, signor Ottaviano, do you think is more fitting for the prince?"

Signor Ottaviano replied, laughing: "Perhaps you think that I imagine myself to be the excellent Courtier who must know so many things and make use of them to the good end I have described; but remember that these gentlemen have fashioned him with many accomplishments that are not in me. Therefore let us first try to find him, and I will abide by his decision in this as in the other things that pertain to a good prince."

Then signor Gasparo said: "I think that if there be wanting in you any of the accomplishments which have been attributed to the Courtier, then they are music and dancing and some others of little importance, rather than those belonging to the education of the prince and to this part of Courtier-ship."

Signor Ottaviano replied: "None are of little importance that serve to gain the prince's favor, which is necessary (as we have said) before the Courtier may venture to try to teach him virtue; which, as I think I have shown you, can be learned, and is as beneficial as ignorance is harmful, from which all sins stem, and especially that false esteem which men conceive of themselves. But I think I have said enough, and perhaps more than I promised."

Then the Duchess said: "We shall be the more indebted to your courtesy, the more your performance surpasses your promise; hence, be pleased to tell us what you think of signor Gasparo's question; and, by your faith, tell us also everything that you would teach your prince if he had need of instruction – and let us assume that you have won his favor completely, so that you are free to tell him whatever comes to mind."

[26] Signor Ottaviano laughed and said: "If I had the favor of some of the princes I know, and if I were to tell them freely what I think, I fear I should soon lose that favor; moreover, in order to teach him, I myself should first have to learn. Yet since it is your pleasure that I answer signor Gasparo on this point also, I will say that it seems to me that princes ought to lead both kinds of life, but more especially the contemplative, because this in them is divided into two parts: one consists in seeing rightly and in judging; the other in commanding reasonable things (justly and in the proper manner) in which they have authority, and in requiring the same of those who rightly should obey, at appropriate times and places; and of this Duke Federico was speaking when he said that he who knows how to command is always obeyed. And whereas commanding is always the chief office of princes, often also they must witness with their own eyes and be present at the execution of their commands according to the times and needs, and must sometimes take part themselves; and all this pertains to action; but the contemplative life ought to be the goal of the active as peace is of war and as repose is of toil.

18

Pierio Valeriano (1477–1558)

Originally from a small town in northeastern Italy, Valeriano rose to prominence in Rome, especially after the election of the first Medici pope, Leo X (1513–21). Serving as tutor to the Medici heirs Ippolito and Alessandro, Valeriano spent a number of years in Florence, but in January of 1529 he returned with them to Rome, which he had not seen since before the city was sacked in May 1527.

His Latin dialogue *On the Ill Fortune of Learned Men*, from which the following selection is drawn, is set in Rome in 1529 during Lent, the period of penitence preceding Easter. The interlocutors are humanists that Valeriano had earlier known in Rome – surviving members of a group that had gathered often to study and to imitate the literary culture of antiquity. In the past, they had enjoyed drinks and dinner, reciting their own poetry and delivering speeches based upon classical models – in effect, sharing in their revival of ancient Roman culture. But after the sack of Rome, the literary community, like the city itself, lay in ruins.

Questions

1 In Castiglione's *Book of the Courtier*, the characters disagree at times, challenging and correcting one another. To what extent is that true of Valeriano's dialogue? Is the degree of consensus consequential?
2 Both this dialogue and Castiglione's have been described by some as "nostalgic." Do you agree? In each instance, why or why not?
3 What significance might there be to Valeriano's dialogue being set in Lent? In what ways might the religious importance of Rome be a key to the dialogue's meaning?

On the Ill Fortune of Learned Men I, 1–14

[1] Recently, when talk and groundless rumors ran everywhere about the imminent death of Pope Clement VII, his nephews Ippolito and Alessandro set off for Rome in great haste, and I followed more slowly with their domestic entourage. The day after I entered the city my first concern was to pay a call on Gasparo Contarini, the Venetian ambassador, a man distinguished for intelligence, learning, and the highest degree of wisdom, whom I had held in honor unceasingly from my earliest youth. But as it happened, on the very day I approached his house, he had gone on a pilgrimage to visit and pray at the seven holy shrines of the saints; for it was Lent, the period of forty days our religion has set aside for purification each year.[1] I had scarcely knocked at the door and learned that the master was not at home and where he had gone, and turned away at the same moment to go to Pietro Mellini, who lived not far from that very house, when I met my good friends Lorenzo Grana, the bishop of Segni, and Angelo Colocci, a man of peerless integrity and extremely learned in Greek and Latin.

[2] When I had greeted them and asked where they were going, they smilingly replied, "To see this most extraordinary man," and pointed to the house.

"It's no use coming here today," I told them. "I had come here to greet him, too, but his servants say he's gone to visit the seven shrines, and so we have no hope left of enjoying his company today. But please tell me – what business do you have with him? And yet I feel foolish for asking, since I'm questioning upright and learned men about the nature of their business with a man preeminent in every field of knowledge."

"To be sure," replied Grana, "you could guess for yourself the purpose of our visit – indeed it was for no other reason than to depart happier in some

1 Contarini was making the standard pilgrimage to the seven major basilicas (S. Paolo fuori le mura, S. Sebastiano, S. Giovanni Laterano, Santa Croce, S. Lorenzo fuori le mura, S. Maria Maggiore, and S. Pietro).

way from his company. This always happens, and yesterday and the day before we felt especially heartened when he freed us of a great error – for we had begun to suspect that all men of learning, and at this time especially, are born to trouble and misfortune. He demolished this idea by his wise conversation and made us no longer regret our studies."

Having learned from our long association that Grana was not in the habit of speaking rashly or falsely, at this point I began to surmise that the conversation had been of the kind I remembered going on in Padua thirty years earlier in the house of the Contarini – now with Gasparo himself, now with his cousin Marcantonio Flavo, and sometimes even with Andrea Navagero.[2] Excited by the recollection of it, I said, "Please, my dear Pontifex Grana and you, too, Colocci, don't begrudge me an account of this conversation by which you claim Contarini encouraged you, so that I may have it as a consolation for not finding him."

[3] At this point Colocci spoke. He had been eager to burst out for some time, as I saw from his expression, but he was keeping quiet out of respect for the Pontifex, who had begun the story. "What conversation do you want, Pierio," he said, "if not one that from our perspective is full of calamities, woe, and misfortune, but, insofar as it concerns Contarini's wisdom, is an easing and cure for all distress?"

"But of whatever kind it was," said I, "how long will you torment me with longing for it?"

"To speak for Pontifex Grana as well, we will tell you," replied Colocci, "and we will set out in detail the whole story in order, from the beginning and just as it proceeded; for we are eager to fulfill your desire. But since the Piazza Agonale[3] is no place for such a long recital, let's go into the house of the Mellini over there and sit in the courtyard of our friend Pietro, where we will tell you the whole thing right from the beginning."

"Splendid!" cried Grana. "Where indeed would we be happier to repair, since we have been kept from our conversation with Contarini?"

"What a timely suggestion!" said I. "For I was going straight back to Mellini's since I hadn't found Contarini at home."

2   Marcantonio Flavo Contarini (ca. 1485–1544) seems to have had a humanist education and to have frequented humanist circles in Padua and Venice around 1500, but little is known of his youth except for this passage. He enjoyed a distinguished diplomatic career. The Venetian patrician and diplomat Andrea Navagero (1483–May 8, 1529) was one of the most highly regarded poets and humanists of his day. He was both the official historian of Venice and Sabellico's successor as librarian of San Marco, as well as editor of the Aldine Virgil, Lucretius, and Ovid. He died at the French court in Blois while on an embassy to King Francis I.
3   i.e., the Piazza Navona, which stands on the site and preserves the shape of the stadium for Domitian's Capitoline games (*agones capitolini*). The name Navona is a corruption of its medieval designation (*in Agone*) but was also popularly associated with its shiplike shape.

At this point Colocci raised his face and hands to the sky and intoned, "O the power and harmony of our guardian spirits, always with a single thought and stirred by the same enthusiasm! For the same idea invites us to do things at the same time, and as the most ancient poet says, 'God brings like to like.'[4] But, look – there's Mellini inviting us from his doorstep. What perfect timing!"

[4] We went in, and when Mellini had ordered chairs to be brought and we had sat down, he asked, "Where were you going? And what chance or design has brought you together, the spirits dearest to me?"

"We have repaired to you," said Grana, "after not finding Contarini at home when we had gone to see him to continue yesterday's conversation."

"I'm glad you mentioned yesterday's conversation, Pontifex," Mellini replied. "For today I was eagerly longing for one of you to question who might tell me the whole thing, since late yesterday evening Giovanni Antonio Pollio explained the gist of it to me in the same way as I was standing on this very threshold; but because he had to hurry to be in attendance on the pope as he dined, he could stay no longer with me and I didn't like to put him out just for my benefit. He did say, though, that he had taken part in your conversation, and he so set me on fire with a single spark that I was restless last night with eagerness. I was just going to send a boy to one of you, since I couldn't come to you myself – for you know why I keep to the house and what enemies secretly threaten my life.[5] But come now, explain the whole thing."

[5] "I will tell," replied Grana at once, "and I will be the first to speak, since just a little while ago you had invited me to visit you with a note in your own hand, and since Colocci is worn out from his journey, because he has come here today from his villa, and is suffering from his feet besides.[6]

"Yesterday Colocci and Giovanni Antonio Pollio and I had all gone to see Contarini, as we had done quite often during these days in which the pope has lain so gravely ill, since we have found him with more time to spare from his official duties; and we had run through many topics, including literature and men of letters in every age. In this connection we took up the question of what age since the decline of the Roman Empire seemed preeminent in letters, and we discovered none that seemed preferable to the era that is

4 The "most ancient poet" is Homer (*Od.* 17.217–18). But the expression had become proverbial.
5 It is not clear what enemies and danger Mellini is referring to.
6 Colocci had several houses in and around Rome, including one not far from Mellini's in Parione; but Grana is probably referring to his most famous property, the villa and gardens at Acqua Vergine near S. Andrea delle Fratte generally called Orti coloziani. Some of Colocci's houses were burned or severely damaged in the sack of Rome; the villa at Acqua Vergine may have been one of them. Colocci's feet hurt because he suffered from gout.

now passing away. Such illustrious men have emerged in the last eighty years who are found to rival antiquity – some in talent, others in learning, others in eloquence. And when we had come to the point of naming them, other cities were found to have had scarcely one or two, or three at the most, whom it seemed fitting to enter into this list. We saw that the city of Rome, however, as the common homeland of the whole world, was so fertile and abounding in a multitude of men of letters (whether she displayed her own citizens or boasted that she had taken foreigners to her bosom and nurtured and cherished them among her own) that here indeed for some years there has been a greater supply of learned men than in all the rest of Italy.

"When we had agreed on this, Pollio asked Contarini whether he was of the same opinion and (since he was someone who knew the customs of many men and had traveled through various cities and nations) whether or not he had found it to be true. And when Contarini agreed that it was so, Pollio went on to ask him how he liked the talented men in Rome and what profit or enjoyment he took from their society.

[6] "At this point Contarini drew a deep sigh and said, 'There has been no time, I swear, from the moment that I began to take pleasure in the study of literature, when I did not have this as my chief desire – to be given a chance someday of visiting Rome, so that I might see for myself the gifted men that I had heard everyone say flourished here and enjoy their most welcome companionship. But it happened last year that I had barely returned to my senate from my embassy to Spain at the court of the emperor Charles when the senators and my fellow citizens appointed me ambassador to the pope. I understood that this duty, to be sure, was being entrusted to me at the worst possible time, since the affairs, not only of all Italy but of the whole world, were in disarray, and since the pope himself was a virtual exile after his flight from the Aelian stronghold.[7] Yet I was somewhat more cheerful about accepting the assignment because I had high hopes that he would be moved by his own wisdom or else persuaded by my advice and that of others to return to his seat when things in Rome finally settled down, and that in this way I would be granted an excuse and an opportunity of seeing Rome.[8] And so, when the pope decided to go back to Rome, we immediately followed him. But he was attacked at once by a serious illness and has caused us great anxiety over and over again.[9] In an attempt to relieve this worry somehow, since with the pope so ill there was no place for business, public or private, I

---

7 i.e., Castel Sant' Angelo, the mausoleum of Hadrian, which Valeriano calls *arx Aelia* from Hadrian's gentile name, Aelius. Clement had taken refuge there in May 1527. He was allowed to escape to Orvieto on the night of December 6, 1527, and returned to Rome only on October 6, 1528.

8 In fact, Contarini opposed Clement's return.

9 Clement fell ill on January 8, 1529 and did not fully recover until March.

had turned to entertaining myself with the acquaintance and society of your talented men. But – good God! – as soon as I began to seek out the philosophers, orators, poets, and professors of Greek and Latin literature I had written down in my notebook, what a great and cruel tragedy I encountered! For I found that the men of letters I was hoping to see had perished wretchedly in great numbers, carried off by the savage cruelty of fate and afflicted with the most undeserved misfortunes. Some had been cut off by the plague; others were in exile and crushed by poverty. Some had been slaughtered by the sword, others killed by slow torture; and some had brought death on themselves – which I think is the most dreadful calamity of all. I would never be able to express how much pain at that first shock these disasters of so many outstanding men caused me. But if I had not found you, at least, and a very few others, I would already have begun to regret my journey here and this eagerness of mine to see Rome.'

[7] "Pollio then picked up Contarini's theme. He said, 'It is wretched and lamentable (I don't deny it) that so many distinguished men of letters in Rome have perished in such a short space of time and – what is still more unfortunate – that almost all suffered a miserable death. Indeed, disasters of this sort are the more dreadful when they are inflicted on greater numbers. Thus, it is far more wretched and lamentable that throughout all of Europe in our lifetime, literature has been so persecuted by the pitiless Fates that now there is not a province, not a city, not a village in which some memorable calamity has not befallen men of this kind in the last forty years. And so in our time this last storm has broken, and especially on the best men, depriving not only our own country, but the whole world, of luminaries in every field of learning. Indeed, you see and hear everywhere that all the good men have been visited most undeservedly with afflictions of every kind, and we can list only a tiny number who enjoyed a fortunate life or old age and died an easy death. And to tell you the truth, since these shafts of unjust Fortune seem to destroy literary men especially – even though I admire and esteem their virtues and hard work more than any man in the world – still, when I am faced with their losses, I believe that being learned is the greatest of all calamities.

"'In our time, moreover, all good men have been harried by incessant calamity and have had as their lot the greatest misery in life or death. For I am thinking only of those whose virtue, as long as they lived, was bright and renowned as far as we could see – and yet if we should reflect on their career and death, we will find that they almost all had a hard life or died wretchedly.

[8] "'And, to begin with the best, Ermolao Barbaro, your own excellent ambassador and senator, Contarini, was generally acknowledged to be the most outstanding man of letters of his day. Yet at the very time when he

thought he had achieved a quiet life for his studies – while he was ambassador for the Venetian nobility to Pope Alexander VI in Rome and by the greatest efforts was restoring the moribund glory of literature and the academic disciplines – he was exiled for accepting the patriarchate of Aquileia without consulting the Venetian senate. His property was confiscated, and he dragged out his life for a while in poverty, supported to some extent by a dole from Pope Alexander. But a few months later he contracted the plague and died a terrible death, deserted by everyone. Thus, the man who had glorified countless men of his time with the eloquence of his praise was cheated of both a funeral and the honor of a tomb, so that no one knows where he was buried or where his corpse was thrown.

[9] "'Recently, moreover, Cristoforo Marcello (to survey men of our own order),[10] a particular ornament of your aristocracy, and a man of such ability, such learning, such eloquence, but above all of such unblemished character, was snatched away from us by a very different fate from the one his piety and rank deserved and by a death unworthy of such virtue and learning. As archbishop of Corfu he was highly regarded by our Pope Clement for his outstanding intellectual gifts, but while he was in daily expectation of receiving far greater honors from him,[11] he was caught up in the recent catastrophe of Rome. Consequently, he was led off as a prisoner by the Spaniards who recently attacked the city of Rome by stealth, captured, and plundered it. He was despoiled of not only his own property but that of all his family; and after they had tortured him in a dozen ways (such was the cruelty of these monsters because of their hatred of the Italian nation), when he could not pay the unbearable tribute they kept demanding and, being destitute, had no hope and no aid or resources to sustain him, he breathed his last in misery at Gaeta.[12] For they say that the Spaniards, after seeing that they had no hope of the gold they had demanded, bound this distinguished man with chains and left him naked under the open air by the trunk of a tree. Every day they pulled out one of his fingernails, and at last they killed him amid these terrible torments, when his sufferings had been compounded by hunger and lack of sleep and exposure to the elements by day and night.

[10] "'Now as for Camillo Porzio [Camillo Porcari] (to bring my own citizens,[13] too, onto this stage) – everyone knows what a reputation he had, whether he was bringing distinction to the University of Rome to the amazement and admiration of all or declaiming before the rostra in such a way that nothing was considered more pleasant, polished, or agreeable than the way

10   i.e., aristocrats.
11   i.e., Marcello expected to be named a cardinal.
12   Gaeta, a port city on the Bay of Naples, was under Spanish control.
13   Apparently an error on Valeriano's part, since Porcari was a Roman and Pollio a Sicilian.

he spoke. But no sooner had he been appointed by Pope Leo X to head the church of Abruzzo[14] than he was suddenly overcome by a long and agonizing illness that none of the doctors recognized. After he had lain stricken with terrible suffering for many months, worn down at last by the violence of the disease and by pain over his whole body, he died still in the prime of life, leaving everyone with an extraordinary sense of loss.

[11] " 'Nor would anyone say that Marco Musuro had a happy fate. He had taught Greek literature for many years in Padua and Venice in the presence of your nobility, with universal favor and applause; and he was esteemed and respected by everyone, since Pope Leo X had honored him for his learning with both a bishopric and an archbishopric, and Pope Leo's cousin Giulio,[15] then a cardinal priest and now pope, had taken him into his circle. Nevertheless, he was secretly eaten up by unhappiness, since not only did he not value any office or income of a benefice in the kind of life that people think most magnificent, but he even considered his disgrace and affliction unsurpassed, since he had been accustomed to go about in the greatest liberty. From this distress he fell into an obscure malady whose cause was unknown to any of the doctors, and after being buffeted back and forth between unspoken anxieties and pitiable complaints about his long ill fortune, he breathed his last.'

[12] "When these words had tumbled out in a greater torrent than respect for such a great man required and I had asked him to excuse my lack of restraint, Contarini said, 'On the contrary, go ahead, and if you have any cases of this kind that you consider unfortunate, put them all before us.'

"Emboldened, I asked, 'What happiness was ever possessed by the impeccable authority on Latin style, Cardinal Adriano of Corneto [Adriano Castellesi]? He was raised to this high office by the favor of Pope Alexander VI, whose secretary he had been; but not long afterward he was exiled and blasted with harsh edicts under Pope Julius II and took shelter abroad, living an obscure and squalid existence for some years in the German Alps of the Raetians.[16] Then after Leo succeeded to the papacy on Julius' death, he was a party to a conspiracy that was especially sacrilegious against such a prince. After it had been exposed, and he had obtained a pardon from the merciful pope and received a letter of absolution, he was stung by the pricking of his conscience and fled secretly in the night; and no one for these fourteen years has been able to find out where he went or where he is. Nevertheless, the

14   Porcari was elected bishop of Téramo in 1517.
15   Giulio was Leo's first cousin, the illegitimate son of Giuliano de' Medici, the brother of Leo's father, Lorenzo the Magnificent. After Giuliano's murder Lorenzo took Giulio into his house and brought him up with his own children.
16   i.e., in Austria at the court of Emperor Maximilian I.

opinion persists that he was carrying a load of gold stitched inside his coat and that he was treacherously struck down by the servant traveling with him, his gold stolen, and his corpse left hidden in some lonely place.

[13] "'And I must add the similar case of Alfonso Petrucci, the son of Pandolfo, who had governed Siena under a rule of unbroken peace as long as he lived. Thoroughly trained in Greek and Latin literature by the monk Severo[17] and destined by his father for the church because of his aptitude for study, Alfonso was decorated by Julius II with senatorial purple and a cardinal's hat. As a young boy he was attacked with a knife by his brother Borghese (a boy himself, who aspired to his father's rule) and nearly had his throat cut. (Indeed, he was never able to conceal the ugly scar on his neck.) When he grew up and began to govern the state in the sacred senate at Rome,[18] in the time of Leo X he became estranged from the pope because of suspicion over the affairs of Siena and was denounced not only as a participant but as the ringleader of the monstrous conspiracy that was formed against Leo's life. After this had been uncovered and he himself had been caught and thrown into prison and found guilty of the crime, he was strangled to death in Hadrian's pile[19] when he was not yet past his twenty-eighth year.

[14] "'But – to seek no further into this mockery of Fortune – Pope Leo X, educated in every sort of learning, splendidly trained in Greek and Latin letters, both a man of the most subtle taste and one who won equal praise whether he wrote prose or composed in verse, might seem to have escaped the snares of misfortune because when he was hardly out of his youth he was exalted to the highest priesthood when it was flourishing in authority and wealth. But even disregarding what he had endured in the past – exile, poverty, wandering, captivity, and countless other troubles – if anyone should look only at what he continually suffered as pope, I greatly fear that he would place him among the most unfortunate of literary men, since he seemed to have his life exposed to every dart of Fortune. For – to begin with his private misfortunes, and with those raging in his own body – because of a suppurating anal fistula from which he had suffered almost constantly, he never had a single hour of rest by day or night. Next, he was wounded by the death of his dearest sisters and deeply grieved by the premature death of his brother Giuliano, whom he loved as much as his own eyes, and soon after that by the funeral of his only nephew, the son of his brother Piero.[20] This

17 In addition to being Petrucci's teacher, the Cistercian monk Severo Varini (d. 1549) was well known among the Roman humanists.
18 i.e., the papal consistory, the assembly of cardinals about the pope.
19 i.e., Castel Sant' Angelo.
20 Leo's brother Giuliano died in 1516; his brother Piero, in 1503. Piero's son was Lorenzo de' Medici (1492–1519), duke of Urbino.

nephew, then already duke of Umbria and already considered worthy of a connection by marriage with the king of France, was reduced to despair of his life after receiving a deadly wound during the siege of some castle, and a few months later he was carried off in the flower of his youth after rotting away with prolonged elephantiasis.[21] And finally the pope was brought more than once into mortal danger by the conspiracies of many, including even his intimates. When he was drawn into the terrible war against the king of France, he not only exhausted the treasury but also pledged his patrimony; and when his own resources were running out he even used up almost all those of his friends. Then when he was cut off by a premature death as he had just begun to hope that the war could be concluded by the ability of his cousin Cardinal Giulio, he left everything at sixes and sevens since he had been caught up by a short and sudden illness. And – a still greater misfortune for an excellent prince – when he had been defamed from the moment of his death by the most slanderous pamphlets you can imagine, actions were taken repeatedly in the senate through his enemies in the opposing faction to efface his good name and rescind his acts. Neither have we read nor do we remember that such a thing ever happened before to any pontiff after his death. Consider in addition the laments of almost all his cultured friends – each of whom had imagined for himself a life of tranquillity under the cultivated prince – when they were cheated of this hope and all (with but two or three exceptions at the most) lay destitute in misery and calamity.'

[15] "Here Grana had fallen silent,[22] as if he were reflecting on the misfortunes of others who came to mind; the rest were all silent, too, while each one pondered to himself in silence Fortune's great jest in the case of Leo, sighing to think that such a great man and such a pontiff, born to be a benefactor to the whole human race, had been cut off at the very moment when, if he had lived just a little longer, he would have easily fulfilled the desires of all."

21   Grana's account is misleading. Three years (not "a few months") after being seriously wounded in the siege of Mondolfo in April 1516, Lorenzo died of syphilis, which was often confused or compared with leprosy (elephantiasis) in the early sixteenth century. In April 1518 he married Madeleine de la Tour, a close kinswoman of the king of France, who died shortly after giving birth to a daughter, Caterina (Catherine de Médicis), in April 1519. Lorenzo died only a few days later, on May 4, 1519. His funeral oration was pronounced in Rome by Camillo Porcari. Leo banned the celebration of the satirical Feast of Pasquino (April 25) in 1519; it seems likely that he feared lampoons on the illness of his unpopular and dissolute nephew.
22   The reference to Grana in the third person suggests that Valeriano has forgotten that he was the narrator. The first-person narrative is later resumed.

Index

Page numbers in **bold** type indicate a main or detailed reference. Page numbers in *italic* indicate illustrations. Continuous page numbers ignore any intervening illustrations. In the interest of emphasis and clarity, some minor references have been omitted.

Abruzzo, 285
Accolti, Benedetto, 249
Adrian VI, pope, 7
Albano, Taddeo, 242–3
Albizzi, Filippo degli, 121
Alcibiades, 195n
Alcionio, Pietro, **206**
  An Oration Concerning the Sack of Rome,
  207–18
Alexander the Great, 153, 155–6
Alexander IV, pope, 215
Alexander VI, pope
  as a cardinal (Rodrigo Borgia), 63n
  character, 129
  politics and territorial expansion, 7,
  76, 78–9, 175, 284–5
Alfonso I, king of Naples (Alfonso V of
  Aragon), 111, 176
Alighieri, Dante, *see* Dante
Ambrose, 60
Ancona, 52, 56
Andrew, St., 52–70
Anguissola, Sofonisba, **138**

*A Game of Chess, involving the painter's
  three sisters and a servant, 138*
Anthony, St., 25, 31–3
Ardinghelli, Niccolò, 120
Ardinghelli, Piero, 129
Arezzo, 24, 43
Aristotle, 150, 176, 192, 206, 262
Arquà, 47
Ascent of Mont Ventoux (Petrarch), 5, 25,
  26–34
astrology, 187
Athanasius, 31
Attila, 186n
Augustine of Hippo, St., 24–5, 33, 60,
  150, 163n
  Confessions, 24, 30–1, 245
Augustus, emperor (Octavian), 17, 35,
  45, 64, 162
Avicenna, 189
Avignon, 24

Baglioni, Orazio, 246, 247n, 250–1,
  253n, 255–6

Baglioni family, 79
balance of power, 3, 51
Bandinelli, Baccio, *Hercules and Cacus*, 223
banishment, *see* exile
bankers, 66, 96
Barbaro, Ermolao, 283
Barbaro, Francesco, **150**
  On Wifely Duties, 150, **151–61**
Barcelona, 112–13
Baroncelli, Antonia, 123
Beazzano, Agostino, 261
Becharo, Vittorio, 243
Bellini, Giovanni, 225–30
Bembo, Pietro, 228–30, 261
Bene, Alessandro del, 245–6
Bene, Pietro del, 245
Bene, Tommaso del, 131
Bentivoglio, Giovanni, 87
Bertini, Paolo, 133
Bessarion, Cardinal, 33, 53–4, 56, 67–9
Bibbiena (Bernardo Dovizi), 130
Bible, citations from
  New Testament, 5, 28–9, 31, 62, 175, 179–80, 184n, 185–6
  Old Testament, 17n, 20n, 29, 88n, 95, 140, 179, 192n
Black Death, *see* plague
Boccaccio, Giovanni, 7, 13, 43, 47, **96**, **139–40**, 198, 199n, 200n, 201n
  Decameron, **96–107**, 139–40, **141–9**
Bologna, 24, 51, 87, 144, 243
Boniface VIII, pope, 3
Book of the Courtier (Castiglione), 7, 260–2, **263–77**, 278
Borgia, Cesare, 71, 73, **76–81**
Borgia, Rodrigo, *see* Alexander VI, pope
Bosnia, 51
Botticelli, Sandro, 231
  Punishment of Korah, 175
Bourbon, Charles de, 206, **207–14**, **216–17, 245–6**
Braccio da Montone, 215
Brandolini, Matteo di Giorgio, 116, 124
Brescia, 7, 197

Bruni, Leonardo, 3, 13, **43**, 44, 153, 197
  Histories of the Florentine People, 43
  Life of Dante, 46
  Life of Petrarch, **44–7**
Brutus, 35
Buonarotti, Michelangelo, *see* Michelangelo
Burckhardt, Jacob, 3

Caesar Augustus, *see* Augustus, emperor
Caesar, Julius, 17, 35
Caligula, emperor, 45
Calixtus III, pope, 7, 52, 63
Capponi, Gino di Neri. 120n
Capponi family, 126
Careggi, 187
Carpaccio, Vittore, **33**
  St. Augustine in His Study (Vision of St. Augustine), 32
Carracci, Annibale, **5**
  Hercules at the Crossroads, 5, 6
Carrara, Francesco da, 72
Casa, Cecchino della, 246
Casavecchia, Filippo da, 133
Castellesi, Adriano, 285–6
Castiglione, Baldassare, **260–2**
  Book of the Courtier, 7, 260–2, **263–77**, 278
Castiglione, Bernardo Antonio di, 232
Cataline, 35
catasto, 122
Cato the Elder, 159, 164, 166
Cato the Younger, 167
Cavalcanti, Ginevra, 150
Cavalcanti, Giovanni, 195n
Cellini, Benvenuto, 206, 223, **244–5**
  Autobiography, **245–56**
  Perseus with the Head of Medusa, 222
Ceresara, Paride, 235–6
Cereta, Laura, 1, 7, **197**, 198, 207, 225
  two "familiar" letters, **198–205**
Ceri, Renzo da, 246–7
Cesena, 78
Charlemagne, 46n

Charles V, emperor, 7, 8, 207n, 211n, 213n, 245n, 260, 282
Charles VIII, king of France, 3, 8
children, 108–21, 141, 144–51, **163–8**
Christ Handing the Keys to St. Peter (Perugino), *174*
Cicero, Marcus Tullius, 5, 34–8, 44–5, 47, 72, 84n, 153n, 158n, 180, 201
Claudius, emperor, 45
Clement IV, pope, 215
Clement VII, pope, 207–12, 214–16, 245–9, 251–5, 260, 279, 281–2, 284–6
  as a cardinal (Giulio de' Medici), 129
  criticisms of, 217–18
  election as pope, 175, 206
  patronage, 206, 244
  political alliances, 7–8
Colocci, Angelo, 279
Colonna, Giacomo, 29n
Colonna, Giovanni, 80
Colonna, Pompeo, 246n
Colonna family, 76–7
Commentaries (Pius II), 52, **53–70**
Constantine, emperor, 45, 66, 175, 178, 180–2, 184
Constantinople, 51–2
Cornaro, Francesco, 229–30
Contarini, Gasparo, 279–83, 285
Contarini, Marcantonio Flavio, 280
Colonna, Pompeo, 246n
Cornelia, 201, 202n
costume
  of emperors and popes, 178–81, 183–4
  of women, 160–3
Council of Ferrara-Florence, 56n
court life
  Book of the Courtier (Castiglione), 263–77
  Vettori on the Roman court, 128–30
courtesans, 128
Cremona, 138
Crusade, 7, 52, 54, 56n
  see also Turks
Cyrus, 154, 158, 161

da Vinci, Leonardo, *see* Leonardo da Vinci
Dante, **14**–15, 24, 43, 46–7, 96, 132
  Divine Comedy, 14, **15–23**
Darius I, king of Persia, 75, 182
Dark Ages, 24
Davizzi, Tommaso, 119
Demaratus of Corinth, 156
Demosthenes, 43, 158, 206
Diogenes Laertius, 189n
Dionysius, tyrant of Sicily, 161
Dioscorides, 194n
Divine Comedy (Dante), 14, **15–23**
Domitian, emperor, 45
Donatello, 95
  Judith and Holofernes, *94*
Dovizi, Bernardo, *see* Bibbiena
dowries, 109–10, 112, 115, 119–20, 139, 145–6
  funding, 110, 113, 115
  legislation on, 110n

economy, 8–9, 259
Eleonora of Aragon, 224
England, 7, 8
Epaminondas, 160
Epicurus, 36
Este, Ercole d', duke of Ferrara, 224
Este, Isabella d', **224**, 225–43, 260
Eugenius IV, pope, 63, 65, 70, 176
Euripides, 156
exile, 14, 108, 117n, 119
Ezzelino III da Romano, 215

Fabius Maximus, 83
Faenza, 76
family, 108–25, 137–8, 150, 163–7
Farnese, Alessandro, *see* Paul III, pope
Farnese, Odoardo, 5
Fedele, Cassandra, 202
Ferdinand, king of Aragon, 8, 85n
Ferrara, 224, 244
Ficino, Marsilio, 33, **187–8**
  Three Books on Life, **188–96**
Fiesole, 96
Findlen, Paula, 1–2

Florence, 13, 79, 81, 95–6, 110–12,
    121–2, 124–6, 168, **223**
    Bruni and, 43
    Dante and, 14, 19
    Machiavelli and, 71–2
    Medici family and, 71, **95**, 114,
      223
Florentino, Giuliano, 247
France, 7, 8, 51, 76–8, 86–7, 211
Francis I, king of France, 8, 213, 244,
    245n, 280n, 287
Frederick II, emperor, 2, 215
Frederick III of Austria, 52
Fregoso, Ottaviano, 263
friendship
    literary, 25, 197, 261
    literary and social, 151–4, 168–9
    political, 79, 82

Gaddi, Niccolò, 249
Gaeta, 78, 284
Galba, emperor, 45
Galen, 189n, 194
*Game of Chess, involving the painter's three
    sisters and a servant, A* (Sofonisba
    Anguissola), *138*
Gellius, Aulus, 159n, 164n, 165n
gender roles, 137–8, 150–69
Genoa, 253n
Germany, 61, 86
Ghibellines, 100n, 246n
Ginori, Filippo, 131
Ginori, Lionardo, 121
Ginori, Tommaso, 119n
Giorgione, 242
Giotto, 221
Giovio, Paolo, 247n
Girolami, Giovanni, 129
golden age, 259, 273, 279
Gonzaga, Federico, 243, 262
Gonzaga, Francesco II, marquis of
    Mantua, 224, 260
government, forms of, 273–5
Grana, Lorenzo, 279
Granada, Treaty of, 8
Gratian, *Decretum*, 178

Greece, 53, 60, 67, 75
Guarino da Verona, 168
Guelfs, 44, 100
Guicciardini, Antonio, 131
Guicciardini, Battista, 131
Guicciardini, Francesco, 9
Guicciardini family, 108

Habsburg rule, 259
Hannibal, Carthaginian general, 82
Henry VII, emperor, 3
Hercules at the Crossroads (Annibale
    Carracci), 4, 5
Herzegovina, 51
Hadrian, emperor, 45
Hadrian VI, *see* Adrian VI, pope
Hebrews, ancient, 88
Herodian, 129
Herodotus, 151
Hildegard of Bingen, 189n
Hippocrates, 189
Holy League, 8
Homer, 150, 156, 181, 281n
Horace, 182n
human nature, 72, 97
humanism, 33, 150, 168–9, **173**, 197,
    262
    civic, 43
Hungary, 7

illegitimacy, 3
imitation
    of literary style, 24, 173
    of moral behavior, 139, 262
    of political accomplishment, 72, 88,
      207
individualism, 2, 221
indulgences, 62, 114
Innocent IV, pope, 215
Ippoliti, Matteo, 243
Isocrates, 159
Italy, 7, 86, **87–90**, **259**, 263, 284

Jerome, St., 189n, 228
Jerusalem, 59
Judith and Holofernes (Donatello), *94*

Julius II, pope, 7–8, 79, 126, 129n, 261, 285
   character, 87
   election, 80, 175
   politics and territorial expansion, 8, 87

Kelly, Joan, 137
Kent, Dale, 95n
King, Margaret, 202n
Klapisch-Zuber, Christiane, 139n
Kohl, Benjamin G., 72n

Lactantius, 45, 180
Lampridius, 129
Landino, Cristoforo, 14
Lannoy, Charles de, viceroy of Naples, 211
Latin language, 24, 36, 43–7, 139, 176–84, 285
Leo I, pope, 186
Leo X, pope, 71, 93, 128, 129n, 261, 285, **286–7**
   election, 88n, 126
Leonardo da Vinci, 238–42
   Portrait of Isabella d'Este, 239
Leontium, 201
libertà d'Italia, 9, **51**, 217
Livorno, 112, 123n
Livy, 26, 71, 83n, 88n, 129, 159n
Lodi, Peace of, 3, 5, 51
Lombardy, 88
Lotto, Pier Maria di, 255
Louis XII, king of France, 8, 71, 76, 78, 240
Lucca, 78
Luna, Antonio della, 121
Luna, Francesco della, 113
Luna, Giovanni della, 112
Luther, Martin, 177, 259
Lysander, 161

Machiavelli, Giovanni, 131
Machiavelli, Niccolò, **71**, 93, 126–7, 130–4, 140, 207, 262
   The Discourses, 71
   Florentine Histories, 71

The Prince, 2, 9, 51, 71–2, **73–90**, 126, 129n, 132
Macinghi, Antonangiolo, 113
Macinghi, Zanobi, 113
Macrobius, 27n
Mahomet, 67
Malatesta, Francesco, 231–4
Manetti, Gianotto, 118
Manetti, Margherita di Pippo, 113
Manfred, 215
Mantegna, Andrea, 226, 228–30, 234–5, 237–8
Mantua, 224, 260
Manuzio, Aldo, 206
Marcellinus, Ammianus, 129
Marcello, Cristoforo, 284
Marius, 214
Maro, P. Virgilius, *see* Virgil
marriage, 109, 118–21, 143, 152–3, 167–9
Martial, 184
Martin V, pope, 3, 215
Maximilian, 8n, 285n
Medes, 88
Medici, Alessandro de', 278
Medici, Bernardo de', 118
Medici, Cosimo de' ("The Elder"), 3, 43, 95, 108, 150, 152, 187, 245
Medici, Cosimo I de', duke of Florence, 223, 244, 259
Medici, Giovanni Bicci de', 152
Medici, Giovanni de', *see* Leo X, pope
Medici, Giovanni de' ("of the Black Bands"), 245
Medici, Giuliano (brother of Lorenzo "The Magnificent"), 7
Medici, Giuliano de', duke of Nemours, 73n, 129, 133, 286
Medici, Giulio de', *see* Clement VII, pope
Medici, Ippolito de', 278
Medici, Lorenzo de' (brother of Cosimo "The Elder"), 150–1, 168
Medici, Lorenzo de' ("The Magnificent"), 7
Medici, Lorenzo de', duke of Urbino, 73–5

Medici, Pallone de', 247
Medici, Piero de' ("The Gouty"), 95,
    120–1, 124n
Medici, Piero de' ("The Unfortunate"),
    286
Medici family, 71–2, 88, 133
Mela, Pomponius, 26
Mellini, Pietro, 279
merchants, 3, 66
Michael, Byzantine emperor, 216
Michelangelo, 221
Milan, 3, 76, 96, 206–7, 213n
Mohačs, 7
Mohammed, see Mahomet
Mohammedans, 67
Monte (public funded debt), 122
Montelupo, Raffaello da, 247n
Moses, 88
motherhood, see women
Musuro, Marco, 285

Nagel, Alexander, 33n
Naples, 3, 51, 78, 87, 111, 177
Nardi, Bernardo, 124
Narni, 56–7
Naso, P. Ovidius, see Ovid
Navagero, Andrea, 261, 280
Nero, emperor, 45, 66, 128
Nerva, emperor, 45
Niccoli, Niccolò, 153
Nicholas V, pope, 61, 176
Nogarola, Isotta, 202

Olympias, queen of Macedon, 156
On the Ill Fortune of Learned Men
    (Valeriano), 279–87
On Wifely Duties (Barbaro),
    151–69
Orange, Prince of, 253n, 254
Orco, Remirro de, 73, 77–8
Orsini, Franciotto, 254–5
Orsini family, 76–7, 79
Orvieto, 282n
Otho, emperor, 45
Otranto, 51
Ottoman Turks, see Turks

Ovid, 28, 30, 132, 193n

Paleologus, Constantine, 55
Paleologus, Demetrius, 55
Paleologus, Thomas, 54–5
Palmieri, Matteo, 14
Pandolfini, Pandolfo, 121, 122n
papacy, 3, 5, 8, 52, 68, **175–86**
Papal States, 5, 76
Parenti, Marco, 109, 113–14, 119
Patras, 53–4
patronage, 127, 221, 244
Paul, St., 57, 59, 66, 68
Paul III, pope, 5, 175, 244
    as a cardinal (Alessandro Farnese),
        175, 250–1
Pavia, battle of, 8
Pazzi Conspiracy, 7
periodization of history, 13, 24
    see also Renaissance, ending
Perseus with the Head of Medusa (Cellini),
    222
Persians, 88, 167
Perugia, 77–8
Perugino, Pietro, 175, 231–2, **234–7**
    Christ Handing the Keys to St. Peter,
        174
Pesaro, 7, 108, 113
Pesellino, Story of Griselda, 140
Peter, St., 52–3, 57, 59, 66–9
Petrarca, Francesco, see Petrarch
Petrarca, Gherardo, 44, 46
Petrarch, 13, **24–5**, 43, 46–7, 72, 90,
    96, 132, 139, 197, 259
    Ascent of Mont Ventoux, 5, 25, **26–34**
    letters to Cicero, **34–8**
    poetry, **38–42**, 47, 90
Petrucci, Alfonso, 286
Petrucci, Borghese, 286
Philip, King of Macedon, 26, 155
Piccolomini, Aeneas Silvius, see Pius II,
    pope
Piccolomini, Francesco Todeschini, see
    Pius III, pope
Pietro da Novellara, Fra, 238–40
Pindar, 160

Piombino, 78
Pisa, 78, 123
Pistoia, 81, 125
Pius II, pope, 7, **52**
    Commentaries, **53–70**
Pius III, pope, 129n, 175
plague, 96, 112, 116n, 121–2, 242,
    255, 283–4
Plato, 43, 192, 195n, 262
Platonism, Renaissance, 33, 187
Plautus, 180
Pliny, 180
Plutarch, 129, 150, 153n–66n
Pompey the Great, 35, 65
Porcari, Camillo, 284
Portrait of Baldassare Castiglione
    (Raphael), *261*
Portrait of Clement VII (Sebastiano del
    Piombo), *208*
Portrait of Isabella d'Este (Leonardo da
    Vinci), *239*
Portrait of Niccolò Machiavelli (attrib. to
    Rosso Fiorentino), *74*
Pragmatic Sanction, 63
Prato, 19, 124–5
    sack of, 132
pregnancy, 113, 163
Prince, The (Machiavelli), 2, 9, 51, 71–2,
    73–90, 126, 129n, 132
Proba, 201
Procopius, 129
Propertius, 37
Pythagoreans, 159

Raphael, 243, 261–2
    Portrait of Baldassare Castiglione, 261
Ravenna, battle of, 89
Reformation
    Catholic, 9, 259
    Protestant, 8
    see also Luther
relics, 52–70, 212
religious beliefs and practices, 5, 109,
    116–18, 167, 173, 187–8, 218,
    275, 279
    see also papacy; Reformation; relics

Renaissance
    ending, 259, 279
    see also humanism
Riario, Raffaelo, 80
Rimini, 76
Robin, Diana, 203n
Romagna, 76–9, 81
Rome, ancient, 17, 37, 43, 45, 71, 162
Rome, Renaissance city, 54–6, 58, 61–5,
    87, 128–30, 206, 244–55, 282–3
    sack of, 8, 72, **206–18**, 244–55, 259,
    284
Rossi, Roberto, 153
Rovere, Francesco Maria della, duke of
    Urbino, 7, 249
Rubinstein, Nicolai, 95n
Rucellai, Donato, 113
Rucellai, Giovanni, 129

Sabellico, Marcantonio, 280n
sack of Rome, *see* Rome, sack of
*St. Augustine in His Study (Vision of St.
    Augustine)* (Carpaccio), *32*
Sallust, 129, 201n
Salutati, Coluccio, 43
Saluzzo, 139
Salviati, Jacopo, 245, 250
Sanluzzo, *see* Saluzzo
Santacroce, Antonio, 248, 254
Sappho, 200, 201n
Scholastic theologians, 24, 176
Scipio, 83, 266
Sebastiano del Piombo, *Portrait of
    Clement VII, 208*
Semiramis, 201
Sempronia, 201
Seneca, 31n, 36, 45, 130n
Serbia, 51
Severus, emperor, 45
sexual practices, 87, 189
Sforza, Ascanio, 80
Sforza, Francesco, 76
Shearman, John, 223, 262n
Sicily, 177
Siena, 78, 286
Sixtus IV, pope, 7, 175

Socrates, 195
Soderini, Niccolò, 122
Soderini, Piero, 126, 133, 242n
Sophocles, 160
Spain, 7, 51, 78, 86–7, 282
sprezzatura, 260, 262
state, *see* government
Strozzi, Agostino, 236–7
Strozzi, Alessandra Macinghi, 7, **108**,
    109–25, 140, 198, 225
Strozzi, Filippo di Matteo, 108–9, 113,
    116–23
Strozzi, Filippo (16th cent.), 253
Strozzi, Jacopo, 114–15
Strozzi, Lessandra (Alessandra, daughter
    of Alessandra Macinghi Strozzi),
    120
Strozzi, Lorenzo (son of Alessandra
    Macinghi Strozzi), 108, 114–15,
    119, 123
Strozzi, Matteo di Matteo (son of
    Alessandra Macinghi Strozzi), 108,
    111–14, 116–18
Strozzi, Matteo di Simone, 108
Strozzi, Niccolò di Lionardo, 109, 112,
    114
Süleyman "The Magnificent," 7, 51
Sulla, 214
Sylvester I, pope, 176, 178, 181, 185

Tacitus, Cornelius, 129
Terentia, 201, 202n
Theocritus, 165n
Theophrastus, 160, 201
Thucydides, 158
Tiberius, emperor, 45
Tibullus, 132
Titus, emperor, 45
Tornabuoni, Lucrezia, 120
Trajan, emperor, 45
Trevisan, Zaccaria, 150, 152, 154, 168
Turks, 7–8, 51–2, 54–5, 56n, 58–61,
    68, 214

Tuscany, 77, 88, 259

Urbino, 7, 77, 260

Valeriano, Pierio, **278**
    On the Ill Fortune of Learned Men,
    279–87
Valerius Maximus, 156n, 162n
Valla, Lorenzo, **176**, 177–86, 197
    On the Donation of Constantine, 176,
    177–86
Venice and Venetians, 8, 76, 87
Vergerio, Pier Paolo ("The Elder"), 161n
Vespasian, emperor, 45
Vettori, Francesco, 93, **126**, 127–30
Vianello, Michele, 225–7
Vienna, 8
Virgil, 14–15, 17–18, 27n, 34n, 37–8,
    44, 47, 82, 165, 181
    Aeneid, 14, 37, 165
Visconti, Filippo Maria, duke of Milan,
    111
Visconti, Galeazzo, 46
Visconti family, 96

Wallace, William E., 221n
wills, 118
Witt, Ronald G., 1, 72n
women
    comportment, 157–60
    dress, 160–3
    education of children, 163–8
    learning and, 197–205
    as mothers, 93, 120, 150, 163–8
    as patrons, 120, 224–43; *see also* Este,
        Isabella d'
    as widows, 93, 111, 121–2
    as wives, 140, 150–1, 154–7

Xenocrates, 153
Xenophon, 5, 150, 158, 161n,
    266